THE HANDBOOK FOR
Highly Effective Teams
IN A PLC AT WORK®

Essential Actions for Tackling Critical Issues

William M. Ferriter | **Bob Sonju**
Anisa Baker-Busby | **Kim Monkres**

FOREWORD BY ROBERT EAKER

Solution Tree | Press

a division of
Solution Tree

555 North Morton Street
Bloomington, IN 47404
800.733.6786 (toll free) / 812.336.7700
FAX: 812.336.7790
email: info@SolutionTree.com
SolutionTree.com

Visit **go.SolutionTree.com/PLCbooks** to download the free reproducibles in this book.

Printed in the United States of America

FSC
www.fsc.org
MIX
Paper | Supporting responsible forestry
FSC® C008955

Library of Congress Cataloging-in-Publication Data

Names: Ferriter, William M., author. | Sonju, Bob, 1967- author. |
   Baker-Busby, Anisa, author. | Monkres, Kim, author.
Title: The handbook for highly effective teams in a PLC at work® :
   essential actions for tackling critical issues / William M. Ferriter,
   Bob Sonju, Anisa Baker-Busby, Kim Monkres.
Other titles: Handbook for highly effective teams in a professional
   learning community at work
Description: Bloomington, IN : Solution Tree Press, [2025] | Includes
   bibliographical references and index.
Identifiers: LCCN 2024046577 (print) | LCCN 2024046578 (ebook) | ISBN
   9781962188005 (paperback) | ISBN 9781962188012 (ebook)
Subjects: LCSH: Professional learning communities. | Teaching teams.
Classification: LCC LB1731 .F43 2025 (print) | LCC LB1731 (ebook) | DDC
   371.1--dc23/eng/20250401
LC record available at https://lccn.loc.gov/2024046577
LC ebook record available at https://lccn.loc.gov/2024046578

Solution Tree
Jeffrey C. Jones, CEO
Edmund M. Ackerman, President

Solution Tree Press
Publisher: Kendra Slayton
Associate Publisher: Todd Brakke
Acquisitions Director: Hilary Goff
Editorial Director: Laurel Hecker
Art Director: Rian Anderson
Managing Editor: Sarah Ludwig
Copy Chief: Jessi Finn
Senior Production Editor: Tonya Maddox Cupp
Proofreader: Jessica Starr
Text and Cover Designer: Abigail Bowen
Content Development Specialist: Amy Rubenstein
Associate Editor: Elijah Oates
Editorial Assistant: Madison Chartier

For my mom, whose unwavering joy, inspiration, and encouragement have been the foundation of all I've achieved—this is for you. With nothing but love and gratitude.

—BILL

To Leslye, the rock of our family: Thank you for your love, support, and encouragement on life's ride. To my four amazing daughters, Macey, Madi, Halle, and Andie: You are my endless source of happiness and joy. To my mom: Your love and kindness continually teach and shape me. And to my dad: Your boundless heart and belief in family mean everything. This book is a tribute to all of you—my foundation and my reason.

—BOB

To my sons, Antonio Jr. and Ashton—you are my greatest blessings. You inspire your dad and me daily to be the best versions of ourselves. To my mother, family, and incredible support system—your love and sacrifices have been my foundation. To my dear friends, my mentors, and the faculty and staff of Lindsey Elementary and Shirley Hills Elementary—your trust and dedication fuel this work.
To Bill and Bob—thank you for inspiring me to believe in the impossible.

—ANISA

To Blaine and Kylee for showing me endless love, patience, and support of all my crazy ideas and journeys.
To my mentor and friend Bob Sonju: Your belief in me and your encouragement motivate me to keep learning, growing, and plowing through life's barriers.

—KIM

Acknowledgments

Highly effective teams are the engine that drives the work of professional learning communities. As coauthors, we are deeply grateful to the many incredible individuals who made *The Handbook for Highly Effective Teams in a PLC at Work®* a reality.

To Rick and Becky DuFour, along with Bob Eaker, who established the foundation of professional learning communities in schools and districts around the world. Their passionate commitment to educators learning together challenged our profession to think and do differently. Their work and legacy continue to inspire us daily.

Jeff Jones and the Solution Tree staff deserve our deepest appreciation for their visionary leadership and unwavering support of educators. We are grateful for their collective ability to navigate the constantly changing landscape of education. Special thanks to Tonya Cupp, our editor, whose kindness, patience, and feedback brought clarity and focus to our words and ideas.

To Douglas Rife and the entire publishing team at Solution Tree, who have been incredible partners throughout our work, bringing expertise and a refining touch to this book, and Claudia Wheatley, our friend and thought partner, for always listening to ideas and providing insightful feedback as we continue to learn and grow. Writing this book has been a genuine team effort, and we are profoundly grateful for the contributions, encouragement, and belief each of you has provided.

Finally, to educators throughout the world. We are grateful for you. We are honored to call you colleagues, working side by side with you in this life-changing work called education.

Solution Tree Press would like to thank the following reviewers:

John D. Ewald
Education Consultant
Frederick, Maryland

Louis Lim
Principal
Bur Oak Secondary School
Markham, Ontario, Canada

Christie Shealy
Director of Testing and Accountability
Anderson School District One
Williamston, South Carolina

Steven Weber
Assistant Principal
Rogers Heritage High School
Rogers, Arkansas

Jacqueline Yu
Doctoral Student
University of Calgary
Calgary, Alberta, Canada

Visit **go.SolutionTree.com/PLCbooks** to download the free reproducibles in this book.

Table of Contents

Reproducibles are in italics.

About the Authors

William M. Ferriter uses his twenty-nine years of experience as a full-time classroom teacher to design professional development sessions for educators on topics ranging from establishing professional learning communities (PLCs) and effective systems of intervention to integrating meaningful differentiation, extension, and student-involved assessment opportunities into classroom instruction.

What Bill brings to audiences is practical experience gained through extensive work with his own professional learning teams and the students in his classrooms. Teachers appreciate the practicality of both his writing and his presentations, knowing that the content shared is content that was developed and implemented by a career classroom teacher. Every book that he writes and session that he delivers is designed to give participants not just a clear understanding of the whys behind the ideas that he is introducing, but tangible examples of how to turn those ideas into classroom and collaborative practices that work.

Bill is also the coauthor of several Solution Tree titles, including *Building a Professional Learning Community at Work*®: *A Guide to the First Year*; *Making Teamwork Meaningful: Leading Progress-Driven Collaboration in a PLC at Work*; *Creating a Culture of Feedback*; and *You Can Learn! Building Student Ownership, Motivation, and Efficacy With the PLC at Work Process*. Finally, he is the author of *The Big Book of Tools for Collaborative Teams in a PLC at Work*.

Bill earned a bachelor of science and master of science in elementary education from the State University of New York at Geneseo.

Bob Sonju is an award-winning educational leader, author, and speaker who is nationally recognized for his energetic commitment to coaching teacher teams and educational leaders in simple, doable processes and systems that create the conditions for lasting success. Bob has led two separate schools to national Model PLC at Work® status, and one of his schools also received the prestigious National Breakthrough School Award from the National Association of Secondary School Principals.

As a district leader, Bob led the implementation of the PLC process in a district composed of over fifty schools. He is committed to making the work of collaborative teams and school leaders both simple and doable, as evidenced in his coauthored book *Simplifying the Journey: Six Steps to Schoolwide Collaboration, Consistency, and Clarity in a PLC at Work.*

Bob was named Principal of the Year by the Utah Association of Secondary School Principals and was selected as one of three finalists for National Principal of the Year by the National Association of Secondary School Principals. He has appeared in various resources and books, including *It's About Time: Planning Interventions and Extensions in Secondary School*; *Best Practices at Tier 2: Supplemental Interventions for Additional Student Support, Elementary* (and *Secondary*); *Help Your Team: Overcoming Common Collaborative Challenges in a PLC at Work*; and *Women Who Lead: Insights, Inspiration, and Guidance to Grow as an Educator*. His work has also been featured in the magazine *Principal Leadership*.

Bob earned a bachelor's degree, a master's degree, and an endorsement in school leadership from Southern Utah University.

Anisa Baker-Busby, EdD, is a highly regarded educational leader, speaker, and author with over twenty years of experience as an elementary teacher and administrator. Known for her unwavering commitment to fostering high levels of learning for all students, Anisa excels in helping schools build systems of support for collaborative teams. Her dedication to maintaining a climate of care, compassion, and celebration while cultivating a learning-focused culture for teachers and students led her to successfully lead two schools to become national Model PLC at Work schools and Georgia PBIS Distinguished Schools, with one also recognized as a Title I Distinguished School.

As an elementary teacher, she was honored as the 2008–2009 Teacher of the Year at Miller Elementary School in Warner Robins, Georgia. Anisa thrives on the challenge of collaborating with teacher teams and leaders to enhance learning outcomes through PLC at Work practices and assessments. She specializes in guiding teams to develop robust Tier 1 instructional and assessment practices and uses assessment data to inform real-time instructional decisions. Her expertise ensures a sharp focus on the foundational principles of PLCs: collaboration, learning, and results.

Anisa holds a bachelor's degree and a master's degree in elementary education from Alabama State University, a K–12 educational leadership certification from Albany State University, and both a specialist and doctoral degree in K–12 educational leadership from Argosy University. Committed to lifelong learning, she has earned additional certifications and endorsements in K–12 special education, preK–12 English for speakers of other languages, teacher leadership, multitiered systems of support, positive behavioral interventions and supports, and dyslexia.

Kim Monkres is the principal of Crimson Cliffs High School located in St. George, Utah. She began her career twenty-four years ago as a high school English language arts and communications teacher and has coaching experience as well.

Kim has been fortunate to work in many capacities and has a passion and appreciation for the collaborative process in education. She has served as a learning coach, assistant principal, athletic director, middle school principal, and state activities director. Kim has experience with creation of high-functioning collaborative teams, PLCs, curriculum development, curriculum design and mapping, instructional coaching, and response to intervention (RTI).

Kim earned a bachelor's degree in English education and communications/journalism from Weber State University and a master's degree in school leadership from Southern Utah University.

To book William M. Ferriter, Bob Sonju, Anisa Baker-Busby, or Kim Monkres for professional development, contact pd@SolutionTree.com.

Foreword

BY ROBERT EAKER

The use of collaborative teaming is not a new idea. For example, my first encounter with the concept of teams, other than in sports, was in 1962, when I joined the United States Marine Corps and was quickly on my way to Parris Island, South Carolina. Early in our training, we were addressed by an officer who emphasized that the entire U.S. Marine Corps was based on one overarching idea—the idea of a Marine rifle squad, a team composed of twelve Marines who worked together as one cohesive unit, supporting each other in the attainment of each mission, depending on each other, and holding each other responsible.

My first academic encounter with collaborative teaming came in the 1980s when I became familiar with the work of W. Edwards Deming, frequently referred to as founder of the *total quality management* movement—although he rarely, if ever, used the term. Collaborative teams were central to Deming's (1982) ideas for improving organizations. It wasn't difficult to see how a school, an organization characterized by individual teachers working in isolation, could benefit from teachers working with their fellow teachers through collaborative teaming.

In 1998, with the publication of *Professional Learning Communities at Work*®, Richard DuFour and I called on schools to, among other things, improve student learning by moving from a culture of teacher isolation to a culture of collaboration through the use of collaborative teams. To add specificity of the term *collaborative teaming*, in 2008, Rick, Rebecca DuFour, and I defined professional learning communities as those "whose members work *interdependently* to achieve *common goals*—goals linked to the purpose of learning for all— for which members are held *mutually accountable*" (p. 14; emphasis in original). This was not unlike what I had heard about teaming in the Marine Corps in 1962!

While the use of teams is not new, remarkably, the idea is relatively new for schools. In fact, teacher isolation remains very much the norm. Although educators are not opposed to the idea of collaborative teaming, there remains the daunting question of just *how* to embed collaborative teaming deep into the day-in-and-day-out life of schools.

Developing the structures, processes, and practices through the use of *high-performing* teams is difficult and complex. Fortunately, much has been learned as teaming in schools has increased. And, importantly, successful practitioners are sharing their insights, practices, and materials with their fellow educators. *The Handbook for Highly Effective Teams in a PLC at Work* by William M. Ferriter, Bob Sonju, Anisa Baker-Busby, and Kim Monkres is an excellent example. The most striking aspect of the authors' work is the fact that they move beyond an attempt to *inform* and *convince* educators of the benefits of collaborative teaming. They drill deep into *how* educators can tackle the critical issues associated with developing high-performing collaborative teams.

The outstanding characteristic of *The Handbook for Highly Effective Teams in a PLC at Work* is the specificity along with the practitioner-developed tools that enable teams to organize and manage their work and their students' work. Simply organizing a school into teams will do little, if anything, to improve student learning. The immediate question faced by those who seek to embed teaming practices deep into school culture is this: What should our teams do and *how should they do it*? In short, student learning improves when teams engage in the *right* work and focus on the critical issues associated with student learning. That's exactly what readers will find in this handbook.

Chapter topics address such issues as developing team norms, dealing with adult behavior that is incongruent with effective teaming, setting goals effectively, monitoring each team's effectiveness, and identifying essential student learning outcomes along with the prerequisite knowledge for each. Chapters also cover how to provide more time for teams to focus on essential content, how to sequence and pace lessons in each course or subject, how to monitor student learning on a frequent and timely basis through common formative assessments, how to use the results of formative assessments to make collaborative decisions regarding additional time and support for individual students as well as extension of student learning, and importantly, how to use these data to improve instructional strategies. This book's specificity and depth comes from how the coauthors address each of these topics. Each chapter details *why* and *how* educators can effectively address each issue, as well as provides tools teams can use to guide their work.

Most importantly, this book is a call to action to drill deeper into the work of teams. For collaborative teaming to positively impact both student and adult learning, leaders must take action, moving beyond applying a simple veneer of a few structural changes that covers the practices that have characterized traditional schools for decades.

In short, leaders must lead the movement from *knowing* to *doing*. For those who embark on the journey of improving student learning through high-performing teams, *The Handbook for Highly Effective Teams in a PLC at Work* will prove to be a valuable asset. My recommendation is this: Read it, think about it, underline key points, fold down important pages, make notes, share it, and discuss it, but most importantly, *use it—again and again*!

References

Deming, W. E. (1982). *Out of the crisis*. MIT Press.

DuFour, R., DuFour, R., & Eaker, R. (2008). *Revisiting Professional Learning Communities at Work: New insights for improving schools*. Solution Tree Press.

DuFour, R., & Eaker, R. (1998). *Professional Learning Communities at Work: Best practices for enhancing student achievement*. Solution Tree Press.

The Promise of Highly Effective Teams

Few moments are as energizing as the beginning of a new school year. Those first weeks are a fresh start for everyone, full of anticipation and enthusiasm. Why? Because each new school year is full of possibilities, holding the promise of growth and discovery. We see hope in the faces of our students and know that it is *our job* to create learning spaces that turn that hope into social and academic success for every learner. That's the charge we accepted when we decided to teach.

But that charge is impossible to meet when teachers work in isolation. There are simply too many academic, social, and emotional needs in our rooms for any one educator to "successfully teach *all* [their] students" (DuFour, DuFour, Eaker, Mattos, & Muhammad, 2021, p. 125). Instead, delivering social and academic success for every learner depends on one critical practice: effective collaboration. We must work systematically with one another, targeting our efforts and relying on our shared expertise, with the understanding that when we *lean on* or *lend a hand to* our peers, we increase our collective capacity to meet the challenges of increasingly diverse classrooms.

Logically, this makes sense. We all have students we struggle to support each year. Those are the students who keep us up at night looking for strategies that we haven't yet tried because the stakes are too high to give up on any learner. And we all have colleagues who make us better by challenging our practice and teaching us skills that we haven't already mastered. Those are the peers we turn to first when we are looking for new ways to reach the students we struggle with, and the support they provide is the only proof we need that collaboration is a strategy worth investing in.

But the promise of highly effective teams is more than just something that makes sense logically. Instead, it is a strategy for accelerating learning that has been overwhelmingly confirmed by research time and time again. Take the work of John Holt (1964), an early advocate for child-centered education, for example. Summarizing the differences between effective schools—defined as schools that ensured students living in poverty made the same academic progress as students from middle-class or affluent homes—and ineffective schools, Holt (1964) identified two factors as crucial in effective schools:

> (1) If the students did not learn, the schools did not blame them, or their families, backgrounds, neighborhoods, attitudes, nervous systems, or whatever. They did not alibi. They took full responsibility for the results or non-results of their work. (2) When something they were doing in class did not work, they stopped doing it and tried to do something else. They flunked unsuccessful methods, not the children. (p. 8)

Holt's ideas are echoed in the seminal research done by John Hattie (2023a), a prominent researcher whose work focuses on identifying and synthesizing the most impactful influences on student learning. Drawing from meta-analyses of thousands of studies, Hattie quantified the effect sizes of various teaching strategies, interventions, and other influences affecting learning. The most powerful influence on student learning is collective teacher efficacy. Collective teacher efficacy has consistently been at the top of Hattie's (2023a) rankings of practices with "the potential to considerably accelerate student learning," having an effect size three times greater than the average impact of other influences on student learning. How does Hattie define collective teacher efficacy? In a manner that is remarkably similar to Holt:

> Collective teacher efficacy is not just rah-rah thinking. . . . *It's the combined belief that it is us that causes learning.* It is not the students. It's not the students from particular social backgrounds. It's not all the barriers out there. Because when you . . . *believe that you can make the difference*, and then you feed it with evidence that you are, that is dramatically powerful. (Hattie, 2018, emphasis added)

Why does collaboration matter so much? Because when teachers work together, they expose one another to instructional strategies they may not have otherwise discovered (Saka, 2021). Teachers who work in isolation tend to remain dependent on "previously acquired skills," while teachers who work collaboratively "can improve their skills, competence and resourcefulness to guarantee their continued relevance on their jobs" (Saka, 2021, p. 34). And the competence that comes from opportunities to work collaboratively directly impacts student achievement. As university professor Adewale Owodunni Saka (2021) notes after researching the impact of collaboration on mathematics instruction in junior high schools:

> A teachers' group . . . had a significant effect on students' achievement in mathematics. Multiple classification analysis showed that *students whose teacher engaged in collaborative activities performed better than those taught by a teacher that did not engage in collaboration* (isolated teacher). (p. 42, emphasis added)

Odds are that nothing here is new to you. The argument that collaboration can improve outcomes for students is a common refrain in education. In fact, you are far less likely to find a school where teachers continue to work in isolation than you are to find a school that has restructured itself as a professional learning community (PLC) to prioritize collaboration. *It's the results of those collaborative efforts that often seem hard to come by.* Time and again, we hear educators say, "We've been working together for years, but we haven't seen any real gains in student learning."

Does that sound like your school? Have you begun to question the value of working together simply because the time and energy that it requires far outweigh the returns you are seeing in student learning? If so, you may have settled for what Richard DuFour and Douglas Reeves (2016), two of the most influential figures in education—particularly in the areas of leadership, school improvement, and PLCs—describe as "the futility of PLC Lite":

> Although many schools around the world have claimed to embrace the professional learning community (PLC) process, it would be more accurate to describe the current state of affairs in many schools as PLC Lite. Educators rename their traditional faculty or department meetings as PLC meetings, engage in book studies that result in no action, or devote collaborative time to topics that have no effect on student achievement—all in the name of the PLC process.

We shouldn't be surprised that simply renaming traditional meetings as PLCs or engaging in book studies doesn't produce results for students. Like anything worth doing, success in schools or on collaborative teams is a function of intentionality. Just as a pilot couldn't deliver passengers from point A to point B without consistently implementing a set of well-designed steps necessary for flying a plane, teachers can't move students forward unless they embrace a set of essential actions that have been systematically defined by schools that are successfully using the shared study of practice to advance learning. As the architects of the PLC at Work® process argue, "Collaboration does not lead to improved results unless people are *focused on the right work*" (DuFour, DuFour, Eaker, Many, Mattos, & Muhammad, 2024, p. 19, emphasis added).

How This Book Is Organized

Divided into four parts detailing fifteen essential actions that collaborative teams must take to turn the shared study of practice into increased student learning, *The Handbook for Highly Effective Teams in a PLC at Work* is designed to help you focus on the right work. Inspired by both the critical issues for team consideration outlined in *Learning by Doing: A Handbook for Professional Learning Communities at Work, Fourth Edition*, (DuFour et al., 2024) and the firsthand experience of the four practitioners who have coauthored this text, each chapter introduces one essential action. Readers learn *what* highly effective teams do when implementing the essential action, *why* highly effective teams do this, and most importantly, *how* they can embed the action into their daily work. The four parts of *The Handbook for Highly Effective Teams in a PLC at Work*, with their respective essential actions, are as follows.

- **Part 1: Highly Effective Teams Have a Common Foundation**—Highly effective teams are built on a strong cultural foundation that supports their work. The first part details the essential actions that teams must take to build this foundation. Readers learn explicit strategies to help teams define their roles, set norms, develop protocols, address interpersonal dynamics, analyze achievement data, and regularly evaluate their effectiveness. By solidifying these critical elements, teams create the groundwork for meaningful collaboration and success.
  - **Action 1.1:** We Identify Team Roles, Norms, and Protocols to Guide Us in Working Together
  - **Action 1.2:** We Have a Process for Addressing Moments When Personalities Interfere With the Team's Work

- **Action 1.3:** We Use SMART Goals to Drive Our Work
- **Action 1.4:** We Regularly Evaluate Our Team's Effectiveness

- **Part 2: Highly Effective Teams Focus on Learning for All Students**—At the heart of every highly effective team is a shared commitment to ensuring *all students* learn. The second part explores the critical actions teams take to clarify essential learning outcomes, define what it looks like when students meet the standards, and align instructional strategies. By focusing on clarity and consistency, teams can help students meet and exceed expectations while ensuring that collaborative time and energy are devoted to what matters most.

  - **Action 2.1:** We Collectively Identify Essential Learnings and Define What Success Looks Like in Student Work
  - **Action 2.2:** We Identify the Prerequisite Knowledge and Skills Needed to Master Our Essentials
  - **Action 2.3:** We Identify Course Content and Topics We Can Minimize or Eliminate to Devote More Time to Our Essentials
  - **Action 2.4:** We Agree on How to Sequence Content and Pace Our Course

- **Part 3: Highly Effective Teams Effectively Use Assessments and Data**— Assessments and data are powerful tools for driving improvement for students and teacher teams alike. The third part outlines how highly effective teams create and use assessments to monitor student learning, study instruction, and identify areas for intervention or extension. With a focus on both formative and standardized data, teams can ensure their efforts lead to measurable progress.

  - **Action 3.1:** We Develop and Deliver Frequent Common Formative Assessments Throughout Our Units of Instruction
  - **Action 3.2:** We Use Team Assessment Data to Identify High-Impact Instructional Strategies
  - **Action 3.3:** We Teach Students the Criteria We Will Use to Judge Their Work
  - **Action 3.4:** We Create Exemplars Students Can Examine to Evaluate Their Own Progress Toward Mastery

- **Part 4: Highly Effective Teams Provide Extra Time and Support for Learning**— Meeting all students' needs requires intentional planning to provide both initial interventions and extensions around grade-level essentials. The fourth and final part addresses how teams provide additional time and targeted support to help students master prerequisite skills, accelerate their learning, and reach their full potential. By acting together, highly effective teams ensure all students grow—and that high achievers are challenged to go further.

  - **Action 4.1:** We Create Flexible Time During Our Units of Instruction to Provide Extra Time and Support to Learners
  - **Action 4.2:** We Deliver Targeted Interventions to Support Students Who Have Not Yet Reached Grade-Level Expectations
  - **Action 4.3:** We Deliver Targeted Extensions to Students Working Beyond Grade-Level Expectations

The four parts of *The Handbook for Highly Effective Teams in a PLC at Work* closely parallel the four critical questions of learning outlined in the PLC at Work process:

a. What knowledge, skills, and dispositions should every student acquire as a result of this unit, this course, or this grade level?

b. How will we know when each student has acquired the essential knowledge and skills?

c. How will we respond when some students do not learn?

d. How will we extend the learning for students who are already proficient? (DuFour et al., 2024, p. 44)

While collaborative teams typically address these questions sequentially, there is no single correct way to read *The Handbook for Highly Effective Teams in a PLC at Work*. Some readers may choose to work through the book from beginning to end, gaining a complete understanding of the essential actions required for effective collaboration. This can provide a clear picture of the work of high-performing teams and allow readers to assess their current practices against that benchmark. Others may use this book as a reference, diving into specific essential actions that address their team's immediate needs. Doing so can offer just-in-time strategies to support progress and growth.

Who This Book Is For

Similarly, there is no single ideal audience for this book. Principals, instructional coaches, and team leaders can use this resource to deepen their understanding of the essential work of collaborative teams and to guide the job-embedded professional learning of the teams they support. And teachers on any collaborative team—grade-level teams in elementary schools, subject-specific teams in middle or high schools, vertical teams of singletons in smaller rural schools, and interdisciplinary teams of specialists in larger urban schools—can turn to this text to gain clarity about the purpose and processes behind the work they are asked to do together.

No matter how you choose to tackle this book, we encourage you to use it to *learn together*. Building a culture of learning in your school or on your team starts with developing a shared understanding of—and commitment to—the essential actions that make collaboration a powerful tool for improving student outcomes. Just as with students, the most meaningful learning for adults happens when it is "active, social, contextual, and engaging" (Cornell University Center for Teaching Innovation, n.d.). Stated more simply, wrestling with the ideas in this text as a group can help you maximize the impact on your work.

And no matter how you choose to tackle *The Handbook for Highly Effective Teams*, the most important step is this: get started! Collaborative teams in professional learning communities exist for more than simply delivering curriculum. They are dedicated to ensuring that *all* students learn at high levels. Achieving this goal requires stepping away from isolation, ineffective group practices, and the trap of PLC Lite. Instead, achieving this goal depends on your commitment to embracing a well-defined set of research-based actions that drive significant improvements in student outcomes, enhance teacher satisfaction, and build team efficacy.

Only then can you deliver on the promise of highly effective teams.

PART 1

Highly Effective Teams Have a Common Foundation

Highly effective teams are built on a strong cultural foundation that supports their work. This part of *The Handbook for Highly Effective Teams in a PLC at Work* details the essential actions that teams must take to build this foundation. Readers learn explicit strategies to help teams define their roles, set norms, develop protocols, address interpersonal dynamics, analyze achievement data, and regularly evaluate their effectiveness. By solidifying these critical elements, teams create the groundwork for meaningful collaboration and success.

- **Action 1.1:** We Identify Team Roles, Norms, and Protocols to Guide Us in Working Together (page 9)
- **Action 1.2:** We Have a Process for Addressing Moments When Personalities Interfere With the Team's Work (page 29)
- **Action 1.3:** We Use SMART Goals to Drive Our Work (page 39)
- **Action 1.4:** We Regularly Evaluate Our Team's Effectiveness (page 49)

We Identify Team Roles, Norms, and Protocols to Guide Us in Working Together

All schools have cultures: the assumptions, beliefs, expectations, and habits that constitute the norm for a school and guide the work of the educators within it. Perhaps it is more accurate, however, to say that educators do not have school cultures but rather that the school cultures have them.

—RICHARD DUFOUR, REBECCA DUFOUR, ROBERT EAKER, THOMAS W. MANY, MIKE MATTOS, AND ANTHONY MUHAMMAD

How do we create learning spaces that turn hope into social and academic successes for every learner? One thing is for certain: It's not as simple as setting up desks, making a seating chart, handing out materials, and starting class. We have yet to meet an effective teacher who brings learners together on the first day of school or the first day of a semester and says, "Come on in and have at it!" Instead, effective teachers set aside time during those first weeks to establish clear expectations for how learning will take place in their classrooms. They introduce important routines and procedures. They emphasize the habits they hope students will demonstrate. They teach students how to interact with teachers, with peers, and with the materials in their room, knowing that establishing positive patterns of participation early is the key to ensuring that purposeful work happens moving forward.

Now, think about the work of your learning team.

- Do you invest time early in your work to establish positive patterns of participation?
- Do you talk about what you need from one another for your collaborative time to be worthwhile?
- Do you establish routines and procedures that will help you function efficiently?
- Have you clarified how you will interact with one another when asking questions, challenging ideas, or making decisions?

On struggling teams, the answer to these questions is almost always, "No. We are adults. We don't need routines and procedures," or "We've worked together for so long that we already know those things about each other." And those answers explain why those teams rarely engage in meaningful work. When teams fail to invest time into articulating a clear set of expectations for one another, "things like working at cross-purposes, working on different problems, and even focusing on individual status within the group (ego) over the goals of the group emerge" (Russell, 2019).

Highly effective teams, on the other hand, recognize that a shared understanding of the expected outcomes for collaboration combined with clear routines and explicit behaviors to govern the work of the group can turn collaboration into a more positive experience for all.

Why Highly Effective Teams Do This

Let's start with a simple truth: There's never enough time in education. While teaching students is often rewarding, the remaining parts of our jobs can become completely overwhelming. No matter how long we stay at school each day, there are always more lessons to plan, interventions to develop, families to contact, papers to grade, hallways to supervise, dances to chaperone, meetings to attend, and emails to answer. In fact, while teachers in the United States work fifty-seven hours a week on average, less than half of that time is spent delivering lessons (Will, 2024). Nothing is more frustrating to classroom teachers than wasted time—and the best way to prevent time from being wasted is to have *clarity of purpose*. That "clarity is instrumental in defining goals and creating steps to [achieve] them while making effective decisions. Without this, there may be a lack of motivation, indecisiveness and a lack of direction or focus" (Nash, Ashford, & Collins, 2023).

That's interesting, isn't it? Time spent without clarity of purpose doesn't just leave us frustrated; it can make us less motivated. While this statement is powerful, we would go even further. We argue that a lack of clarity around *what teams will work on* and *how they will work together* is the primary reason that teachers in PLCs question the value of collaboration. When a team lacks clarity of purpose, its members become convinced that they could get more done on their own than with their peers—and those people are probably right. As the architects of the PLC at Work process write in *Learning by Doing* (DuFour et al., 2024), "It is difficult to overstate the importance of collaborative teams in the improvement process. It is even more important, however, to emphasize that collaboration does not lead to improved results unless people are focused on the right work" (p. 19).

The skepticism regarding the value of collaboration that arises within teams lacking clear goals, expectations, and patterns of participation is discouraging, considering the pivotal role collaborative teams play in improving schools. In his research on the influences impacting student learning, John Hattie (2023b) identifies *collective teacher efficacy*—defined as the "shared belief by a group of teachers in a particular educational environment that they have the skills to positively impact student outcomes"—as the influence with the greatest potential to accelerate student learning. What Hattie confirmed in his research is something that educators know: When a group of teachers gathers evidence that they *can* find solutions to help struggling students learn at higher levels, they are more likely to do three things—(1) persist, (2) set challenging goals for themselves, and (3) try new practices (Donohoo, 2017). More importantly, they become more determined to ensure that all students learn at the highest levels. Why? Because there is no reason to give up on challenging students when you have proof of your shared capacity to overcome challenges.

Teams are more powerful than individuals because they can tap into the experiences, talents, tools, and insights of multiple members. Think of it this way: On a learning team, each teacher acts like a unique piece of a collaborative jigsaw puzzle. To create a complete picture of learning for all, every piece of that puzzle is important—and every piece must be carefully arranged to build off one another. When we stand alone—or are forced into the wrong place—we are an incomplete picture and fall short of our promise to some of the students in our classrooms. But when we use focus, structure, and shared purpose to join together, our collaborative whole becomes more powerful than the sum of its parts. Figure 1.1.1 offers a comparison of language between ineffective groups and highly effective teams around this topic.

The Language of Ineffective Groups	The Language of Highly Effective Teams
"We keep having the same issues over and over."	"What norms can we establish to avoid repeating the same mistakes?"
"These meetings are a waste of my time."	"What actions can we take to make sure that your needs are met and your time is honored?"
"Why am I the only one doing this work?"	"What if we tried reviewing our roles to make sure tasks are balanced and clear?"
"We never get anything done when we work together. Everything takes so much longer."	"How can we structure our time and define our roles to be more productive?"
"We don't need a protocol for this; let's just get started."	"Let's use a protocol to structure our discussion so everyone has a chance to contribute."

FIGURE 1.1.1: Language comparison.

Can you spot the differences between the language of ineffective groups and the language of highly effective teams? Lacking clear structures and processes to guide their work, ineffective groups see little value in collaboration and are not convinced that working together can improve their practice. On the other hand, highly effective teams recognize that they can have a direct impact on the quality of their collaborative time by embracing explicit structures that focus their work.

How Highly Effective Teams Do This

Carefully designed norms, roles, and protocols are essential tools for ensuring that collaboration leads to meaningful outcomes. However, mention them at your next team meeting and you are likely to get a collective groan from your colleagues. Why do teachers doubt the value of the very structures that can make them more productive as a group? It's not because writing norms or establishing roles is an overwhelming task. In fact, when we work in schools, many teams have already taken the time to draft norms, assign roles, and select protocols intended to guide their collaborative efforts. But these tools are often poorly understood and rarely woven into the day-to-day practices of a team's work. When norms are merely written as a task to complete, roles are assigned but not embraced, and protocols are selected but inconsistently followed, collaboration turns into just another meeting. A closer look at these structures— what they are, how to develop them, and why they are critical—can provide insight into their potential to help teams engage in meaningful work.

Norms

Team norms are the first essential structure highly effective teams use to bring clarity to their work. *Norms*—defined as "agreements about how members will work with each other and how the group will work overall" (Nawaz, 2018)—are designed to address the common patterns of participation that exist in any group. Sometimes, those participation patterns are positive, facilitating the team's work. Other times, those patterns are negative, preventing collaboration from feeling productive (Ferriter, 2020). To ensure that those patterns facilitate meaningful work, highly effective teams engage in explicit conversations to articulate the actions they will take to meet the individual needs of their members.

That's an important point to remember about norms: They *are statements of our needs* (Ferriter, 2020). Some members need meetings to start and end on time, while others are less concerned about whether meetings begin late or run long. Some members need time to carefully think through decisions before moving forward, while others adopt an act-fast-and-correct-later approach. Some members need their peers to table their devices to avoid distractions during meetings, while others see multitasking as a way to maximize their time.

When members' expectations for how groups will function aren't met, they end up doubting the value of the time they spend together. On the other hand, writing and then consistently following a set of explicit norms "increases trust, saves time, and decreases backbiting and politics" (Nawaz, 2018).

Writing Norms

Daniel R. Venables (2011), in *The Practice of Authentic PLCs: A Guide to Effective Teacher Teams*, introduces a powerful tip for writing norms. Venables (2011) argues that to write good norms, teams need to have an open conversation about the "peeves and traits" of individual members (p. 29). *Peeves* are the meeting behaviors that frustrate individual members, making it difficult for them to fully invest in the team's work (Venables, 2011). *Traits* are the unique behaviors of individual members that others need to understand (Venables, 2011). For example, a team member may share that their personal peeve about working in groups is when colleagues spend more time looking at their devices than they do one another, and their trait is that they need little to no think time to make decisions. This conversation alone can help teams discover clear patterns in their frustrations with collaboration or help them better understand the behaviors of colleagues they have worked with for years.

Discussing peeves and traits raises awareness of both *who we are* and *what we need*, but we have not yet written norms. To write norms, we need to define *the actions that we will take to honor the needs of our peers*. For example, imagine that you work on a team with a colleague named Andie who needs time to process before making important decisions. Your team could write a norm that reads, *To honor Andie, we will never make an important decision at the end of one meeting. Instead, we will table our decision and make it at the beginning of the next meeting.*

Note the following things as you keep the example in mind.

- **Start each norm with the phrase, "To honor _____":** Here's why: When people see a connection between your norms and the needs of individual team members, those norms become more important. We aren't taking this action because it matters in some general sense. Instead, we are taking this action because it is important to a colleague who is sitting right next to us.

- **Each norm should describe a specific action that you will take to address a member's expectation for how your collective will work:** General statements like *be respectful* or *be prepared* are ineffective because they can be interpreted in different ways by different people. Instead, explicitly describe what being respectful or being prepared looks like in action—*To honor Antonio, we will list items necessary for each week's meeting in our agenda and in an email to members the day before we meet. That way, we can all come prepared to participate.* The more specificity you include in a norm statement, the more likely members are to honor their commitments to one another. As vulnerability researcher Brené Brown (2018) reminds us, "Clear is kind. . . . Not getting clear with a colleague about your expectations because it feels too hard yet holding them accountable or blaming them for not delivering is unkind" (p. 47).

There are no firm rules about the number of norms that a team should write—but we recommend that you have no more than four or five. The goal is to ensure that every member has their needs met, but that doesn't always require a one-to-one relationship between number of norms and number of members. Often, members have the same needs, so one norm can honor more than one person's needs. As global CEO coach Sabina Nawaz (2018) explains, "Focusing on fewer norms increases your chances of remembering them and practicing them regularly."

What's more important is reviewing your norms regularly until they become habits. Simple statements from the team lead at the beginning of every meeting like, "Remember, team: We are going to make an important decision today—so we will honor Andie by tabling that decision until the start of next week's meeting to give her plenty of processing time," remind members that there are expectations for participation and that those expectations represent the needs of specific colleagues. It is equally important to end every meeting with moments of gratitude, where members acknowledge when their needs have been met. To extend the example, Andie might say, "Thanks for giving me a chance to think a little more about this decision. I know you are ready to move on, but I really need that time."

Addressing Violations of Norms

The final question that you likely are thinking about is, "How do we hold members accountable for breaking a norm?" We argue that the best strategy for ensuring that members adhere to norms is to follow four steps.

1. Connect norms to individual members' needs.

2. Write specific actions that you will take to meet those needs.

3. At the beginning of each meeting, remind members of the norms that will play an important role in your current meeting.

4. End each meeting with moments of gratitude, where members acknowledge when their needs have been met.

In our experience, teams that consistently and intentionally take these steps rarely see norms broken because members understand the importance of the actions that they have written with—*and for*—one another.

Roles

Team roles are another structure that highly effective teams use to bring clarity to their work. While some teachers believe that establishing roles to govern their work is overcomplicated and unnecessary, establishing roles is the only way to ensure that tasks important to the team's efficient functioning aren't overlooked. More importantly, roles help members recognize that they are part of something bigger than themselves. If team members "understand their role and how their actions contribute, they will know how to invest time in the things that really matter and will try to produce the best results" (Forbes Business Council, 2022). Consultant Jean Paul De Silva Clauwaert says, "It makes people happy to know that they are doing something right that contributes to the bigger picture" (Forbes Business Council, 2022).

While there is no set list of roles necessary on all teacher teams, we suggest that it is difficult to collaborate effectively without people filling the following roles (Ferriter, 2020).

- **Team leader:** Responsible for organizing agendas for weekly meetings, keeping the team focused on yearly goals, and leading consensus-building conversations

- **Team challenger:** Responsible for constantly questioning the team's current practices and brainstorming alternatives worth considering

- **Team producer:** Responsible for creating first drafts of team documents, developing a system for organizing team files, and communicating team decisions

- **Team encourager:** Responsible for providing words of affirmation and encouragement during weekly meetings and monitoring individual members' attitudes and workloads

- **Team realist:** Responsible for evaluating the team's decisions against their current workload and voicing concerns that might otherwise go unspoken

To fill each of these roles, teams identify the member with the right personal and professional skills to complete the task. For example, your team's leader should be a detail-oriented person with strong relationships, your team's producer should be fluent in the technologies that you will use to create shared content, and your team's encourager should be an optimist who finds joy in lifting others up.

Whitney Johnson (2018), CEO of Disruption Advisors, calls this *finding your superpowers*—the "things we do effortlessly, almost reflexively, like breathing." When members fill roles that align with their superpowers, they "feel strong," and that feeling of strength brings both confidence and competence to the work (Johnson, 2018). On the other hand, when members fill roles for which they are not well suited, teams get little done and lose faith—in one another and in the value of collaboration.

We would go so far as to argue that once team roles have been assigned, *they should rarely change*. While the notion of rotating roles monthly or yearly to give members opportunities to build capacity beyond their current skill set is a common practice that seems good in theory, it results in wasted time during weekly meetings as members muddle through tasks they are poorly suited to complete—and nothing kills collaborative momentum faster than wasted time. Teachers must be convinced that their team will accomplish something together every single week if they are going to embrace the notion that collaboration is worthwhile, and the best way to accomplish something every week is to have people fill roles that align with their skill sets.

The final question you are probably thinking about is, "What if we have three people on our team but five roles to fill?" Because each role is essential to the functioning of highly effective teams, members working on small teams must take on more than one role. If we choose roles based on our skill sets, though, this shouldn't be overwhelming. For example, most teams have one or two members who are empathic. You know who they are. They stop by your room every Monday morning to see how your weekend went and send you texts when they think you need words of encouragement. They remember your birthday and show up with cookies to celebrate. Filling the encourager role will come easily to those members. In fact, they are already doing that work without being formally assigned it. Those members could pick up a second role that aligns with their professional skill set without feeling like they are being asked to do extra work.

Or you might be thinking about the opposite question: "What if we have eight people on our team but only five roles to fill?" Philosophically, we would argue that you don't need more roles. Instead, you need a smaller team. The most effective teams have between three and five members simply because conversations on larger teams are harder to coordinate efficiently; and, again, efficiency is essential to maintaining support for collaborative work. We would rather see large teams meet as a whole on school or district professional learning days to identify essentials, establish pacing, and write common assessments, and then break into smaller teams that meet weekly to study their practice together. Doing so increases the likelihood that members feel seen and heard in their collaborative work. Practically, teachers don't always have the organizational influence to make this decision. If you are on a large team with no chance of making it smaller, consider sharing particularly demanding or important roles with one another. Maybe you can have two producers or encouragers. Doing so ensures that those roles are filled even if members are absent. It also ensures that members filling those roles won't feel overwhelmed by the work they are asked to do.

Protocols

Protocols are a third structure that highly effective teams use to bring clarity to their work. Described by the National School Reform Faculty (n.d.) as "guidelines to promote meaningful, efficient communication, problem solving, and learning," *protocols* help create a working environment that facilitates clear expectations and shared understanding. These guidelines can cover topics ranging from how teams will conduct meetings and make decisions to how they will communicate information and resolve conflicts.

Think of protocols as recipes for positive interactions. Just as a recipe provides cooks with a set of instructions and guidelines to create a specific dish, a protocol offers teams a set of guidelines to consistently achieve a particular outcome. Over time, teams build a collection of protocols in much the same way that a cook builds a collection of recipes. And like cooks with recipes, teams will follow protocols closely at first, customize them over time based on their preferences, and update them to ensure that they remain current and fresh.

Figure 1.1.2 is an example of a protocol that a team could use to revisit their norms with one another.

Context: Norms are statements of our needs. When our needs aren't being met, our meetings will feel frustrating to us. When meetings are not productive, it is most often a result of norms that are in need of revision. It is important to periodically re-examine our norms to ensure that they continue to serve us well.

Frequency: We will work through this protocol at the beginning of each new quarter.

Process: The team follows these steps.

1. The team encourager reminds the team that they created norms to honor one another and then reads their current list of norms to the group.

2. The team encourager asks, "Based on our current list of norms, what kinds of behaviors does our team value?"

   - Members restate essential behaviors and traits that are valued by the group. The following are sample responses.
     - "We value hearing from all members of our group."
     - "We value being fully present while we are working together."

3. The team encourager asks, "From your perspective, which norm have we, as a team, lived well?"

   - Members share examples of norms that they believe are being honored.

   - As you listen to each other's responses, ask questions that help you understand one another's perspectives.

   - If disagreement arises, the team encourager asks for evidence, perhaps in the following ways.
     - "Can you give me an example of when you have seen that norm in action on our team?"
     - "Can you remember a time when that norm wasn't honored on our team?"

4. The team encourager asks, "From your perspective, what changes do we need to make to our norms to ensure that everyone's needs are met in our meetings?"

- Participants can consider starting a response with "What if we tried . . . ?" and then proposing a revision to one existing norm.
- Remember that norms are specific actions, not general statements of hoped-for behaviors.
- As you listen to responses, ask questions that help you understand one another's perspectives.

Next Steps: The team encourager thanks the group for their willingness to think alongside one another, summarizes the conversation, and volunteers to use the information to revise the team's norms. The team reviews the revised norms at the beginning of the next meeting.

FIGURE 1.1.2: Tool: Protocol for reviewing team norms.

Visit go.SolutionTree.com/PLCbooks for a free reproducible version of this figure.

When teachers new to collaboration look at their first protocols, they wonder why they need such explicit directions. Having clear guidelines to structure common collaborative conversations offers four main benefits to highly effective teams.

1. **Standardization:** Protocols detail a set of procedures for common tasks and situations, ensuring that all team members are on the same page and that activities are carried out consistently.

2. **Efficiency:** By providing clear guidelines, protocols reduce the need for decision making on routine matters, allowing team members to focus their energies on more important issues.

3. **Clarity:** Protocols clarify roles, responsibilities, and expectations, reducing confusion and potential conflicts among team members.

4. **Equity:** Protocols encourage active listening and reflection, ensuring that every voice within the group—not just those of assertive members—is both acknowledged and respected.

While there are no hard-and-fast rules for writing protocols, we suggest the following process.

1. **Define the purpose:** Begin by identifying the need for the protocol. Discuss what you hope to achieve or improve through this protocol, such as streamlining communication, decision-making processes, or conflict resolution.

2. **Review sample protocols:** Use protocols like those found in this book, in the free tools of other books found on Solution Tree's website (https://go.solutiontree.com), or in the open-access collection on the National School Reform Faculty's website (https://nsrfharmony.org/protocols) to examine samples. Identify protocols with promise, and consider adapting them for your work.

3. **Draft the protocol:** Based on the discussions and reviews, draft an initial version of the protocol. Assign this task to one or two team members, or work on it together in a collaborative meeting. Ensure the draft includes clear steps, roles, responsibilities, and expectations rather than general suggestions.

4. **Monitor and review:** Set a timeline for reviewing the protocol's effectiveness. Monitor its implementation and gather feedback about its impact on team collaboration and productivity. What works in the protocol? What doesn't work? How has it impacted the interactions on your team?

And we *do* recommend that you write some of your protocols together rather than always using protocols written by others. Like all the work done by highly effective teams, writing protocols is a learning opportunity for *you*. As you think through the steps that you will take to make important decisions, you establish clarity of purpose with one another—and teams with clarity of purpose are always more effective. More importantly, when teams collaboratively develop their own protocols, teachers are more likely to see the importance of using structure to achieve team goals.

If you are interested in writing protocols together but aren't sure where to start, consider asking artificial intelligence (AI) chatbots like ChatGPT (https://chatgpt.com), Gemini (https://gemini.google.com), or Claude (https://claude.ai) to generate initial drafts your team can consider. AI chatbots are digital tools that can answer questions, generate ideas, and analyze information for users. For example, teams interested in using chatbots to develop protocols for common collaborative processes can try asking prompts like the following.

- Can you create a protocol that a team of K–12 teachers can use to review their norms to determine whether they are still working for the group? Include steps that remind the team to consider the needs of individual members when developing norms for their group. Also, include steps that encourage the team to reinforce their norms in positive ways rather than in ways that involve calling out members of the group.

- Can you create a protocol that a team of K–12 teachers can use to analyze data from a common formative assessment? Include steps that encourage the team to use data to identify students who need additional time and support for learning and that encourage the team to study the efficacy of their instructional strategies.

- Can you create a protocol that a team of K–12 teachers can use to review student work samples with one another? Include steps that encourage the team to look for evidence of mastery and of student misconceptions in the work samples they are examining. Finally, include steps that encourage the team to draw conclusions about their instruction from the evidence that they gather.

Did you notice how detailed each of those prompts is? That is an important strategy for using AI chatbots to support your team's learning. The more detailed your prompts, the more likely you are to receive responses that align with your needs. Write a good prompt for a protocol and you can count on receiving a thoughtful response that accelerates your thinking. Then, your team can review, revise, or refine that response until you have a protocol that you are ready to use to guide you through your most important conversations.

Tools and Resources for Highly Effective Teams

The following tools and resources will help you accomplish the work for this essential action.

- **"Tool: Developing Team Norms" (page 20):** We genuinely believe that it is impossible for a team to function at the highest levels without using norms correctly. Until a team establishes positive patterns of participation that honor the needs of individual members, meetings will feel like a frustrating waste of time. Use this tool to develop a set of norms that can help move your team forward.

- **"Tool: Developing Specific Actions to Address the Needs of Our Peers" (page 23):** The most common mistake that teams make when writing norms is generating general statements that leave room for individual interpretation. Norms like *be on time* and *be respectful* are ineffective because notions of punctuality and respect vary among individuals. Effective norms outline specific actions teams will take to address the common behaviors that interrupt productive work. Use this tool and its corresponding **"Sample: Developing Specific Actions to Address the Needs of Our Peers" (page 24)** to practice writing better norms.

- **"Tool: Establishing Team Roles" (page 26):** To ensure that collaborative meetings are productive, highly effective teams identify specific roles that individual members will fill for the group. Those roles are best chosen based on the personal and professional skill sets of each member. Use this tool to identify the right person to fill the roles that are essential to the success of collaborative teams.

- **Solution Tree's PLC tools (go.SolutionTree.com/PLCbooks):** A lesser-known fact about Solution Tree is that they make nearly every tool from every book they publish available for free download to registered users of their website. Why does that matter in the context of this book? After logging in, you can explore those tools to find samples of protocols your team can adapt to meet your own needs. There are entire collections of tools sorted by both topic and book on Solution Tree's website—so you can search through the content in texts on assessment, texts on professional learning communities, or texts on response to intervention (RTI) to find potential protocols for your team.

PART ONE
Common Foundation

Tool: Developing Team Norms

Step 1: Sharing Your Pet Peeves and Essential Traits

Instructions: In a team meeting, all members should share one pet peeve that they have while working in groups with others and one essential trait that others will notice while working in a group with them. Those peeves and traits should be recorded in the following chart by your team's notetaker. They will be used to develop norms in step 2.

Team Member	Pet Peeve	Essential Trait
Sample: Bill Ferriter	*Sample:* It drives me nuts when people are on their devices while we are engaged in important conversations.	*Sample:* I make decisions quickly and am almost always ready to move on. That can drive people who need more think time than me crazy.

Questions for Team Reflection

Do you notice any patterns in the behavior of other team members that are pet peeves for you? What are they and why do you think they bother you?

What patterns in your own behavior are likely to bother other members of your learning team? Why?

What are some common actions you will need to take to make sure that your meetings feel productive to all team members?

Step 2: Brainstorming Your Norms

Instructions: Now, brainstorm four to six norms that describe how your team will respond when working through common team processes. Remember that norms are explicit statements designed to address the peeves and traits that your team detailed in step 1. If followed, your norms should create a working environment that honors and respects the needs of the individual members of your learning team.

Common Team Behaviors and Processes Brainstorm a norm for each of the following common team behaviors and processes.	Sample Norm	Our Norm
Making Shared Decisions	We will use our fist-to-five rating scale to give everyone the opportunity to express their level of agreement with shared decisions.	

page 2 of 3

Handling Disagreements	We won't move forward with important decisions until everyone has had the chance to be heard and to offer alternatives to the ideas we are considering.	
Showing Respect to One Another	We will be active contributors in every meeting, adding thoughts, offering suggestions, and sharing our opinions.	
Structuring Our Meetings	We will have a clear agenda for every meeting, with no more than three items.	
Other: Use this space to create a norm for other common behaviors or processes that your team addresses on a regular basis.		

Questions for Reflection

Which of your team's norms will be the easiest for you to follow? Which will be hardest?

Based on your team's unique set of peeves and traits, which of your norms will be the most important to ensure that your collaborative work feels productive for everyone?

How will you hold each other accountable for adhering to your team's norms? How will you celebrate moments when members are following your team's norms?

Source: Ferriter, W. M. (2020). The big book of tools for collaborative teams in a PLC at Work. *Solution Tree Press. Adapted from Venables, D. R. (2011).* The practice of authentic PLCs: A guide to effective teacher teams. *Corwin Press.*

Tool: Developing Specific Actions to Address the Needs of Our Peers

Instructions: Working with your learning team, examine the statements listed in the first column of the following table. These statements outline ten of the most common behaviors that interrupt collaborative teams' productive work. Then, in the second column, craft a specific action that teams can implement to address each behavior. Use the following format to write your norms: "To ensure that *[insert desired pattern of participation]*, we will *[insert specific action]*."

Common Behaviors That Derail Collaborative Teams	Norm Designed to Address This Behavior (Written as a specific action statement)
Sample: *One person dominates the conversation.*	**Sample:** *To ensure everyone has an equal voice in our conversations, we will ask everyone to speak once before anyone speaks twice.*
People are distracted by their digital devices rather than tuned in to the team's ongoing conversations.	
Team meetings are unfocused.	
Team never gets anything done.	
There is a lot of complaining about problems and very little time spent finding solutions.	
Members come to meetings unprepared.	
Members show up to meetings late.	
Members engage in sidebar conversations.	
Members have negative attitudes about the team's collective work.	
Decisions are made before everyone has enough time to think about the options.	
Members don't share their thoughts during team meetings.	

Source: Ferriter, W. M., Mattos, M., & Meyer, R. J. (2025). The big book of tools for RTI at Work. Solution Tree Press.

Sample: Developing Specific Actions to Address the Needs of Our Peers

Instructions: Review the sample actions detailed in the second column of the following table. Compare them to the actions that your team generated while working together on the previous page. What do you like best about your own answers? What do you like best about the sample answers? Does your team need to borrow any norms from either of these two lists?

Common Behaviors That Derail Collaborative Teams	Norm Designed to Address This Behavior (Written as a specific action statement)
Sample: One person dominates the conversation.	*Sample: To ensure everyone has an equal voice in our conversations, we will ask everyone to speak once before anyone speaks twice.*
People are distracted by their digital devices rather than tuned in to the team's ongoing conversations.	To ensure everyone is tuned in to our team's conversations, we will turn our devices off or over unless we are working on a shared document together.
Team meetings are unfocused.	To ensure our work stays focused, our team's facilitator will share our agenda two days before our meetings, and we will assign a "team rounder" who will hold us accountable for sticking to it during our meeting.
Team never gets anything done.	To ensure we complete work together, we will set a timer whenever we are creating a shared product. When the timer goes off, our shared product is finished. Our timekeeper will remind us of the timer whenever we get bogged down in wordsmithing or conversations that seem to be going in circles.
There is a lot of complaining about problems and very little time spent finding solutions.	To ensure our work is focused on finding solutions, we will list all our concerns at the beginning of each meeting and generate "what if we tried" statements for each one. Example: Concern—We don't have enough time to collaborate. "What if we tried" statement—What if we tried collaborating around just one essential until we establish positive work routines?
Members come to meetings unprepared.	To ensure we all arrive with the materials we need to participate in our meetings, our team encourager will send a text message reminder on the morning of our meetings listing the items we need to bring with us.
Members show up to meetings late.	To ensure all members show up to our meetings on time, we will leave a ten-minute buffer at the beginning of our planning period to allow members to get any last-minute things finished before we start our work together. That way, unexpected changes to our personal schedules won't interfere with our collaborative work.
Members engage in sidebar conversations.	To ensure we can fully invest in thinking together, we will begin every meeting with a moment of sharing—each member can share one thought that is at the forefront of their minds and likely to prevent them from giving their complete attention during our shared conversations.

page 1 of 2

Members have negative attitudes about the team's collective work.	To ensure we all see the positives in the work we are doing together, we will add an "our latest win" item to every agenda when we celebrate something positive we have accomplished together.
Decisions are made before everyone has enough time to think about the options.	To ensure everyone has had enough time to process, we will never make important decisions in one meeting. Instead, we will talk through the decision together, table it, and finish the discussion at the beginning of the next meeting.
Members don't share their thoughts during team meetings.	To ensure everyone shares their thoughts about important decisions, we will create a Padlet (www.padlet.com) and ask members to share a post with their thoughts before our meetings begin. Then, our facilitator will summarize the ideas shared at the beginning of our team meetings.

Source: Ferriter, W. M., Mattos, M., & Meyer, R. J. (2025). The big book of tools for RTI at Work. *Solution Tree Press.*

PART ONE
Common Foundation

①

Tool: Establishing Team Roles

Instructions: Listed in the following template are five roles—(1) team leader, (2) challenger, (3) producer, (4) encourager, and (5) realist—that all collaborative teams need if they are going to be productive. Working together, record all members of your team who have the skills and dispositions to fill each role. That way, you can maximize your collaborative potential by ensuring that all members are doing work that matches both their personalities and their professional abilities. Remember that on small teams, some members may need to fill more than one role.

Name of Role	Description of Role	Skills Necessary for Filling Role	Members Suited for Filling Role
Team Leader	• Organizes agendas for weekly meetings • Addresses conflict between team members • Leads consensus-building conversations • Keeps the team focused on yearly goals	☐ Strong relationship builder ☐ Good sense of the over-all direction of both the team and the school ☐ Willingness to listen to all perspectives ☐ Commitment to seeing everyone move forward together	
Team Challenger	• Challenges the current practices of the learn-ing team • Contributes to or leads brainstorm-ing of new alterna-tives and approaches worth considering • Regularly asks, "What if we tried _____?" when the team is working to generate new ideas	☐ Strong professional knowledge base and learning network to draw ideas from ☐ Good sense of the professional strengths and weaknesses of the learning team ☐ Ability to look at data summarizing the team's current reality and offer logical suggestions for next steps	

The Handbook for Highly Effective Teams in a PLC at Work® © 2025 Solution Tree Press • SolutionTree.com
Visit **go.SolutionTree.com/PLCbooks** to download this free reproducible.

Team Producer	• Takes notes during meetings • Develops a logical system for organizing the team's shared documents • Produces first drafts of shared documents for the team's review • Finds ways to accurately communicate team decisions	☐ Skilled with all kinds of document creation: Google Docs, PowerPoints, PDFs, and so on ☐ Logical thinker with strong organizational skills ☐ Good at listening to and summarizing ideas generated in group conversations ☐ Able to participate in conversations and create content at the same time	
Team Encourager	• Provides words of encouragement and affirmation both during and beyond weekly meetings • Moves the team forward during moments of stagnation or apathy • Monitors the attitudes and workloads of individual members and provides support when necessary	☐ Generally optimistic; skilled at finding things worth celebrating regardless of the circumstance ☐ Strong relationships with—and genuine concern for—all members of the team ☐ Willingness to always find time to lend a hand when others need help	
Team Realist	• Evaluates team decisions against the current workload of the team • Questions team decisions that seem unrealistic or impossible to pull off • Gives voice to concerns that might otherwise go unspoken	☐ Ability to understand the work capacity of the learning team ☐ Strong sense of all the different projects and initiatives that the team is currently tackling ☐ Ability to express skepticism, concern, and doubt in a professional way	

The Handbook for Highly Effective Teams in a PLC at Work © 2025 Solution Tree Press • SolutionTree.com
Visit **go.SolutionTree.com/PLCbooks** to download this free reproducible.

Questions for Reflection

Are there any roles that your team will have no trouble filling? How will that help your team?

Are there any roles that will be difficult for your team to fill? How might that hurt your team?

Do you think that rotating team roles is important? Why or why not? How would rotating team roles help your team? How would rotating roles hurt your team?

Are there any roles that aren't listed here that you think your team will need in order to be successful? What are they? Why are those roles important for your team?

Source: Ferriter, W. M. (2020). The big book of tools for collaborative teams in a PLC at Work. Solution Tree Press.

We Have a Process for Addressing Moments When Personalities Interfere With the Team's Work

Simply putting people in groups does not ensure a productive, positive experience for participants. Most educators can remember a time when they worked in a group that was painfully inefficient and excruciatingly ineffective. But teams increase their likelihood of performing at high levels when they clarify their expectations of one another regarding procedures, responsibilities, and relationships.

—RICHARD DUFOUR, REBECCA DUFOUR, ROBERT EAKER, THOMAS W. MANY, MIKE MATTOS, AND ANTHONY MUHAMMAD

One of the consistent mistakes that schools make when trying to implement the PLC at Work process is rushing into the technical work of collaboration. "If we can get teams to identify essential standards and write common assessments for those essentials," the thinking goes, "we can ensure higher levels of learning for all students." While there is no doubt that collaborative teams of teachers working together to study their practice are the best way to improve outcomes for students (DuFour et al., 2024; Visible Learning Meta^X, 2023), those teams are effective only when they attend to the cultural elements that support the highest-functioning groups. To put it another way, *the technical work of collaborative teams is the easy part.* Teachers have done that technical work—identifying essentials, planning lessons, developing assessments, and delivering instruction—independently for generations. Your teachers did that work, and so did the teachers who taught your parents and your grandparents. What makes collaboration difficult is that *you must do it with other people*—and working with other people brings social challenges that can derail teamwork before it ever begins.

While teams begin building a strong cultural foundation for collaboration by writing norms, creating roles, and using protocols to guide their work—ideas detailed in action 1.1

(page 9)—highly effective teams must also develop a clear process for *addressing moments when personalities interfere with the work of the group*. Now, you may be thinking, "We've done personality-typing activities a thousand times. They never work." And you are right: Schools ask teachers to engage in personality-typing activities all the time. Odds are that if you have spent any time in education, you have completed the Myers–Briggs personality test, identified the True Color that represents you, found where you land on the personality compass, or discovered your Enneagram. And if you are a seasoned vet, odds are you have completed *all those tests* at some point or another. But here's the point: We aren't simply suggesting that you do another personality test. Instead, we are encouraging you and your team to have open, honest conversations about how personalities—the qualities that explain how you interact with others and respond to circumstances—can either move a group forward or hold a group back, and then use those conversations to intervene when a person's interactions are keeping your team from doing meaningful work together.

Why Highly Effective Teams Do This

In the spring of 2022, Deb Mashek, who researches the impact of collaboration in businesses, surveyed 1,100 full-time employees in the United States about the impact of collaborative relationships on their workplace productivity and satisfaction. Her findings probably won't surprise you: The quality of collaborative workplace relationships positively predicted job satisfaction—and yet over 70 percent of respondents reported being involved in at least one relationship that was "absolutely horrendous" (Mashek, 2022). Sounds familiar, doesn't it? When we work alongside people we enjoy and respect, we are more likely to embrace collaboration as a strategy for improving our professional practice. On the other hand, when we clash with colleagues we don't understand or appreciate, we wonder whether collaboration is even worth the time and energy we invest in it.

What may surprise you are the consequences of workplace conflict. As Mashek (2022) writes, "Having even one low-quality collaborative relationship may drive undesirable outcomes, including poor mental health that contributes to burnout, and job dissatisfaction that contributes to turnover." Still more surprising is how little professional development employees report receiving in how to develop positive workplace relationships. Thirty-one percent of respondents to her Workplace Collaboration Survey have never received any training in developing relationships with colleagues—and another 20 percent report receiving anywhere from a few minutes to an hour of training in this essential collaborative skill (Mashek, 2022).

Our argument is that the consequences of poor collaborative relationships in schools are too great to leave to chance. We must develop systems for better understanding the interactions that we have with our peers. Figure 1.2.1 offers a comparison of language between ineffective groups and highly effective teams around this topic.

One thing to notice about the differences in how ineffective groups and highly effective teams address the impact that personalities have on performance is that ineffective groups actively avoid conversations about interpersonal dynamics. There is a sense of resignation in ineffective groups, assuming that there is nothing they can do when individual members

The Language of Ineffective Groups	The Language of Highly Effective Teams
"Not another personality-typing activity. We did that last year."	"Let's take the time to talk about our collaborative strengths and weaknesses together. It will make us more productive in the long run."
"Everyone on our team gets along just fine except for Bill. He doesn't get along with anyone."	"Hey, Bill. You add tons of value to the work that we do together, but sometimes, your personality gets in the way of what we are trying to do. Can we give you an example?"
"One of our colleagues is hard to work with, but we're not going to say anything. There's no point. They aren't going to change anyway."	"Let's recognize that we are all hard to work with once in a while, and then come up with a safe way to call out one another when it happens."
"Remember: We don't have to like each other. We just have to work together."	"What really matters is that we recognize that we all move our group forward and we all hold our group back—and that's OK. If we understand and appreciate each other, it makes it easier to keep going when the going gets tough."

FIGURE 1.2.1: Language comparison.

derail the work of their team. Highly effective teams, on the other hand, acknowledge the challenges that personalities can bring to collaboration, but address those challenges with constructive feedback, mutual understanding, and proactive problem solving. As a result, all team members feel valued and supported.

How Highly Effective Teams Do This

One strategy for establishing a process to address moments when personalities interfere with the work of the group is to ask members of your collaborative team to think metaphorically, comparing the strengths and weaknesses of their personality to a tool found in a common toolbox (Holloway, Martin, & Shaddix, 2007). For example, members who take an assertive "act first, think later" approach to decision making might describe themselves as *hammers*, while detail-oriented colleagues who are more likely to "measure twice and cut once" might describe themselves as *rulers*.

As members share, remind them that everyone brings both strengths and weaknesses to collaborative teams and that every member needs to identify ways that they move collaborative work forward and hold collaborative work back. For example, people who are hammers are likely to do a lot of heavy lifting for teams, developing materials and moving ideas forward quickly—but because of their confidence in their ideas, they can also dominate conversations and make others who need time to process uncomfortable. And while rulers will always ensure that teams are doing the right work the first time around, their deliberate approach to action can make others impatient.

If a team stopped after having these initial conversations, their work would be no different from any other personality-typing activity teachers are used to completing. Members may have been open with one another about who they are and what they bring to the group, but there is a difference between *being open with one another* and *establishing a process* for addressing moments when personalities interfere with the group's work. After members identify the tools that best represent them, highly effective teams refer to those tools to check one another when their personalities interfere with the work. For example, a team could say, "Bill, you are being a hammer right now," when a colleague is taking over a conversation and preventing others from getting a word in. Doing so serves as an in-the-moment reminder to Bill that a part of how he interacts with others—which isn't a character flaw but instead a part of who he is as a person—is preventing the group from moving forward together. Bill can now more actively monitor his behavior and protect his relationship with his peers.

We have conducted this activity with hundreds of teams, and it is almost always productive—but if you are worried about starting this conversation with your peers or using personalities as a code to interrupt one another when behaviors are derailing the work of your team, consider the following recommendations.

- **Begin the conversation by thinking about others before thinking about yourself:** Questions like, "What tool best represents your significant other, your child, or your boss?" can sometimes be safer entry points to the conversation— particularly for teams with low levels of interpersonal trust.

- **Remember that tone matters:** Messages that address difficult topics like the personalities of our peers are better received and acted on when delivered without overt negativity. Addressing difficult topics with a critical tone can trigger defensiveness, undermining trust on the collaborative team (Lisitsa, 2024).

- **Model the behavior for others:** Calling out peers, or being called out by others, can feel intimidating. To make this practice more comfortable, openly invite your peers to point out moments when *your* actions may hinder group progress. This helps teachers practice observing behaviors and allows you to demonstrate the constructive responses to being called out that you hope to see as colleagues begin using this approach with one another.

- **Encourage teams to conduct this activity with students:** Most teachers instantly recognize the value in teaching students to recognize how their personalities affect the work they do in groups, and once teams use this task with students, it becomes natural to extend the concept to the work they do with one another.

Whatever you do, take personalities seriously. It is impossible to ensure higher levels of learning for students when we don't recognize the impact that our interactions have on our shared work together.

Tool for Highly Effective Teams

The following tool will help you accomplish the work for this essential action.

- **"Tool: Personality Typing" (page 34):** If you need more structure for your discussion on the impact personalities have on highly effective teams, ask teachers to complete this individual reflection about the strengths and weaknesses they bring to collaborative work before engaging the entire team in conversation with one another. This tool offers several sample answers as scaffolding for members. Remember, however, that teachers can pick any tool to represent them—not just tools on this sample list. We have heard teachers self-identify as everything from sandpaper to a plunger!

Tool: Personality Typing

Everyone has a unique personality that helps define who they are. Some people are easygoing, and some are intense! Everyone has individual personality strengths and challenges. Learning who you are and who the people you work with are can improve your teamwork.

What Tool Are You?

Follow these three steps.

1. To better understand the personalities of your peers, we are going to look for the similarities between people and tools. Start by finishing the following sentence.
If I were a tool, I would be a _____ because:

Examples follow.

If I were a tool, I would be a hammer because I tackle all kinds of difficult tasks—and I get my work done quickly.

If I were a tool, I would be a pencil because I like to dream up lots of neat new ideas that are worth pursuing.

If I were a tool, I would be a ruler because I like to work carefully and deliberately, and I always want to follow the directions.

2. Determine what strengths and weaknesses you bring to the team. Every member brings both. Spend a few minutes brainstorming the ways your personality could help your group move forward and could potentially hold it back.	
People who are _____ can move their group forward when they . . .	People who are _____ can hold their group back when they . . .

An example follows.

People who are hammers can move their group forward when they are always willing to tackle challenging tasks, and they get those tasks done quickly. Hammers are capable doers. To get our work done, we need doers.

People who are hammers can hold their group back when they are too assertive. Sometimes, hammers work so quickly that they lose patience with people who need time to process their thinking. Also, when a hammer makes a mistake, it is hard to fix. Their errors can be more permanent and painful than the errors made by people with other personalities.

The Handbook for Highly Effective Teams in a PLC at Work® © 2025 Solution Tree Press • SolutionTree.com
Visit **go.SolutionTree.com/PLCbooks** to download this free reproducible.

3. Now that you have a better idea of how your personality will influence the members of your collaborative group, reflect on how the personalities of other members of your collaborative group will influence you.

Questions	Your Response
What about your own personality will you have to keep in mind when working with others to make sure that your group is successful?	
Which tool makes you the most uncomfortable when you are working in a group? What is it about others' traits that you struggle with? What is it about their traits that you can admire?	
What do you notice about the balance of personalities in your group? Does the team have a variety of strengths and challenges, or do most people have the same strengths and challenges? How will this balance help and harm your team?	
What type of personality is your collaborative group currently missing? How will this impact your work together?	
If you could create the perfect collaborative group, what would it look like? What personalities would you require to have a perfect group? What personalities could you live without?	

Remember the following important points as you do this work.

- **There are no such things as "good" and "bad" personality types:** Everyone brings strengths to collaborative groups, and everyone brings weaknesses to collaborative groups. The key is to always see the value that people who work differently bring to your team.

- **You can't change someone's personality:** For better or worse, people are who they are. That means you aren't going to change anyone's personality to make them "better" to work with. Instead, you need to understand the personalities of the people you are working with and recognize that the traits that frustrate you about other people are just part of who they are.

- **You frustrate others, too:** Here's an uncomfortable truth—you are probably frustrating someone else in your collaborative group. That's because we all work differently. So, keep your weaknesses in mind, and be on the lookout for moments when your weaknesses are getting in the way of other people's learning in your collaborative group. If we are all honest about how our behaviors can hold back our team, we will start to be more tolerant of the peers we struggle to work with.

Tool Types: Sample Answers

The following are sample strengths and weaknesses for each tool type.

Tool	Strengths	Weaknesses
Saw	Cuts away extra ideas Cuts to the main point quickly Divides big tasks into manageable pieces Can find small points hidden in bigger ideas Doesn't waste time	Can be rough around the edges Can sometimes work too fast Can sometimes cut the wrong stuff Can't fix their mistakes If not careful, can sometimes hurt people's feelings
Drill	Breaks through barriers Speeds up group work Makes the most of group efforts; knows a little work goes a long way Targets very specific ideas accurately and carefully Can look past the surface and get to the hidden ideas underneath	Can be a little bit old-fashioned Is not always the coolest tool in the box Can't fix their mistakes If not careful, can sometimes hurt people's feelings Prefers to keep things simple
Wrench	Tightens up loose parts Brings people together Connects the separate parts Strengthens weak parts and helps repair broken parts	Can only work on one type of part Is very rigid and hard, not flexible at all Struggles with doing careful or delicate work Doesn't like to undo their work Can sometimes rub other pieces the wrong way
Pencil	Is creative Can do very careful work if sharpened Is a common tool that everyone enjoys and knows how to use Has an eraser—is willing to start over again Can be used to communicate Is good at many tasks	Can break easily Doesn't necessarily make bold decisions Is somewhat ordinary—doesn't always see exciting new opportunities Can get lost easily
Hammer	Is a bold tool Can do the difficult work Can get to the bottom of things quickly Can fix some of their mistakes Brings the point home Is probably the most frequently used tool when you're building something	Can do a lot of damage if they're not careful Can break things easily Sometimes does damage that can't be fixed Is not particularly good at doing careful work

Screwdriver	Is a persistent tool; doesn't stop working until the job is done	Is a slow tool; takes awhile to get jobs done
	Stays focused on one task at a time	Is a somewhat old-fashioned tool; is not necessarily interested in newer ways of doing things
	Keeps working even when they meet resistance	Can only do one task at a time
	Joins other things together	
Ruler	Is a precise tool	Is a slow tool that wants to work carefully
	Can be used to measure things exactly	Struggles to be creative; is not designed to make new things
	Tends to follow rules	Instead is designed to see how new things measure up against expectations
	Is a smart tool; does the thinking for projects	
	Measures how well you are meeting your project goals	

Source: Adapted from Holloway, M. E., Martin, J., & Shaddix, L. (2007, July). Under construction: Building communities from the ground up *[Presentation]. National Staff Development Council Third Annual Summer Conference for Teacher Leaders and the Administrators Who Support Them.*

We Use SMART Goals to Drive Our Work

We have found that the best way to help people throughout a school district truly focus on results is to insist that every collaborative team establish SMART goals that align with school and district goals.

—RICHARD DUFOUR, REBECCA DUFOUR, ROBERT EAKER, THOMAS W. MANY, MIKE MATTOS, AND ANTHONY MUHAMMAD

Please reread the epigraph. It's a powerful statement, isn't it? The original architects of the PLC at Work process make it clear: If you want to successfully focus on results in a school or district, every collaborative team must write SMART goals. For school leaders, that's probably no surprise. After all, using SMART goals to drive change has been a cornerstone of school-improvement efforts for years. But for classroom teachers? Let's be honest. This recommendation might just be met with *another* collective groan.

Why do teachers groan about a strategy that the strongest voices in the school change movement insist is essential? The answer is simple: Like the training teams receive around norms, roles, protocols, and the study of personalities, teams' professional development in what SMART goals are and why they are important is rarely effective. The result: While many teams are already writing SMART goals, those goals have been awkward, unrealistic, task oriented, or vague for so long that they have little real impact on the work of the team. How many of the following examples sound familiar to you?

- By the end of the second semester, 80 percent of students will demonstrate at least a 5 percent increase in reading comprehension scores on the STAR Reading Assessment compared to their fall baseline.

- By the end of the quarter, 75 percent of students will achieve proficiency on at least 80 percent of the grade-level mathematics standards as measured by unit assessments and classroom exit tickets.

- By June, 80 percent of students who began the year reading below grade level will demonstrate at least one year of growth on the DIBELS Benchmark Assessment.

- By December, we will hold four collaborative team meetings focused on analyzing student performance data from common assessments, with meeting notes documenting action plans for addressing learning gaps.
- By the end of the semester, the percentage of students actively participating in Socratic seminars will move from 60 percent to 70 percent as measured by weekly observation checklists.

Write enough goals that are difficult to understand, difficult to achieve, or difficult to invest in, and you will doubt their overall value, too.

Dig into *Learning by Doing* (DuFour et al., 2024)—the core text of the PLC at Work process—however, and you will learn that a team is a "group of people working *interdependently* to achieve a *common goal* for which members are *mutually accountable*" (p. 50). That means it is the team's job *by definition* to collaborate toward achieving goals. When teams collaborate to create goals, they foster ownership and collective responsibility, ensuring that every team member feels invested in the work and understands their role in moving the group forward. They also build a shared understanding of and accountability for the students they serve and the actions necessary to help those students learn at the highest levels. And the good news is that the number of goals you set is not what determines how successful you will be. In fact, schools that set fewer goals often see greater success because they stay focused and can clearly communicate their priorities to stakeholders (Conzemius & O'Neill, 2014).

So, what does that mean for you? It means that understanding why SMART goals matter and how to use them to move student learning forward really is an essential action of highly effective teams.

Why Highly Effective Teams Do This

As we dive deeper into the why of goal creation, it is important to be clear about what we mean by goals. *Goals* are the outcomes or objectives that individuals or teams work to achieve in a set time frame. In schools, SMART goals play a crucial role for several reasons.

- **Clarity and focus:** SMART goals help educators and administrators define clear objectives and priorities, ensuring everyone is aligned on what needs to be achieved.
- **Measurable progress:** SMART goals allow teams to track and evaluate progress, making data-driven decisions easier and more effective.
- **Alignment with the mission and vision:** When aligned with the school or district's mission and vision, SMART goals ensure every team's efforts contribute to shared objectives.
- **Accountability:** SMART goals create a sense of accountability among team members, driving collective action toward achieving established targets.
- **Continuous improvement focus:** SMART goals promote reflection and adaptability in teachers and teams, two professional traits that are essential for supporting ongoing growth in student outcomes.

For successful teams, goals act as a compass, providing direction, focus, and motivation to guide their actions and decisions. This targeted direction is especially important for teams new to collaboration, who sometimes struggle to see meaningful changes in student outcomes no matter how many times they meet. More often than not, the problem isn't the collaboration itself. Instead, it is a lack of focus in the team's work. Writing SMART goals helps a team ensure that its efforts are targeted and intentional. When teams clearly define what they want to achieve and how they will measure success, they shift from simply meeting together to producing measurable results for students. Simply put, SMART goals are what turn collaboration into a results-driven process.

SMART goals, which were first proposed by corporate planner George T. Doran (1981) in a paper titled "There's a S.M.A.R.T. Way to Write Management's Goals and Objectives," have become a widely accepted format for writing goals both in and beyond education. Here is a breakdown of each component of a SMART goal (Conzemius & O'Neill, 2014).

- **Strategic and specific:** Goals should be well defined and focused, clearly stating what needs to be accomplished.

- **Measurable:** Goals should include criteria for measuring progress and determining when the goal has been achieved.

- **Attainable:** Goals should be realistic and doable with the available resources and constraints.

- **Results oriented:** Goals should be focused on student learning.

- **Time bound:** Goals should have a defined time frame or deadline for completion, providing a sense of urgency and accountability.

Educators and authors Sharon V. Kramer and Sarah Schuhl (2023) take SMART goals even further by distinguishing between two types.

1. **Program goals:** Program goals are designed to help teams improve *learning outcomes within a specific grade level or course over time*. For instance, an eighth-grade English language arts team might set a SMART program goal focused on increasing their current students' proficiency on the end-of-year state assessment, using data from the previous year's eighth graders as a baseline. These goals can strengthen teachers' collective efficacy by demonstrating their ability to identify instructional practices that advance student learning.

2. **Cohort goals:** Cohort goals, on the other hand, are designed to address *the specific needs of the students you are teaching right now*. For example, a fourth-grade team might review the third-grade state assessment results for their incoming students. Using those data, they can craft a SMART cohort goal, setting clear targets for how their current fourth graders will perform on this year's end-of-year state assessment. Cohort goals build a shared commitment to helping every student in a unique group of learners achieve success.

Taken together, program and cohort goals can help a collaborative team focus on both long-term systemic improvements to instruction and immediate outcomes for current students. This dual focus allows teams to work more effectively toward meaningful, data-driven achievements. Figure 1.3.1 offers a comparison of language between ineffective groups and highly effective teams around this topic.

The Language of Ineffective Groups	The Language of Highly Effective Teams
"Let's list some tasks and call it our SMART goal."	"Let's ensure our SMART goal is specific enough to clearly define what we are hoping to achieve and how we will know if we have met our goal."
"Our SMART goal doesn't need to be measurable; as long as we think we're making progress, it's fine."	"Measurability is key. Tracking our SMART goal allows us to evaluate progress and celebrate when we succeed."
"Let's make our SMART goal really vague so that it's open to interpretation."	"Our SMART goal should be results oriented, focusing on improving student learning and supporting our team's priorities. Otherwise, what's the point of working on it together?"
"Why bother setting a deadline for our SMART goal? We'll get to it when we get to it."	"Setting a deadline helps us stay focused and ensures we hold ourselves accountable for reaching our SMART goal."

FIGURE 1.3.1: Language comparison.

One of the key differences to notice between the language of ineffective groups and the language of highly effective teams is the purpose behind their goals. Ineffective groups focus on creating goals that are easy to implement and hard to monitor, prioritizing compliance over impact. For them, SMART goals are a task to complete because they are required, not a tool that guides their ongoing teamwork and that drives student learning forward. Highly effective teams, however, understand that SMART goals can bring structure to their work. This shift—from seeing SMART goals as a requirement to recognizing them as an essential strategy for keeping collaborative efforts aligned and effective—is a clear indicator that a group is becoming a team.

How Highly Effective Teams Do This

Our first recommendation for writing effective SMART goals is a *don't*: Don't write goals that emphasize task completion over improvement in student achievement. For example, a goal like, *By the end of the year, we will integrate three new technology tools (Kahoot!, Google Slides, and Flip) into our lesson plans, with at least one tool used each month to increase student engagement*, might make teams feel productive because they are completing tasks together, but it misses the real priority: making measurable progress in helping more students learn at high levels.

Instead, develop results-oriented goals that are centered on helping students achieve specific outcomes tied to your essential standards. For example, imagine that you are on a kindergarten team that wants to increase the percentage of students in your building who are reading on grade level. Knowing that understanding digraphs (the combinations of letters that work together to make common sounds) is essential to developing young readers, you might write a SMART goal that reads like this.

> *By the end of the school year, 80 percent of kindergarten students will accurately identify and produce the sounds of the digraphs* sh, ch, th, *and* wh *in isolation and within simple words as measured by classroom observation checklists conducted during the final quarter.*

Your next step is to identify the actions that you will take as a team to help students reach that goal. It might look like this.

> *To achieve this, we will do the following.*
>
> - ***Deliver a phonics lesson of the week that targets an essential digraph:*** *Last year, we weren't as consistent or intentional as we could have been in teaching digraphs. By being more deliberate and explicit in our instruction, we can help our students build a stronger foundation in decoding skills.*
>
> - ***Use more small-group practice sessions:*** *Last year, we primarily taught digraphs in whole-class lessons. This year, small-group practice sessions will help us in two ways—(1) We will get a clearer picture of what each student can do, and (2) we will be able to provide immediate corrections when students make errors with the digraphs we are studying.*
>
> - ***Research and implement one new instructional strategy per month:*** *Last year, we ran out of ways to teach digraphs before every student had mastered digraphs. To tackle this, we will dedicate time to identifying and implementing new strategies for teaching digraphs. This will ensure we have a variety of approaches to draw from if students continue to struggle.*

Notice a few important things in this example. First, the most effective SMART goals for collaborative teams focus on specific essentials, like mastering digraphs, rather than broad topics, like improving schoolwide reading results. Here's why: Broad goals can be so general that they don't lead teams to take specific actions. Think about improving reading results, for instance. Where would a team begin? There are so many possible areas to focus on and actions to take that the sheer number of options can become a barrier or an excuse to starting. For teams to fully engage with a goal, they need to believe both that it is important and that they can succeed. Focusing SMART goals on specific grade-level or course essentials helps create that belief by giving teams a clear path forward.

That doesn't mean a school or district shouldn't have broader goals like improving reading results, mathematics results, or graduation rates. In fact, those school- and district-level goals should establish a framework for each collaborative team when writing their own SMART goals. When the goals written by collaborative teams align with a school or district's broader goals, it ensures that each team's work contributes to *a systemwide effort* to support higher levels of learning.

It is also essential that your team identify a small set of actions you will take to achieve that result. These actions should be shaped by your current context: Where are the gaps in your professional expertise? What do your data reveal about your students' needs and the effectiveness of your current instruction? Why do you think your students struggled to master the essential skill or concept tied to your SMART goal? How will school priorities influence your work?

Detailing specific actions is what turns a goal into an actionable plan. By breaking a SMART goal into targeted steps, teams can prioritize their efforts, discuss progress, and address challenges with greater precision. Specific actions ensure that every meeting has purpose and that every conversation is tied to moving student learning forward. Specific actions also create accountability among team members, ensuring that the work is both shared and aligned with the team's overall goal. This focus turns collaboration into a strategic process.

Here are a few final reminders about writing SMART goals for your collaborative team.

- **Document your goals:** Highly effective teams document their SMART goals in formal templates that they use to maintain clarity, alignment, and accountability. It is, however, important to remember that documentation isn't about compliance. You are not creating a record of your work to prove to administrators that you are doing what they asked you to do. Instead, you are creating a record of your work for your team—a tool you can review and reference to track progress toward your goals.

- **Assign responsibility for leading individual actions:** One common mistake ineffective groups make when developing SMART goals is failing to assign responsibility for individual actions. They often think, "Why do we need someone in charge? Can't we all just work on these actions together?" Highly effective teams know that when everyone is in charge, no one is. Assigning specific responsibilities ensures that work gets done and builds commitment among team members. When responsibilities are explicitly defined, team members are more likely to remain focused and committed to achieving the goals, leading to greater success (Dagher, 2024).

- **Monitor progress and celebrate achievements:** Monitoring progress toward SMART goals is essential for keeping teams motivated. Using common formative assessments to track short-term progress helps teams see whether they are on track or need to adjust their strategies. Just as important, using common formative assessments to track short-term progress shows teams that their efforts are paying off, reinforcing their belief in the work they are doing. Celebrating milestones, no matter how small, boosts morale and builds collective efficacy (Chiprany & Page, 2025).

Writing SMART goals is one of the most essential actions that collaborative teams can take. The clarity and accountability that come from working toward a goal is part of what helps move student learning forward. Collaboration can only deliver meaningful results for students when teams fully embrace this process.

Tools and Resources for Highly Effective Teams

The following tools and resources will help you accomplish the work for this essential action.

- **"Tool: SMART Goal Template" (page 46):** This template is a tool your team can use to document your SMART goals, helping you develop a shared plan for your work that you can reference throughout the year to track progress, adjust strategies, and stay focused on priorities. Remember that this documentation isn't about compliance. Instead, it is about giving your team a shared direction, which increases your chances of achieving meaningful results for students.

- **"Sample: Elementary SMART Goal Template" (page 47):** This sample demonstrates how an elementary team can use the "SMART Goal Template" to document their work. One key feature to notice is the inclusion of a list of essential standards that students will need to master to achieve the team's goal. By identifying these standards up front, the team establishes a clear direction to guide their next steps. This approach ensures that their everyday actions are directly tied to helping students master critical content, making their planning more targeted and effective.

- ***Celebrating in a PLC at Work: A Leader's Guide to Building Collective Efficacy and High-Performing Collaborative Teams*** **(Chiprany & Page, 2025):** This book is a valuable resource for teams looking to build stronger collaboration through meaningful celebrations. The authors offer practical ideas for boosting morale and keeping teams motivated. Remember—Celebrations aren't just about making teams feel good. Instead, they are a powerful way to remind teams that *they have been successful*. This guide provides strategies to make celebration an intentional part of your team's work.

Tool: SMART Goal Template

SMART Goal Worksheet

School:

Team Name: Team Leader:

Team Members:

District Goals:

School Goals:

Team SMART Goal	Strategies and Action Steps	Who Is Responsible	Target Date or Timeline	Evidence of Effectiveness

Source: DuFour, R., DuFour, R., Eaker, R., Many, T. W., Mattos, M., & Muhammad, A. (2024). Learning by doing: A handbook for Professional Learning Communities at Work (4th ed.). Solution Tree Press.

Sample: Elementary SMART Goal Template

SMART Goal: English Language Arts

Grade: Fourth   **Date:** August 16   **Team Members:** Smith, Flowers, Bush

School Goal: By the end of the school year, 100% of students will achieve a growth and achievement percentile of 65 or higher, as measured by the end-of-year standardized assessment, indicating both high growth and high achievement for each student.

During the winter administration of MAP Growth, students will achieve a minimum RIT score of 204 or higher in reading to align with our school goal of increasing each student's achievement and growth percentile to 65 or higher, indicating high growth and high achievement for each student.

Essential Standards:

RL.4.1: Refer to details and examples in a text when explaining what the text says explicitly and when drawing inferences from the text.

RL.4.2: Determine a theme of a story, drama, or poem from details in the text; summarize the text.

RI.4.2: Determine the main idea of a text and explain how it is supported by key details; summarize the text.

L.4.4: Determine or clarify the meaning of unknown and multiple-meaning words and phrases.

W.4.4: Produce clear and coherent writing in which the development and organization are appropriate to task, purpose, and audience.

Plan of Action (Short- and Long-Term Goals)

Team SMART Goal	Strategies and Action Steps	Who Is Responsible	Target Date or Timeline	Evidence of Effectiveness
Our Current Reality: Looking at i-Ready benchmark scores, our students are currently performing well below grade level in reading. • Smith—82% of students are below grade level. • Flowers—100% are below grade level. • Bush—30% are below grade level. **Our Goal:** By the winter administration of MAP Growth, 100% of students will achieve a minimum RIT score of 204 or higher in reading, as measured by the MAP Growth assessment.	We will focus on preteaching prerequisite skills and addressing the knowledge gaps students have carried over from previous years during our schoolwide intervention period.	Smith	Yearlong	We will reassess student mastery of the prerequisite skills that we preteach. Students must score 80% or higher on these assessments to reach mastery.
	We will develop small-group lessons that focus on both guided reading that meets students where they are and strategy groups that meet the Lexile grade-level band needed to reach achievement goals.	Flowers	Yearlong	Teacher observation and assessment of reading and strategy levels through running records
	We will implement weekly vocabulary lessons with an acquisition goal of four terms per week.	Bush	Yearlong	Biweekly "show what you know" vocabulary quizzes with scores of 80% or higher for understanding and application of new terms

Source for standard: National Governors Association Center for Best Practices [NGA] & Council of Chief State School Officers [CCSSO]. (2010a). Common Core State Standards for English language arts and literacy in history/social studies, science, and technical subjects. Authors. Accessed at https://corestandards.org/wp-content/uploads/2023/09/ELA_Standards1.pdf on September 29, 2024.

Source: DuFour, R., DuFour, R., Eaker, R., Many, T. W., Mattos, M., & Muhammad, A. (2024). Learning by doing: A handbook for Professional Learning Communities at Work (4th ed.). Solution Tree Press. Adapted from Bailey, K., & Jakicic, C. (2023). Common formative assessment: A toolkit for Professional Learning Communities at Work (2nd ed.). Solution Tree Press.

PART ONE
Common Foundation

We Regularly Evaluate Our Team's Effectiveness

We remain convinced . . . that when educators learn to clarify their priorities, to assess the current reality of their situation, to work together, and to build continuous improvement into the very fabric of their collective work, they create conditions for the ongoing learning and self-efficacy essential to solving whatever problems they confront.

—RICHARD DUFOUR, REBECCA DUFOUR, ROBERT EAKER, THOMAS W. MANY, MIKE MATTOS, AND ANTHONY MUHAMMAD

When preparing for flights, airline pilots invest tons of time, energy, and effort into planning the coordinates for the best route to their final destination. These routes are chosen based on the shared knowledge of their airline, collected and organized over time; the pilot's individual experience with similar flights; and anticipated circumstances: "Where are we trying to go? Has anyone else taken this trip recently? What conditions do we expect to encounter along the way? What strategies will we use to address those conditions safely and effectively?"

While this initial route planning is an essential first step in getting a plane off the ground, it isn't the *only* planning that pilots engage in; they constantly check their progress during a flight, assessing whether their initial plans are appropriate given what they are experiencing moment by moment throughout their journey (Page, 2019). They check their fuel load against the weather conditions, knowing that changes in headwinds, tailwinds, or their altitude can affect aircraft efficiency; they check their route, looking for the best destinations for diversions in case of mechanical failures or medical emergencies; and on longer flights, they check the crew's mental health, rest levels, and operational readiness, knowing that mental or physical exhaustion can lead to disaster (Page, 2019). Perhaps most importantly, they check to ensure that their plane remains on their original course—or that they find efficient paths around unexpected changes in weather systems or flight traffic—knowing that on long flights, even small deviations from their initial plans can cause them to miss their final destinations completely if left uncorrected (Cutler, 2017).

Can you see how this applies to the work of highly effective teacher teams? Each school year is like the start of a new long-distance flight, and odds are that you will go into the year with some idea of how best to get from point A to point B. Based on your shared knowledge, your individual experience, and the circumstances you expect to face over the course of the year, you build an initial plan for teaching your students. You plot what you will teach unit by unit through your curriculum. You refer to resources like your standards and curriculum guides. You consult with others who have led the same trips before. But like any trip, school years often come with predictable challenges or unforeseen obstacles that can throw both you and your students far off course if they go unaddressed.

Because of this, a final foundational habit of highly effective teams is to frequently evaluate their collective effectiveness, validating their initial assumptions and shared efforts to move learning forward and making immediate course corrections in response to any current circumstances that might derail their journey. Building "continuous improvement into the very fabric of their collective work," a trait of highly effective teams highlighted in the epigraph at the start of this chapter, depends on a commitment to continuously monitoring where we are against our shared vision for where we want to go next (DuFour et al., 2024, p. 307).

Why Highly Effective Teams Do This

There are often misunderstandings regarding just what a *professional learning community* is. Some educators mistake it for a professional *paperwork* community, spending their time completing required forms, crossing off predetermined tasks from checklists, and fulfilling district or school mandates without carefully considering how those forms, tasks, and mandates are moving learning forward. Others mistake it for a professional "this is how we've *always* done it" or "this is how we're *willing* to do it" community, picking and choosing actions to pursue that will cause the least amount of change to their existing practices or challenge to their existing beliefs.

A reminder of the real *work* of educators in a professional learning community is built right into the term: *professional* educators who are *learning* together in a school *community*. Tom Schimmer (2024), internationally recognized author and consultant, goes so far as to argue that it might be more accurate to think of PLCs as CPLs: communities of professionals learning together. For teams to become a community of professionals learning together, developing an initial plan to guide their work and then frequently reflecting on and monitoring their progress against that plan must become a core collaborative behavior. While ineffective groups see reflection as "one more thing we have to do," highly effective teams embrace reflection as an essential action to drive continued growth, and they build time into their collaborative meetings to engage in this powerful practice. Figure 1.4.1 offers a comparison of language between ineffective groups and highly effective teams around this topic.

Notice the language of ineffective groups seems to "embrace victimhood" by insisting "this won't work here" or accepting the "status quo of your current situation as unchangeable" (Covey, 2023, p. 220). Conversely, the language of highly effective teams is proactive, focusing on reflection, growth, and learning together.

The Language of Ineffective Groups	The Language of Highly Effective Teams
"We have too much to do right now. We don't have time to reflect and evaluate our progress as a team."	"We recognize the importance of reviewing where we've been together. It helps us adjust and get where we want to go."
"Some team members are feeling overwhelmed, and taking time to reflect as a team will just add another thing to their plates."	"We've built opportunities for reflection and evaluation into our team's collaborative time at least three times per year."
"We think somebody who's not part of our team would be better at telling us what we need to do."	"Reflection is like good assessment: It means more when it is done by the learner. It's not about being assessed by others. It's about assessing ourselves to be sure we are still on the right track."
"We don't need a formal tool to help us evaluate our effectiveness; we prefer to have informal conversations."	"Our team understands the need for a consistent evaluation tool that we can compare our progress against."

FIGURE 1.4.1: Language comparison.

How Highly Effective Teams Do This

As teams integrate the essential actions from this book into their collaborative work, regularly setting aside time for reflection becomes an essential part of growing and learning together. At a minimum, highly effective teams engage in intentional reflection three times per year. The frequency for reflection, however, can change depending on the predictability of the tasks that teams are tackling together and their professional expertise at completing those tasks. Here are a few examples of how the frequency of team reflection might vary.

- A team that is unpacking essential standards they have taught for years may not need to reflect regularly on whether their processes for unpacking worked. However, when state or provincial standards are rewritten and the same team is unpacking new standards for the first time, they might pause more frequently to consider whether their current processes are helping them better understand the new standards they are about to teach.

- A team that has worked together for years may not need to reflect regularly on whether their existing norms are ensuring that the needs of individual members are being honored in their weekly meetings. However, when the team adds a new member, they might need to pause more frequently to determine whether their common participation patterns are moving them forward or holding them back.

- A team that has served an unchanging student population for years may not need to reflect on the effectiveness of the proven, high-impact instructional strategies they are using to teach essential grade-level standards. However, if their school's student population becomes more academically, economically, or culturally diverse over time, they may need to pause more frequently to determine whether the practices that they believe in are moving learners with different needs forward.

Notice in these samples that when teams evaluate their collective effectiveness, they are as systematic about reflecting on their *cultural* practices (ensuring that individual member needs are met, that they resolve conflict productively, and that they proactively seek out individual member perspectives) as they are about reflecting on their *technical* processes (unpacking essential standards, designing instruction, and writing assessments). Evaluating both the cultural and technical dimensions of their work enables teams to quickly adjust and overcome any obstacle together.

Highly effective teams also understand that general, ambiguous conversations do little to improve their work. Instead, effective teams identify and use a consistent tool against which they can measure their progress. While there is no right or wrong tool for a team to use to guide this reflection, there are criteria to consider when selecting a tool that will move your team forward.

- **Is the tool easy to use?** Like any practice embraced by collaborative teams, reflection must become a consistent part of the work you do with one another. Consistency for classroom teachers is almost always a function of sustainability. If a tool is easy to use, teams are more likely to use it regularly. Think about pilots performing preflight checks. Those checks are designed to be straightforward and efficient because they must be completed before every flight, no matter the circumstances. Similarly, a reflection tool for teachers should be simple enough to use during a single collaborative team meeting without requiring excessive time or effort.

- **Does the tool give you a point of comparison?** When evaluating our progress, knowing where we stand is valuable only if we have something to measure ourselves against. Pilots use flight plans to compare their current position to their intended destination. Similarly, collaborative teams need a clear expectation or standard to gauge their growth. A good reflection tool should provide criteria that teams can use as a point of comparison, helping them understand whether they are exceeding, meeting, or falling short of expectations. Without this frame of reference, it's impossible to determine whether progress has been made or to set meaningful goals for the future.

- **Does the tool help you take next steps?** When pilots evaluate their progress during a flight, they aren't simply collecting data for the sake of collecting data. Instead, they actively use that information to adjust their course and ensure they reach their destination. The same principle applies to collaborative teams. Evaluation isn't just about understanding where we currently stand. It's about using that understanding to identify actionable next steps that can move us forward. Reflection tools that fail to guide teams toward meaningful action provide little value in improving the work of collaborative teams.

Tools and Resources for Highly Effective Teams

The following tools and resources will help you accomplish the work for this essential action.

- **Continua for team development:** Some of the least commonly used resources in *Learning by Doing: A Handbook for Professional Learning Communities at Work,*

Fourth Edition (DuFour et al., 2024), are a series of continua describing the development of collaborative practices from initiating and implementing through developing and sustaining. These continua cover everything from developing a schoolwide culture to support higher levels of learning to hiring staff members who are well suited for the work in PLCs. There are several continua designed specifically to help teacher teams reflect on and evaluate their current work. Covering cultural topics like responding to conflict and developing norms, as well as covering technical topics like clarifying what every student must learn and turning data into information, these continua are useful for teams that already use *Learning by Doing* to guide their implementation of the PLC at Work process.

- **"Tool: Assessing Our Reality" (page 54):** Published in *Simplifying the Journey: Six Steps to Schoolwide Collaboration, Consistency, and Clarity in a PLC at Work* (Sonju, Powers, & Miller, 2024), this tool provides a framework of the work of highly effective teams and allows teams the opportunity to evaluate the current state of their team's practices. At the conclusion of each section, teams are provided space to identify strengths of the team to celebrate and to articulate an area of focus moving forward.

- **"Tool: Survey—The State of Your Learning Team" (page 57):** First published in *The Big Book of Tools for Collaborative Teams in a PLC at Work* (Ferriter, 2020), this survey asks respondents to evaluate both the personal dynamics and the task development on their current collaborative team. Prompts like, "Our learning team has a process for gathering honest and open input from all members when making key decisions," and "Our learning team analyzes learning results, looking for trends in both student and teacher performance," provide your team a way to compare your current work against the work of highly effective teams.

- **"Tool: Learning Team Quarterly Reflection" (page 60):** This simple tool was initially created to help teams reflect at the end of each quarter during the school year. It prompts members to consider four key questions: (1) What should we keep doing?, (2) What should we start doing?, (3) What should we stop doing?, and (4) What should we improve on? While it isn't designed to provide a comprehensive look at a team's work, its simplicity makes it easy to integrate into regular collaborative practices—encouraging consistent reflection among teachers.

- **"Tool: Critical Issues for Team Consideration—Highly Effective Team Actions" (page 62):** This tool provides teams an opportunity to reflect on their progress, celebrate strengths, and identify next steps worth taking. At the conclusion of each set of actions, teams use a portion of this tool to dialogue about their current practices, to identify strengths and areas of focus, and to identify next steps on their pathway to becoming a highly effective collaborative team.

Tool: Assessing Our Reality

Directions: Your honest evaluation is critical! Please thoughtfully discuss the reality of your team in each of the target practices and behaviors. Use the following scale to rate your team in each target area. At the conclusion of each section, identify areas to celebrate and areas for your team to focus on.

3—This is very true of us! This is embedded in our beliefs and actions.

2—This is true of us some of the time. We need to be more consistent with this.

1—This is not true of us. This is definitely something we can work on.

Rating	The Collaborative Team's Work
	Our team has identified shared norms that guide our collaborative teamwork and reviews the norms prior to each meeting.
	Our team consistently adheres to and honors our team norms and addresses violations in an immediate and respectful way.
	Our team respects and values the input of each team member as part of the team learning process.
	Our team collaboration is focused, productive, and a good use of our professional time.
	Our team uses our time to make decisions about learning with little conversational drift.
	Our team depends on the expertise of each member to ensure all students learn at high levels.

Celebrations:	Areas of Focus:

Rating	Essential Standards and Skills
	Our team has identified the essential standards or skills for each unit of instruction.
	Our team has identified critical academic vocabulary that is shared prior to instruction.
	Our team has defined mastery for each essential standard or skill and shared it with students.
	Our team has agreed on how to best pace the instruction of the essential standards or skills.
	Our team shares examples of *approaching mastery* and *mastery* student work with the class.

Celebrations:	Areas of Focus:

Rating	Team Formative Assessment or Learning From Data
	Our team utilizes a variety of quick, targeted collaborative formative assessments during the unit to determine each student's progress toward the essential standards and skills.
	Our team provides opportunities for students to self-assess their progress and learning.
	Our team uses team formative assessment data to identify which teaching strategies elicit the best results with students.
	Our team analyzes team formative assessment data to determine which students need extra time.

Celebrations:	Areas of Focus:

Rating	Extra Time and Support
	Our team uses the results from the team formative assessments to determine which students need extra time and support in a targeted skill.
	Our team commits to using days as needed during the unit of instruction to provide extra time and support for students.
	Our team reteaches students who have not yet met mastery with the most effective strategies as identified in the collaborative formative assessment data.
	Our team provides extra time and support for students who have mastered the essential standard through extended learning opportunities.

Celebrations:	Areas of Focus:

Rating	

Celebrations:	Areas of Focus:

Source: Sonju, B., Powers, M., & Miller, S. (2024). Simplifying the journey: Six steps to schoolwide collaboration, consistency, and clarity in a PLC at Work. *Solution Tree Press.*

Tool: Survey—The State of Your Learning Team

Instructions: First, please indicate with a checkmark the extent to which you agree with, disagree with, or feel neutral about each indicator in the following survey. Next, please indicate how ready your learning team is to tackle the tasks detailed in each indicator. Finally, answer the reflection questions found at the end of this template. This information will be used to plan customized next steps for each collaborative team in the building.

PART ONE
Common Foundation

Name of Learning Team:						
Personal Dynamics	**Disagree**	**Neutral**	**Agree**	**We Aren't Ready for This Yet**	**We Are Ready for This Now**	**We Are Already Doing This**
Our learning team has a well-developed agenda for every meeting that effectively documents our shared decisions.						
Our learning team has a process for gathering honest and open input from all members when making key decisions.						
Our learning team has clearly defined roles for participation in our meetings.						
Our learning team has a process for sharing the workload.						
Our learning team has a process for resolving conflicts.						
Our learning team has a process for giving and receiving critical feedback among team members.						
Our learning team has a common language to use when working through conflict.						
Our learning team has a process for holding team members accountable for making productive contributions.						
Our learning team has a process for determining when we have reached consensus.						
Our learning team has a process for bringing new and challenging ideas into our group.						

page 1 of 3

Collaborative Task Development	Disagree	Neutral	Agree	We Aren't Ready for This Yet	We Are Ready for This Now	We Are Already Doing This
Our learning team has a SMART (strategic and specific, measurable, attainable, results oriented, and time bound) goal that we set and are working toward together.						
Our learning team has identified essential outcomes for each of the units in the curriculum.						
Our learning team has developed common assessments designed to measure student progress toward mastering our essential outcomes.						
Our learning team has incorporated questions that require higher-level thinking into our common assessments.						
Our learning team uses open-ended assignments for some of our common assessments.						
Our learning team analyzes learning results, looking for trends in both student and teacher performance.						
Our learning team takes action based on the trends that we spot in student learning data.						
Our learning team has developed exemplars that illustrate what student mastery looks like on tasks that are evaluated subjectively.						
Our learning team has practiced grading subjective assignments together to ensure reliability in our scoring.						
Our learning team varies the pacing of our content to support the struggling students and to challenge the most accomplished pupils in our classrooms.						

The Handbook for Highly Effective Teams in a PLC at Work® © 2025 Solution Tree Press • SolutionTree.com
Visit **go.SolutionTree.com/PLCbooks** to download this free reproducible.

Questions for Reflection

Please describe your learning team's greatest success to date. What are you the proudest of about the work that you are doing together?

Please describe the stumbling block that is currently holding your learning team back. What could your group be doing better?

Please describe the practices that your learning team is currently the most comfortable with. What has your team already mastered?

What is the most logical next step for your learning team to take? Why does this step make sense for your team at this time? How will it help you move forward as a group?

Source: Ferriter, W. M. (2020). The big book of tools for collaborative teams in a PLC at Work. Solution Tree Press. Adapted from Ferriter, W. M., Graham, P., & Wight, M. (2013). Making teamwork meaningful: Leading progress-driven collaboration in a PLC at Work. Solution Tree Press.

PART ONE
Common Foundation

Tool: Learning Team Quarterly Reflection

Instructions: As a team, answer the following questions, drawn from the work of leadership expert Dan Rockwell (2017), four times a year.

What do we need to *keep* doing?	What do we need to *improve* on?
Why? What evidence do you have that these efforts are making a difference for teachers? For students?	*Why? What evidence do you have that these efforts could make a difference for teachers and students with a bit of tweaking?*
What should we *stop* doing?	**What should we *start* doing?**
Why? What evidence do you have that these efforts aren't worth the time and energy that we invest in them?	*Why? How would these new actions make a difference for teachers and students? How are they better than the work we have been tackling?*

Reference

Rockwell, D. (2017, March 16). *How to K.I.S.S. lousy operational meetings goodbye* [Blog post]. Accessed at https://leadershipfreak.blog/2017/03/16/how-to-k-i-s-s-lousy-operational-meetings-goodbye on August 5, 2019.

Source: Ferriter, W. M. (2020). The big book of tools for collaborative teams in a PLC at Work. *Solution Tree Press.*

Tool: Critical Issues for Team Consideration— Highly Effective Team Actions

Your honest evaluation is critical!

Please thoughtfully discuss your team's reality in each of the highly effective team indicators. Use the scale to rate your team in each area. At the conclusion of each section, identify areas to celebrate and areas for your team to intensify efforts.

+ This is very true of our team. This belief or action is embedded in our beliefs and actions.

✓ This is sometimes true of our team. We are not consistent about this belief or action.

− This is rarely or never true of our team. We need to work on implementing this belief or action.

Rating	Part 1: Highly Effective Teams Have a Common Foundation
	Action 1.1: We identify team roles, norms, and protocols to guide us in working together.
	Action 1.2: We have a process for addressing moments when personalities interfere with the team's work.
	Action 1.3: We use SMART goals to drive our work.
	Action 1.4: We regularly evaluate our team's effectiveness.

Celebrations:

Next steps:

Rating	Part 2: Highly Effective Teams Focus on Learning for All Students
	Action 2.1: We collectively identify essential learnings and define what success looks like in student work.
	Action 2.2: We identify the prerequisite knowledge and skills needed to master our essentials.
	Action 2.3: We identify course content and topics we can minimize or eliminate to devote more time to our essentials.
	Action 2.4: We agree on how to sequence content and pace our course.

Celebrations:	
Next steps:	

Rating	**Part 3: Highly Effective Teams Effectively Use Assessments and Data**
	Action 3.1: We develop and deliver frequent common formative assessments throughout our units of instruction.
	Action 3.2: We use team assessment data to identify high-impact instructional strategies.
	Action 3.3: We teach students the criteria we will use to judge their work.
	Action 3.4: We create exemplars students can examine to evaluate their own progress toward mastery.

Celebrations:
Next steps:

Rating	**Part 4: Highly Effective Teams Provide Extra Time and Support for Learning**
	Action 4.1: We create flexible time during our units of instruction to provide extra time and support to learners.
	Action 4.2: We deliver targeted interventions to support students who have not yet reached grade-level expectations.
	Action 4.3: We deliver targeted extensions to students working beyond grade-level expectations.

Celebrations:
Next steps:

Source: Adapted from DuFour, R., DuFour, R., Eaker, R., Many, T. W., Mattos, M., & Muhammad, A. (2024). Learning by doing: A handbook for Professional Learning Communities at Work *(4th ed.). Solution Tree Press.*

PART 2

Highly Effective Teams Focus on Learning for All Students

At the heart of every highly effective team is a shared commitment to ensuring all students learn. This part of *The Handbook for Highly Effective Teams in a PLC at Work* explores the critical actions teams take to clarify essential learning outcomes, define mastery, and align instructional strategies. By focusing on clarity and consistency, teams can help students meet and exceed expectations while ensuring they devote collaborative time and energy to what matters most.

- **Action 2.1:** We Collectively Identify Essential Learnings and Define What Success Looks Like in Student Work (page 67)
- **Action 2.2:** We Identify the Prerequisite Knowledge and Skills Needed to Master Our Essentials (page 81)
- **Action 2.3:** We Identify Course Content and Topics We Can Minimize or Eliminate to Devote More Time to Our Essentials (page 91)
- **Action 2.4:** We Agree on How to Sequence Content and Pace Our Course (page 101)

We Collectively Identify Essential Learnings and Define What Success Looks Like in Student Work

Stakeholders expect teachers to teach to a very large number of standards; however, there is no way that teachers can give all standards the same amount of time or emphasis. They must continually decide which standards to prioritize and what learning to target within the standards. In a PLC, teacher teams make those decisions collaboratively.

—THOMAS W. MANY, MICHAEL J. MAFFONI, SUSAN K. SPARKS, AND TESHA FERRIBY THOMAS

Too many standards, too little time! If you work in education, you've likely heard this phrase uttered by teachers and teams nearly everywhere. State and provincial content standards are intended to guide teachers and instruction by outlining the expectations for what they *should teach* at each grade level or course. Often, the sheer number of standards teachers are expected to teach over a school year is overwhelming and nearly impossible given the actual time students spend in the classroom. In response, teachers often plan their instructional year based on furiously teaching all the standards with the goal being simple: covering all the standards by the end of the school year.

The result? A curriculum that feels overwhelming and instruction that can seem rushed, with variations from classroom to classroom regarding what team members are teaching. To remedy this, highly effective teams recognize they must work together to prioritize the standards, identifying those that students *must know* to succeed in the course or grade level and beyond, and those that the team may deem *nice to know*. By identifying these high-leverage standards and skills, teams can *focus* their collaborative time, common formative assessments, and intervention efforts, shifting their practice from merely *teaching* all the standards to ensuring students *learn* a team's agreed-on set of essential standards and skills. Author Maria Nielsen (2016) reaffirms the critical nature of the agreed-on essentials:

> Remember: the standards we have determined as essential are the ones we are going to spend the bulk of our time teaching, assessing, re-teaching and reassessing. These are the standards we can't imagine our students leaving our course of study or grade level without mastering.

It's important to note that we're not advocating for the elimination of some standards. Instead, we encourage teams to allocate their time and resources to ensuring all students learn those deemed essential, giving more time to those agreed-on standards and skills and giving less time to those that may not hold the same value. To illustrate this point, consider figure 2.1.1.

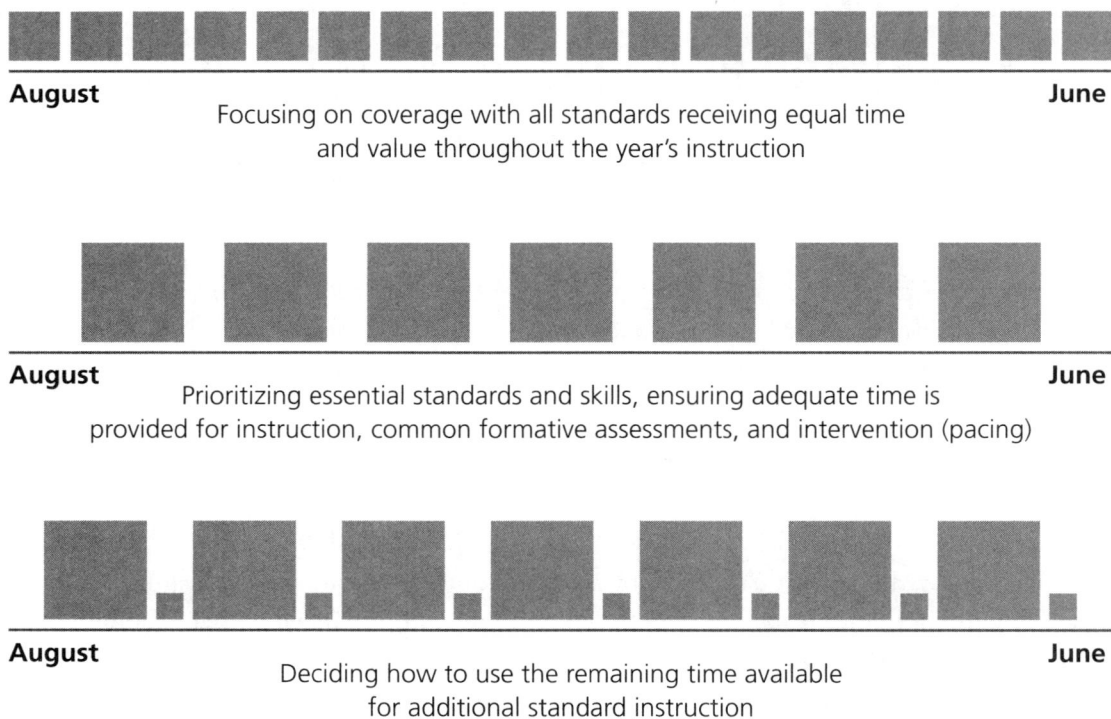

August   **June**

Focusing on coverage with all standards receiving equal time
and value throughout the year's instruction

August   **June**

Prioritizing essential standards and skills, ensuring adequate time is
provided for instruction, common formative assessments, and intervention (pacing)

August   **June**

Deciding how to use the remaining time available
for additional standard instruction

FIGURE 2.1.1: Prioritizing how to spend time.

Keep in mind that identifying essential standards and skills is just the first step—but not the only step. Highly effective teams go further by developing *shared clarity* and defining *what success looks like in student work* for each essential standard and skill. Shared clarity means reaching agreement on exactly what a standard requires students to know and do. Defining success means agreeing on expectations of what mastery will look like when met in student work.

Why Highly Effective Teams Do This

To address the overwhelming nature of covering all standards, highly effective teams prioritize standards based on their significance, allowing for ensured understanding of essential content. As *Learning by Doing, Fourth Edition*, emphasizes, "Perhaps the greatest benefit of prioritizing the standards is that it encourages teachers to embrace more in-depth instruction by reducing the pressure to simply cover the material" (DuFour et al., 2024, p. 149).

Consider this analogy: In a successful restaurant, the head chef is responsible for designing dishes that work in harmony. However, the head chef isn't the only one preparing meals; multiple lead and line cooks work together to ensure a final product that meets the chef's expectations. To maintain consistency, the head chef provides detailed recipes and procedures, ensuring every dish meets the same high standards. Without this clarity—if the recipe lacks precise ingredient measurements, clear cooking instructions, or defined presentation guidelines—customers ordering the same meal may receive completely different experiences.

Like a poorly designed recipe, state and provincial standards are often ambiguous and open to interpretation. When teams identify essential standards but fail to analyze them collaboratively, the result is inconsistency from classroom to classroom, just as different cooks, without shared understanding and expectations, produce vastly different versions of the same dish. This inconsistent instruction leads to inconsistent, often inequitable, learning experiences for students in the same grade level or course.

- Some may experience high levels of instructional rigor, while others face much lower expectations.
- Some may be held to high standards of mastery, while others move forward with minimal proficiency or without proficiency at all.
- Some may receive targeted interventions, while others receive only general, unfocused support.

Highly effective teams prevent this inconsistency by establishing a shared understanding of what each standard means and what proficiency looks like in student work before planning their instruction. Robert Eaker (2020) affirms the importance of developing shared clarity and clearly defined expectations for mastery and explains further that "to harness the full power of that process of clarifying essential standards, [a team] must also answer, What would these learning outcomes look like in student work if they were met?" (p. 72).

When collaboratively performing this essential action, a team's individual and collective practices change in significant ways (DuFour et al., 2024).

- **Intentional instruction:** Daily instruction becomes more focused, with lessons, practice, and feedback intentionally designed to move students toward mastery.
- **Aligned assessment:** Formative and common formative assessments serve as knowledge checks, providing ongoing information about student progress toward mastery.
- **Targeted intervention:** Intervention efforts become more targeted, enabling teachers and teams to address specific skills necessary for mastery.
- **Visible learning:** Students benefit from visible exemplars, allowing them to see various examples of high-quality work that meets or exceeds mastery. Seeing high-quality examples also speeds up the learning process and improves the quality of students' initial work.

Clear communication of essential standards and learning targets to students is crucial for developing a shared understanding among students and teachers. Tim Brown and Bill

Ferriter (2021) emphasize that "one of the fundamental principles of learning that is both common sense and supported by evidence is the notion that students are more likely to hit a target when they know what the target is" (p. 30). By collaborating to define the agreed-on essentials to be learned, clearly defining what success will look like in student work, and sharing exemplars with students, highly effective teams create a highly impactful learning environment through intentional instruction, focused assessment, and targeted intervention. Figure 2.1.2 offers a comparison of language between ineffective groups and highly effective teams around this topic.

The Language of Ineffective Groups	The Language of Highly Effective Teams
"We have to teach every standard. Everything we teach is important."	"Let's find out where students are and determine how in-depth we need to go in this standard."
"We can't decide what to do when we do not agree on certain standards."	"Let's visit with the grade level above ours to assist us in making a decision about a standard that we disagree on."
"We identified essential standards two years ago. We even laminated them and post them on the board at the beginning of each lesson!"	"We revisit our essential learnings at the beginning and end of each unit of instruction to clarify our shared understandings."
"We don't want to provide work samples that demonstrate success to students. If students see what's expected, that's cheating!"	"We provide work samples that demonstrate success and approaching success as part of our instruction, and we allow students to compare and evaluate each."

FIGURE 2.1.2: Language comparison.

Notice that ineffective groups' conversations often emphasize *teaching* all standards, treating the identification of essentials as just another task to check off the list. In contrast, highly effective teams focus on prioritizing the standards, clearly defining what success looks like in student work, and making learning visible for students through work examples that meet expectations.

How Highly Effective Teams Do This

Highly effective teams recognize that identifying essential standards, skills, and learning targets within the required curriculum is a critical first step. However, if teams stop there—without gaining shared clarity or defining success for each essential learning—it is almost guaranteed they will see little to no improvement in student outcomes. Simply identifying essentials does little to advance student learning; rather, how teams *use* these essentials to shape their collective instructional practices is what makes a meaningful difference in student learning and the team's efficacy.

To gain shared clarity and define success for essentials, highly effective teams plan units of instruction together, collaboratively engaging in the following steps.

1. **Identify critical vocabulary.**

   - Determine key vocabulary related to the essential learning students need to understand as part of the unit of instruction.

   - Ensure consistency across classrooms by developing a shared list of critical vocabulary.

   - Introduce these vocabulary terms one or two weeks before the unit begins, helping students build necessary background knowledge.

2. **Agree on formative feedback prompts.**

   - Agree on three or four common formative feedback prompts to use consistently with students throughout the unit to determine their understanding of the essential. For instance, an English language arts team might consistently ask, "How would you summarize what you just read?" A mathematics team might ask, "Is there another way to reach this solution?"

   - Consistently use formative feedback prompts as a common check for understanding and use the information gathered to guide meaningful team discussions about student learning, progress, and instructional next steps.

3. **Identify measurable learning targets.**

   - Because many academic standards are complex and ambiguous, requiring students to demonstrate proficiency in multiple concepts and skills within a single standard, deconstruct each essential standard into smaller, measurable learning targets. This allows teams to assess student understanding skill by skill. Figure 2.1.3 is an example.

   - Identifying each required learning target allows teams to intentionally plan and pace their instruction, assess at the target level, and ensure students receive support in mastering all learning targets that compose the essential standard.

A sixth-grade reading standard states, "Determine a theme or central idea of a text and how it is conveyed through particular details; provide a summary of the text distinct from personal opinions or judgments" (RL.6.2).

To successfully master this standard, a student must demonstrate proficiency in the following learning targets.

1. **Define** the term *theme*.

2. **Determine** the theme of a text.

3. **Identify** details in the text that support the theme.

4. **Define** the term *summarize*.

5. **Provide** a summary without personal opinions or judgments.

Source for standard: NGA & CCSSO, 2010a.

FIGURE 2.1.3: Deconstructing an essential standard into learning targets.

4. **Define what success looks like when the standard or skill is met.**

- Ensure consistency from teacher to teacher and classroom to classroom when teams answer the following key questions.

    - What will student work look like when success in the essential learning or target is demonstrated?

    - How does the work of a student approaching proficiency differ from that of a student who has fully demonstrated success?

    - What examples of varying levels of student work can we share to make learning visible for students and help them assess their own progress?

Figure 2.1.4 is a visual representation of these actions.

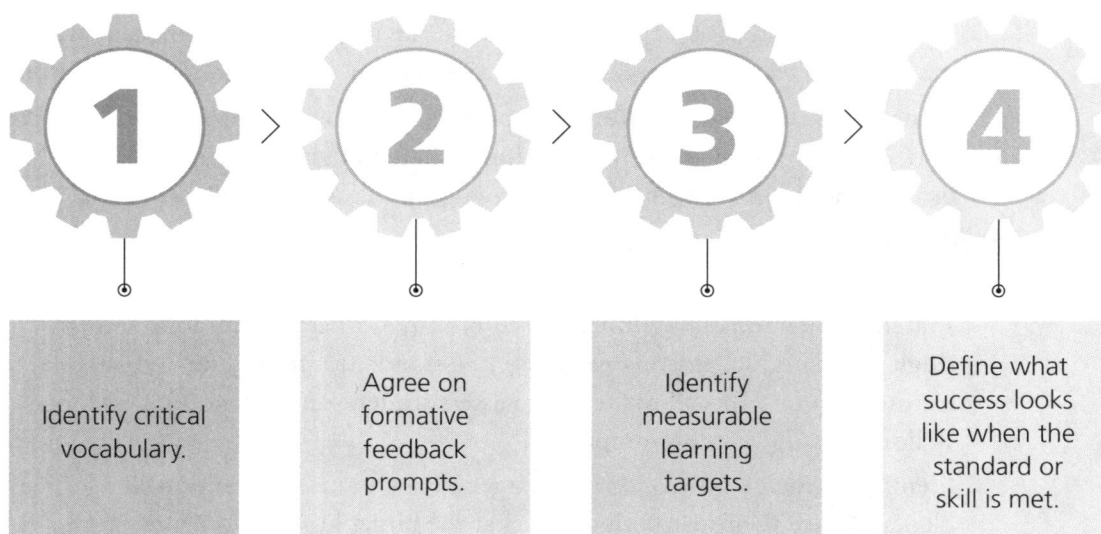

1	2	3	4
Identify critical vocabulary.	Agree on formative feedback prompts.	Identify measurable learning targets.	Define what success looks like when the standard or skill is met.

FIGURE 2.1.4: Steps to gain shared clarity and define mastery.

Sharing these expectations with students through visible targets and student work exemplars, teacher assessment practices become measures of progress. As Brown and Ferriter (2021) observe:

> It appears that much of what assessment for learning is all about, then, is helping students understand as clearly as possible what the learning targets are for a lesson, analyze where they are in relation to hitting those targets, and receive appropriate feedback on how to improve. (p. 31)

By addressing these clarifying steps in planning units of instruction, highly effective teams move beyond simply identifying essentials to creating a clear, shared understanding of success for the team and the students.

AI can help teams to complete this work if they view it as *another member of their collaborative team* that can offer assistance and ideas. By streamlining the process of defining success, highly effective teams can spend their valuable collaborative time engaged in deep instructional conversations. It's important to note that when using these powerful tools, the more specific the prompt, the more concise the answer. Consider the following examples.

- We are a grade-level or subject-specific collaborative team. What are the key vocabulary terms students will need to know in order to master this standard: [*Standard*]?
- We are a grade-level or subject-specific collaborative team. What are the key concepts and skills students will need to know as part of this standard: [*Standard*]?
- We are a grade-level or subject-specific collaborative team. Help us identify the measurable learning targets within this standard: [*Standard*].
- We are a grade-level or subject-specific collaborative team. Help us develop formative questions we can ask during instruction based on this standard: [*Standard*].

A final reminder: Highly effective teams recognize that *identifying* essentials and skills does not mean eliminating standards—rather, it means prioritizing essentials that are absolutely critical for students to know and be able to do. Without team consensus, instruction can become fragmented, leading to inconsistencies in student learning experiences from classroom to classroom. Engaging in professional discussions about the essentials, gaining shared clarity, and defining what success will look like in student work may take time, but ultimately, it streamlines instructional planning, encourages more focused instruction, and ensures adequate time and collective focus on the most important skills for student success.

With this in mind, collaboratively planning units of instruction is a key characteristic of highly effective teams. As discussed, teams identify the essential standards, skills, and learning targets in the unit of instruction; design assessments that measure student progress toward the team's agreed-on expectation of proficiency; and establish a shared pacing plan for instruction, assessment, and extra time and support.

Tools and Resources for Highly Effective Teams

The following tools and resources will help you accomplish the work for this essential action.

- **"Tool: Deconstructing an Essential Standard" (page 75):** Educational expert Paula Maeker emphasizes that the most important step collaborative teams can take is to become students of their standards before ever introducing those standards to their students. To achieve this, teams work together to deconstruct their essential standards. This process helps teachers on highly effective teams develop a shared understanding of the concepts and skills embedded within a standard and establish clear language to communicate mastery expectations to their students. Use this tool to deconstruct an essential that you are responsible for teaching.

- **"Tool: Using AI Tools to Deconstruct an Essential Standard" (page 78):** The simple act of deconstructing a standard into its component parts can take so long that it leaves little time for teams to engage in meaningful conversations about what the standard requires students to know and be able to do. To address this challenge, highly effective teams are using AI chatbots like ChatGPT (https://chatgpt.com) or Gemini (https://gemini.google.com) to accelerate the deconstructing process. This tool includes a set of prompts that you can ask those chatbots to help you deconstruct an essential that you are responsible for teaching.

- **"Tool: Gaining Shared Clarity" (page 79):** Highly effective teams recognize that while identifying the essential standards and skills that all students must master is a crucial step, it is only the beginning. These teams also engage in meaningful discussions to define critical vocabulary, develop formative feedback prompts to use during instruction, establish measurable learning targets in each essential standard, and, most importantly, describe what success looks like in student work. Use this tool to guide your team's thinking and document your collective decisions for each of these key elements.

- **"Tool: Seven Critical Steps for Team Success—Instructional Unit Design" (page 80):** Collaboratively planning units of instruction is a key characteristic of highly effective teams. To do this well, teams identify the essential standards, skills, and learning targets in the unit; design assessments that measure student progress toward proficiency; and establish a shared pacing plan. This tool provides a structured approach to unit planning, helping teams clarify their work and leverage their collective strengths to increase student learning.

Tool: Deconstructing an Essential Standard

Follow the steps to deconstruct an essential standard. Use this tool to deconstruct an essential standard that you are responsible for teaching.

Standard to Deconstruct

Copy and paste directly from your state or provincial standards document.

Step 1: Annotate the Standard

In *Make It Happen*, assessment experts Kim Bailey and Chris Jakicic (2019) recommend that teachers use the following symbols when annotating a standard: **Circle** verbs to indicate the skills students are expected to master when working with the standard; **underline** significant nouns or noun phrases to highlight the concepts, ideas, and facts that students are expected to master when working with the standard; and put **brackets** around words or phrases that suggest the context of the task that students should encounter when demonstrating mastery of the standard.

Use those symbols to annotate your essential standard in the box.

Step 2: Categorize the Standard

Jan Chappuis, Rick Stiggins, Steve Chappuis, and Judith Arter (2012) recommend that to annotate a standard, teachers identify the type of learning defined in the standard by classifying it in one of four categories. Those categories are defined in the following table.

Looking back at the verbs that you circled in the preceding standard, which category do you think this standard fits into the best?

Knowledge	Reasoning	Performance Skills	Product
Requires students to learn factual information, procedural knowledge, or conceptual understandings	Requires students to use thought processes to solve problems or to apply knowledge to new situations	Requires students to use physical processes (running, playing, speaking, using a tool) to demonstrate mastery	Requires students to create a product (a graph, an essay, a map, a table, a chart) to demonstrate mastery
Circle the category that you believe the essential standard you are unpacking fits into the best.			

The Handbook for Highly Effective Teams in a PLC at Work® © 2025 Solution Tree Press • SolutionTree.com
Visit **go.SolutionTree.com/PLCbooks** to download this free reproducible.

Step 3: Reflect on the Standard

Answer the following questions about the essential standard that you annotated in step 1.

Using your annotations in step 1, list the content knowledge that students will need to know in order to master this standard.	
Using your annotations in step 1, list the skills that students will need to demonstrate in order to master this standard.	
Why is it important for students to master this standard?	
How can you assess the progress that students are making toward mastering this standard?	

Step 4: Write Student-Friendly Learning Targets

Finally, create a set of between three and five statements describing exactly what students should know and be able to do in order to master this standard. Remember to write your learning targets in student-friendly language so you can effectively communicate your expectations to your students. Also, consider writing a doing task that students can complete in order to demonstrate mastery of the learning target.

Learning Target	Student-Friendly Learning Target	Doing Task That Serves as a Demonstration of Mastery
Sample: Students will need to know the impact that the Silk Road had on cultural sharing between the East and the West.	*Sample:* I can explain the impact that the Silk Road had on the cultures of both the Eastern and Western worlds.	*Sample:* This means I can name three different ideas that were introduced to the East and to the West by traders who traveled on the Silk Road and rank them in importance from having the greatest impact on culture to having the least impact on culture.

References

Bailey, K., & Jakicic, C. (2019). *Make it happen: Coaching with the four critical questions of PLCs at Work.* Solution Tree Press.

Chappuis, J., Stiggins, R., Chappuis, S., & Arter, J. (2012). *Classroom assessment for student learning: Doing it right—using it well* (2nd ed.). Pearson.

Source: Adapted from Ferriter, W. M. (2020). The big book of tools for collaborative teams in a PLC at Work. *Solution Tree Press.*

PART TWO
Focus on Learning

Tool: Using AI Tools to Deconstruct an Essential Standard

Instructions: When deconstructing your next essential standard, use an AI chatbot like ChatGPT (https://chat.openai.com) or Gemini (https://gemini.google.com) as a collaborative thought partner by posing the prompts in the first column of the following table. Then, assess the responses from your AI chatbot for accuracy and summarize its thinking in the second column of the table. Remember, you should never rely on AI chatbots for original thinking. Instead, use them to give you something to think about. Doing so will accelerate your collaborative work, giving your team more time for meaningful conversations.

Standard We Are Deconstructing:

Start a new chat in your AI chatbot. Then, ask these prompts in order.	Together, review your AI chatbot's response for accuracy. Summarize its thinking here.
Can you deconstruct this standard? *[Paste standard]* **Sample:** *Can you deconstruct this standard? "Choose a variety of transition words, phrases, and clauses to convey sequence, to signal shifts from one time or setting to another, and/or to clarify the relationships among ideas" (CCSS.ELA-Literacy.W.6.3.C).*	
List the three most important prerequisites that *[insert grade level]* students should know before learning this standard. **Sample:** *List the three most important prerequisites that sixth-grade students should know before learning this standard.*	
What are the three most common mistakes that *[insert grade level]* students make when learning this standard? **Sample:** *What are the three most common mistakes that sixth-grade students make when learning this standard?*	
Can you give me a learning progression for teaching this standard to *[insert grade level]* students? **Sample:** *Can you give me a learning progression for teaching this standard to sixth-grade students?*	
Describe two resources that I can create to help *[insert grade level]* students master this standard. **Sample:** *Describe two resources that I can create to help sixth-grade students master this standard.*	

Source for standard: National Governors Association Center for Best Practices & Council of Chief State School Officers. (2010a). Common Core State Standards for English language arts and literacy in history/social studies, science, and technical subjects. Authors. Accessed at https://corestandards.org/wp-content/uploads/2023/09/ELA_Standards1.pdf on September 29, 2024.

Source: Ferriter, W. M., Mattos, M., & Meyer, R. J. (2025). The big book of tools for RTI at Work. Solution Tree Press.

PART TWO
Focus on Learning

Tool: Gaining Shared Clarity

Essential Standard:

List measurable learning targets.
1. _____ 2. _____ 3. _____

Define mastery.
(Define what a student who has mastered the standard will be able to do with the content. These statements should be written in student-friendly language. I can statements are helpful for students to see what they are going to be able to do.)
1. _____ 2. _____ 3. _____ 4. _____ 5. _____ 6. _____

Prior to Unit of Instruction	During Unit of Instruction
Critical Academic Vocabulary	**Formative Prompts**
(Vocabulary front-loaded prior to instruction)	(Feedback for student learning and teaching practices)

Source: Sonju, B., Powers, M., & Miller, S. (2024). Simplifying the journey: Six steps to schoolwide collaboration, consistency, and clarity in a PLC at Work. *Solution Tree Press.*

Tool: Seven Critical Steps for Team Success— Instructional Unit Design

Step 1: Identify essential learnings.	• Identify the essential standards and skills in the unit that all students must know and be able to do. • Break each essential into measurable learning targets that teachers can quickly assess. • Agree on critical vocabulary that students will need to know.
Step 2: Describe success.	• Agree on what success will look like when students meet each learning target. • Develop student self-assessment tools (rubrics, continua, and so on) to facilitate student ownership of learning.
Step 3: Create an end-of-unit assessment.	• Create an end-of-unit assessment. • Include all essential standards and learning targets that are part of the unit.
Step 4: Plan for weekly common formative assessments.	• Create or identify short, weekly common formative assessments that measure student progress toward each learning target. • Agree on what student success looks like for each of those assessments. • Use a quick data protocol to learn from those data.
Step 5: Agree on strategic pacing.	• Determine the number of instructional days for the unit. • Identify days the common formative assessments will be given. • Specify days to use for targeted interventions and extensions.
Step 6: Identify high-impact instructional strategies.	• Identify high-impact instructional strategies to be used throughout the unit. • Share high-impact instructional strategies with the team.
Step 7: Make learning visible.	• Make learning visible by sharing learning targets or *I can* statements with students. • Make learning visible by sharing exemplars of work with students.

We Identify the Prerequisite Knowledge and Skills Needed to Master Our Essentials

Some students don't just need more time to practice; instead, they need reinforcement of immediate prerequisite skills required to master the current essential standard. If a team wants to improve its results, it should consider assessing for immediate prerequisite, or prior, skills as part of the Tier 1 team teaching-assessing-learning cycle.

—MIKE MATTOS, AUSTIN BUFFUM, JANET MALONE, LUIS F. CRUZ, NICOLE DIMICH, AND SARAH SCHUHL

In the second edition of *Taking Action: A Handbook for RTI at Work™*, authors Mike Mattos, Austin Buffum, Janet Malone, Luiz F. Cruz, Nicole Dimich, and Sarah Schul (2025) write, "If there is one thing for certain at the start of every school year, it is this: Educators are going to work hard. The question is whether we will work hard and succeed or work hard and fail" (p. 312). When teams work hard and fail, it causes them to question the value of collaboration. However, such failures are inevitably the result of doing the wrong work. An example of doing the wrong work is beginning instruction in a new essential without identifying the immediate prerequisite knowledge, skills, and vocabulary necessary to master that essential. In fact, one could argue that teaching new concepts without first screening for prerequisites and preteaching them to students who have not yet mastered them is professionally irresponsible, resulting in wasted instructional time and causing struggling students to doubt their ability to learn.

Screening for and preteaching prerequisites, however, is often met with pushback from classroom teachers who say, "That's impossible. I have too much to cover and too little time to teach already! How do you expect me to also introduce students to things they are supposed to already know and be able to do?" If those thoughts have crossed your mind, we understand. There *is* too much to cover and too little time to teach. And well-intentioned district leaders often prioritize curricular coverage in their communications with classroom teachers, hoping students will be fully prepared for standardized tests. "We aren't adapting these materials," they may share. "We are adopting them. We expect you to teach them with fidelity."

But we have both a reminder and a question for you. The reminder is that a team's focus in the PLC at Work model is not just to *teach* important concepts to students. Instead, it is to ensure that students *learn* those concepts: The "goal of a learning-focused school is not to cover curriculum but to ensure students actually learn the skills, content, and behaviors that are critical to their future success" (DuFour et al., 2024, p. 215). And our question is, Have you ever discovered, midway through a unit, that some of your students had knowledge gaps that made it difficult for them to understand your lesson? If you answered yes, you have all the proof you need that working together to identify, screen for, and preteach prerequisite knowledge, skills, and vocabulary is worth the collaborative time that you invest into it.

Why Highly Effective Teams Do This

It shouldn't surprise you that learning new concepts and skills is dependent on mastery of certain prerequisites. That pattern repeats itself in all learning, both in and beyond schools. Think about how some babies learn to walk. They don't start by surprising everyone and standing up on two legs one day. Instead, they work through a series of prerequisites: learning to lift their heads and chests, learning to roll over onto their stomachs, learning to rock back and forth, learning to crawl, learning to pull themselves up and balance, learning to walk while holding on to objects for support, and then, *finally* learning to walk independently. And our job as caregivers is not to rush babies through these prerequisites but, instead, to recognize what our children have yet to learn and to provide the right instruction and intervention to continue their development. For example, if we know that our children can pull themselves up and balance, we can begin to offer hands to hold on to. By doing so, we provide the support they need to take the next step.

This commonsense notion—that learning new skills is dependent on the mastery of prerequisites—is well established in the research. Russian child psychologist Lev Vygotsky (1978), who was studying human learning at the turn of the 20th century, suggested that most learning is gradual and linear, with mastery of more complex skills dependent on initial mastery of simpler skills learned in a logical order. As simpler skills are mastered, new concepts and skills move into what Vygotsky (1978) called a person's *zone of proximal development*—the range of learning possibilities based on what one has already mastered. But here's the thing: It is impossible to effectively and efficiently learn new skills resting outside of your zone of proximal development (Vygotsky, 1978).

Cognitive psychologists David Wood, Jerome S. Bruner, and Gail Ross (1976) worked to apply lessons learned from Vygotsky to the field of education, coining the term *scaffolding* to describe the supports educators provide to students during the learning process. For Wood, Bruner, and Ross (1976), learning was a "hierarchical program in which component skills are combined into 'higher skills' by appropriate orchestration to meet new, more complex task requirements," and success was a function of combining previous knowledge to build new understandings (p. 89). Moving forward, then, requires "matching (and the correction of mismatching)" of previous knowledge to the demands of the new learning we want students to do (Wood et al., 1976, p. 90).

For collaborative teams determined to work hard and succeed, the work of Vygotsky, Wood, Bruner, and Ross means we must articulate the prerequisites essential for mastery of new concepts and skills and then use that articulation to fill gaps for students before instruction begins. Doing so ensures our lessons lie within the zone of proximal development for all students—not just those who come to us having mastered important prerequisites in previous instruction. Figure 2.2.1 offers a comparison of language between ineffective groups and highly effective teams around this topic.

The Language of Ineffective Groups	The Language of Highly Effective Teams
"Why are we talking about prerequisites? Don't we have enough to teach already?"	"What would we want a student to know and be able to do before we even begin teaching our next lesson?"
"If last year's teachers would have done their job, maybe our kids could actually learn what we are trying to teach them."	"Let's look back at the concepts that students should already have learned. Then, we can identify the most important prerequisites and pretest for them."
"Who is responsible for getting kids caught up on all the things they haven't learned yet?"	"We may not be able to get kids completely caught up, but can we find a few prerequisites that we can teach so students are ready for our upcoming essential?"
"I don't have time for preteaching prerequisites."	"Preteaching prerequisites will save us time because more students will master our essential standard during initial instruction."

FIGURE 2.2.1: Language comparison.

What do you notice about the language used by ineffective groups? Their attention is focused solely on the amount of time it will take to preteach prerequisites. Convinced that students should come to class knowing all that they need to master grade-level essentials, they question the logic in committing time to addressing gaps in prerequisite knowledge. Highly effective teams, on the other hand, recognize that preteaching prerequisites is the key to ensuring that students learn new content to begin with. No matter how good you are at teaching grade-level standards, students won't learn if they have gaps in the immediate prerequisite skills necessary to master those standards.

How Highly Effective Teams Do This

The suggestion that highly effective teams should identify, screen for, and preteach prerequisite skills is often interpreted as, "Collaborative teams are solely responsible for taking students who are grade levels behind in their learning and getting them caught up in everything." So, let us be clear: *That is not what we are suggesting.* In fact, to expect teacher teams to catch up students grade levels behind runs contrary to the intervention process articulated in both *Learning by Doing, Fourth Edition* (DuFour et al., 2024), and *Taking Action, Second Edition* (Mattos et al., 2025), the core texts detailing the work of collaborative teams. Instead, both texts suggest that highly effective teams accept lead responsibility for teaching grade-level essentials and some *nearby* prerequisites (DuFour et al., 2024; Mattos et al., 2025).

What we are wrestling with here is the difference between foundational and immediate prerequisites. Here's how Mattos and colleagues (2025) detail that difference:

> *Immediate prerequisite skills* and vocabulary often precede current instruction by a few units, a few weeks, or, at most, the previous year. *Foundational prerequisite skills* come from instruction that should have been learned years ago, usually two or more years previous. (p. 211)

Just as it would be professionally irresponsible for teams to push forward with instruction in new essentials without identifying, screening for, and preteaching *immediate prerequisites*, it would be professionally irresponsible for schools to expect teams to work alone to address gaps in *foundational prerequisites*. Instead, in an effective intervention system, lead responsibility for addressing gaps in foundational prerequisites belongs to instructional specialists working beyond the core classroom (Mattos et al., 2025).

The best way for a highly effective team to identify the immediate prerequisites worth screening for and preteaching is to consider an upcoming grade-level essential and determine the declarative and procedural knowledge necessary to *begin* learning that essential (Mattos et al., 2025).

- *Declarative knowledge* includes the concepts, ideas, facts, and vocabulary that students must already know to master grade-level essentials.
- *Procedural knowledge* includes the skills that students must already be able to do before mastering grade-level essentials.

For example, imagine that a middle school science team is teaching about buoyancy, and the focus question for their upcoming lesson is, *How can cruise ships—which are made from metal and weigh thousands of pounds—float even though their individual parts would easily sink if we dropped them in the ocean?* To understand buoyancy, students are going to rely on both declarative and procedural prerequisites that they ideally have learned in previous units or courses. Some of those prerequisites are in figure 2.2.2.

Declarative Prerequisites	Procedural Prerequisites
Students will need to know that matter is made of individual atoms.	Students will need to know how to calculate the density of a substance.
Students will need to know that atoms are arranged differently in solids, liquids, and gases.	
Students will need to know that density refers to how tightly packed together atoms are in different substances.	

FIGURE 2.2.2: Prerequisite examples.

We encourage teams to keep this process *simple*. While you can certainly refer to the essential standards covered in previous units of your own curriculum or in previous grade levels, those extra steps are often unnecessary. Instead, asking simple planning questions like those in the following list will help teams quickly generate ideas for prerequisites to screen for and preteach.

- "What do we hope students know and are able to do before we start teaching this standard?"
- "What common misconceptions do students always have when we teach this standard?"
- "What vocabulary words do students always stumble over when we teach this standard?"

We also encourage you to keep your list of prerequisites short. While it is true that there are lots of concepts and vocabulary words that we wish students knew by the time they arrive in our rooms, it is also true that we have a limited amount of time to screen for and preteach prerequisites. To ensure that our work is doable, we must keep ourselves focused on the declarative and procedural prerequisites that are truly pivotal to mastering the standard we are about to teach.

Once your team has identified a small handful of essential prerequisites, develop a short prerequisite pretest, and administer it to all students roughly two weeks before beginning new instruction. Keeping your pretest short—three to five questions that you can administer as a warm-up activity or an exit ticket—makes it more likely that you will have time to analyze and act on the data that you collect. Administering the assessment roughly two weeks before new instruction provides you with enough time to plan interventions, whether they happen during a schoolwide flex period or during small-group instruction inside your classroom.

Tools and Resources for Highly Effective Teams

The following tools and resources will help you accomplish the work for this essential action.

- **"Tool: Prerequisite Planning Document" (page 86):** Teams can use this tool to guide their conversations around the prerequisites necessary before teaching an upcoming essential. Notice the addition of common misconceptions to the planning document. Listing common misconceptions can often point teams to gaps in declarative or procedural knowledge that will prevent students from learning a new essential.

- **"Tool Overview: Preparing a Prerequisite Pretest" (page 88) and "Tool: Preparing a Prerequisite Pretest" (page 89):** Once teams have identified prerequisites, they must also develop and deliver a pretest to identify students who need additional time and support to master those prerequisites before beginning new instruction in grade-level essentials. This tool can guide your team through the process of writing a short three-to-five-question pretest covering both procedural and declarative knowledge.

Tool: Prerequisite Planning Document

Instructions: A simple step that teacher teams can take to prevent students from needing supplemental interventions is screening students in the immediate prerequisite skills necessary for mastering grade-level academic essentials. By thinking carefully about and then prescreening for necessary prerequisites, teams can identify and address gaps that will keep students from successfully mastering grade-level essentials before instruction in those essentials even begins. Use this planning tool to develop plans for preteaching prerequisite vocabulary, knowledge, and skills for your next unit of study.

Essential Outcome We Are Planning For:

Prerequisite vocabulary for this essential

Prerequisite knowledge for this essential

Prerequisite skills for this essential

Common misconceptions about this essential

Questions for Reflection

How will we screen our students to assess current mastery levels with these prerequisites?

What resources will we use to preteach these prerequisites to students who have not mastered them?

When will we preteach these prerequisites to students who have not mastered them?

Who will lead this work?

Source: Ferriter, W. M., Mattos, M., & Meyer, R. J. (2025). The big book of tools for RTI at Work. *Solution Tree Press.*

Tool Overview: Preparing a Prerequisite Pretest

In *Taking Action: A Handbook for RTI at Work, Second Edition*, authors Mike Mattos and colleagues (2025) suggest that teams systematically screen students for immediate prerequisite skill mastery before starting a new instruction unit. Doing so allows teams to proactively address knowledge and skill gaps that will prevent students from successfully mastering grade-level academic essentials. Teams can screen for immediate prerequisite skill mastery by delivering short prerequisite pretests one to two weeks before a new unit of study and then using the information gathered from these pretests to target students with preventive instruction designed to ensure they have mastered the knowledge and skills necessary to learn essential academic standards.

To prepare a prerequisite pretest, your team should do the following.

1. **Identify the grade-level essentials you are expected to teach:** Targeted instruction in prerequisite skills starts once a team has a clear, shared understanding of the grade-level essentials they are expected to teach.

2. **Identify declarative and procedural prerequisites:** Mattos and colleagues (2025) recommend that teams identify the declarative and procedural prerequisites required to master grade-level essentials.

   - *Declarative prerequisites* include the concepts, ideas, facts, and vocabulary that students must already know to master grade-level essentials.

   - *Procedural prerequisites* include the skills that a student must already be able to do to master grade-level essentials.

3. **Write three to five questions designed to test student mastery of declarative and procedural prerequisites:** Prerequisite pretests should be intentionally short. Teachers should be able to deliver them quickly. If a prerequisite pretest takes too long to deliver, analyze, or respond to, teachers will begin to question the value of pretesting for prerequisites.

4. **Tie each question to a specific prerequisite:** Like all good assessments, questions on a prerequisite pretest should assess one isolated concept or skill. By deliberately connecting each question to an individual prerequisite, teams facilitate their response to the data they collect. Targeted interventions are only possible when teachers are clear about the exact gaps that individual students are bringing with them to the classroom.

5. **Generate an expected response and identify common mistakes students are likely to make:** When teams discuss the answers they expect students to give to—and the mistakes students are likely to make on—prerequisite pretest questions, they build a shared understanding of what mastery looks like in action. That shared understanding of mastery is essential to high-functioning collaborative teams.

Use "Tool: Preparing a Prerequisite Pretest" on page 89 to complete this work with your collaborative team.

Reference

Mattos, M., Buffum, A., Malone, J., Cruz, L. F., Dimich, N., & Schuhl, S. (2025). *Taking action: A handbook for RTI at Work* (2nd ed.). Bloomington, IN: Solution Tree Press.

Source: Ferriter, W. M., Mattos, M., & Meyer, R. J. (2025). The big book of tools for RTI at Work. *Solution Tree Press.*

Tool: Preparing a Prerequisite Pretest

Instructions: Use the following template to design a short, five-question pretest to assess mastery of prerequisite skills and knowledge that a student must have learned to master your grade-level essentials.

Grade-Level Essential Standard or Standards We Teach:	
Identifying Declarative Prerequisites: List any concepts, ideas, or vocabulary that a student **must already know** to master this grade-level essential standard.	**Identifying Procedural Prerequisites:** List any skills that a student **must already be able to do** to master this grade-level essential standard.

Prerequisite Pretest Questions

Generate five questions to use as a prerequisite pretest. Tie each question to a specific declarative or procedural prerequisite skill to facilitate efforts to address gaps in prerequisite knowledge.

Question	Prerequisites This Question Assesses	Expected Student Response	Common Mistakes Students Struggling With Prerequisite Knowledge Will Likely Make

page 1 of 2

PART TWO
Focus on Learning

②

Questions for Reflection

When will we give our prerequisite pretest?

How will we deliver our prerequisite pretest?

How will we analyze the results of our prerequisite pretest?

When will we intervene for students who struggle on our prerequisite pretest?

Source: Ferriter, W. M., Mattos, M., & Meyer, R. J. (2025). The big book of tools for RTI at Work. *Solution Tree Press.*

ACTION 2.3

We Identify Course Content and Topics We Can Minimize or Eliminate to Devote More Time to Our Essentials

The process of prioritizing the standards has significant benefits. . . . Perhaps the greatest benefit of prioritizing the standards is that it encourages teachers to embrace more in-depth instruction by reducing the pressure to simply cover the material.

—RICHARD DUFOUR, REBECCA DUFOUR, ROBERT EAKER, THOMAS W. MANY, MIKE MATTOS, AND ANTHONY MUHAMMAD

We have said it before, and we will say it again: Every highly effective team's goal is to ensure all students acquire the essential knowledge, skills, and behaviors necessary to succeed in their course or grade level. That can feel like a completely overwhelming task, however, given the sheer number of standards. Imagine you are on a third-grade team. Over the course of a single school year—which covers 178 days and requires a minimum of six hours of instructional time per day (National Center for Education Statistics, 2020) for a total of 1,068 instructional hours—your team would be responsible for teaching 159 complex, multifaceted standards to students across the core subjects of mathematics, English language arts, science, and social studies.

On the surface, this might seem reasonable. Divide 1,068 instructional hours by just over one hundred standards, and you have almost seven hours to teach each standard to your students. But while 1,068 hours may be *allocated* to instruction over the course of the school year, time will be interrupted many different ways. On a broader scale, time is built into every school day to provide students with opportunities for recess and other important subjects like visual arts, music, and physical education (Bureau of Legislative Research, 2022). Additionally, everything from student absences and teacher absences to transitions, classroom management issues, and celebrations steals instructional minutes from the study of grade-level essentials. Research suggests that students lose anywhere from 16 to 25 percent of their allocated instructional time each year to issues like these (Kraft & Novicoff, 2023). If you are on that third-grade team, you now have 45 fewer days of school—270 fewer hours—to teach those standards to your students.

It is also important to remember that the standards assigned to third grade in the core subjects of mathematics, English language arts, science, and social studies often include multiple individual learning targets (a fact addressed in action 2.1, page 67). Take the following third-grade standards as an example.

> **Mathematics:** 3.OA.2—"Interpret whole-number quotients of whole numbers, e.g., interpret 56 ÷ 8 as the number of objects in each share when 56 objects are partitioned equally into 8 shares, or as a number of shares when 56 objects are partitioned into equal shares of 8 objects each. For example, describe a context in which a number of shares or a number of groups can be expressed as 56 ÷ 8." (NGA & CCSSO, 2010b, p. 23)
>
> **English language arts:** ELA.Literacy.RI.3.1—"Ask and answer questions to demonstrate understanding of a text, referring explicitly to the text as the basis for the answers." (NGA & CCSSO, 2010a, p. 12)
>
> **Science:** 3-LS3-1—"Analyze and interpret data to provide evidence that plants and animals have traits inherited from parents and that variation of these traits exists in a group of similar organisms." (Next Generation Science Standards, 2013)
>
> **Social studies:** C.1.3.4—"Investigate origins of state and national symbols, patriotic songs, and mottos: American flag, flag etiquette, Star Spangled Banner, recitation of Pledge of Allegiance, Arkansas motto: *Regnat Populus*" (Arkansas Department of Education, 2022, p. 12)

Even the shortest standard in this list (English language arts) and the standard at the lowest level of cognitive complexity (social studies) require mastery of far more than just one concept or skill. Multiply the individual learning targets in each of the standards that you are required to teach, and the challenge of teaching every standard to mastery during the time you have available for instruction becomes painfully clear.

To accomplish this task, teachers in ineffective groups often plan their instruction based on *delivering* all the standards and learning targets by the end of the school year. *Coverage* becomes the instructional priority. This approach inevitably leaves teachers frustrated and some students lacking the knowledge and skills needed to succeed at grade level or higher. Student learning becomes the casualty in our rush to get everything taught.

Highly effective teams function much differently, acknowledging that the sheer number of standards they are expected to teach is virtually impossible. Knowing this, they work together to develop a guaranteed and viable curriculum by identifying the essential skills and dispositions a student needs to succeed in the course or grade level and beyond (Marzano, 2017). Developing a guaranteed and viable curriculum does two things: (1) It ensures that all students have access to the same essential outcomes regardless of who is teaching the class, and (2) it ensures that all teachers have enough time to teach each essential standard to mastery (DuFour et al., 2024; Marzano, 2017).

Highly effective teams also recognize that the individual team members may value each standard differently. In *Concise Answers to Frequently Asked Questions About Professional Learning Communities at Work*, this need for teams to prioritize standards *together* is reaffirmed:

> Merely providing teachers with a copy of the state standards for their grade level does
> not ensure all students will have access to a guaranteed curriculum that can be taught
> in the amount of time available for teaching. Teachers may ignore the standards, assign
> different priorities to the standards, vary dramatically in how much time they devote to
> the standards, . . . and possess significant differences in their ability to teach the stan-
> dards. (Mattos, DuFour, DuFour, Eaker, & Many, 2016, p. 77)

Nothing in this statement is surprising. This is a critical challenge teachers and teams face each day. Highly effective teams address this challenge by recognizing the following.

- Certain standards are critical for *all students* to master in their current course or grade level and to be prepared for the next.
- There are too many standards to expect *all students* to learn *every* standard.
- Some standards in the required curriculum *are not essential* for students to learn at grade level or higher.
- We must make decisions together about what is essential and what is not.

Look at that list carefully. Notice that as highly effective teams work together to identify and then understand essential grade-level standards, *we are simultaneously identifying content and topics that have less priority.* These "nice to knows"—or standards we will prioritize only after ensuring that all students have mastered our essentials—*can be minimized or eliminated from our instructional planning* to create additional time for teaching or reteaching the most important outcomes in our curriculum.

Why Highly Effective Teams Do This

Have you ever been to a dinner buffet? The sheer variety of food options can be almost overwhelming. Craving pasta? You will find multiple kinds. Prefer chicken? It's there, too. Maybe you are in the mood for beef stir-fry, turkey, barbecue, or pizza. Whatever you choose, it's all hot and ready, sitting alongside lots of soups, salads, cakes, and cookies. The toughest part isn't finding something to eat. The toughest part is deciding what to put on your plate. Odds are that you walk into the buffet with a few priorities—things you know you are going to eat, no matter what. As you move through the line, you probably spot a few tempting items to return for, provided you have the room. And, of course, there are always options you know you are going to skip because they are just not worth the plate space or the strain on your health.

Acknowledging the limited time available for teaching and learning during the school year, most teachers already approach their decision making with the same strategies as a diner attending a buffet. Some standards are non-negotiable and must be added to their instructional plates, others may be revisited if time allows, and some might be left out entirely because they don't significantly contribute to the academic meal they are preparing for students.

What's not familiar to most teams is the suggestion that nice-to-know standards can be minimized or possibly eliminated altogether from their instructional planning to prioritize the agreed-on essentials in their curricula. In fact, for many teachers, the suggestion to minimize or eliminate some standards from their instructional plans can cause great anxiety. After all, every standard in the state or provincial curriculum *could* be included on the end-of-grade exams. If we don't attempt to cover everything in our standards—even if covering everything means moving so quickly that we can't ensure all students master our essentials—aren't we at risk of leaving our students unprepared for the measures used to hold us accountable?

Highly effective teams recognize that investing their collective energies into studying the best ways to teach, assess, and intervene around the highest-leverage outcomes in their standards is far more likely to lead to academic success for both students and schools. They commit to prioritizing those outcomes in every planning conversation and spend little to no time talking about the curriculum nonessentials. They may teach and assess nonessentials if they have the time, but that teaching and assessment is done individually, not collectively. Furthermore, they are as clear about the outcomes they will abandon if they run out of instructional time as they are about the outcomes they will spend more time teaching if their initial attempts don't result in high learning levels for all students. Figure 2.3.1 offers a comparison of language between ineffective groups and highly effective teams around this topic.

The Language of Ineffective Groups	The Language of Highly Effective Teams
"We must cover everything because it could be on the end-of-grade test."	"We need to prioritize our standards and skills, identifying those that all students need to know to be successful."
"Let's teach all the standards; some students will learn them and some won't."	"Let's focus our valuable time as a team on the standards and skills we have identified as essential."
"We each like to teach different things, so you identify what is essential for your class, and I'll identify what is essential for mine."	"We commit to studying the standards together and giving shared priority to those we value together."
"All standards have the same value. They were identified by the government, after all. We've got to teach all of them."	"We recognize all standards are not created equal, with some being nice to know while others are absolutely need to know."

FIGURE 2.3.1: Language comparison.

Notice that ineffective groups focus on the idea that covering standards and skills is more important than ensuring that students learn. Highly effective teams, on the other hand, recognize the importance of prioritization: Some standards and skills are more important than others, and we should spend every moment ensuring that students know them.

How Highly Effective Teams Do This

We are not suggesting that teams simply pick what they do and don't want to teach. Instead, prioritizing begins with conversations focused on exactly what all students need to know and be able to do to be successful in the course or grade level and exactly what can be minimized or eliminated to create additional time for teaching, assessing, and intervening around those essentials. Highly effective teams use the following resources as they begin making these critical decisions (DuFour et al., 2024).

- The state or provincial standards for the course or grade level
- Testing blueprints provided by the state or province

- Essential standards and skills for the grade levels above and below theirs, if available
- District curriculum pacing guides
- Recommended standards from professional organizations such as the National Council of Teachers of Mathematics

These resources are the anchor for team conversations because they provide insight into what other experts see as essential. If a standard never appears on released versions of end-of-grade exams or is given limited time in district pacing guides, for example, there is a good chance that it can be minimized in a team's instructional plans without much consequence. Referencing these external resources, teams sort the standards and skills covered in their required curriculum into one of three groups.

1. Standards and skills all students **must know** to be successful in the course or grade level.
2. Standards and skills **we will teach well** and may use to extend the learning of students who have mastered the essentials.
3. Standards and skills that are **nice to know** that we may briefly address if we have the time.

To assist in this process, authors Thomas W. Many and Ted Horrell (2014) provide a REAL question framework for teams to consider as they prioritize standards.

- **Readiness:** Will the standard provide students with the knowledge they need to be ready for the next course or grade level?
- **Endurance:** Will mastery of the standard provide students with knowledge or skills needed beyond the unit of study?
- **Assessed:** Is knowledge of the standard highly likely to be reflected in a large portion of a high-stakes assessment?
- **Leverage:** Will knowledge of the standard potentially have value in other courses or disciplines?

Ultimately, highly effective teams understand that to ensure all students learn at high levels, they must be *as* clear about the content and topics they can address briefly or not at all as they are about the essentials for the grade level or course. These shared decisions about what is essential and what is not can help teams better allocate their instructional time, their intervention time, and the time they have for shared study of practice.

Tools and Resources for Highly Effective Teams

The following tools and resources will help you accomplish the work for this essential action.

- **"Tool: Identifying Essential Learning Outcomes for a Unit of Study Checklist" (page 97):** A key takeaway from this chapter is the importance of working systematically to identify the essentials and nonessentials in your curriculum. These decisions cannot be left to chance, as they directly impact the work you will do to ensure students are ready to move forward in their learning. This checklist is designed to provide your team with a clear set of criteria when assessing the importance of a standard or skill within your curriculum.

- **"Tool: Using REAL to Identify Essential Standards" (page 98):** The REAL criteria outlined earlier in this essential action have become a widely used framework for prioritizing state and provincial standards. If your school is familiar with these criteria for identifying essential and nonessential standards, you may find this tool valuable. It is designed to guide teams in evaluating individual standards against each of the REAL criteria, generating scores that can be compared across all the standards under consideration.

- **"Tool: A Record of Our Essential Standards and Skills" (page 99):** One common misconception about recordkeeping in a professional learning community is that its primary purpose is to demonstrate to principals that required work is being completed. In reality, recordkeeping is not about accountability. Instead, it provides a reference for the decisions teams make, allowing them to revisit and build on those decisions in future years. Use this tool to document your team's current perspectives on the standards and skills students must learn, the standards and skills you will teach, and the standards and skills you plan to de-emphasize in an upcoming unit of study.

- **Chapter 6 of *Learning by Doing, Fourth Edition*:** The notion of prioritizing essentials is well established in *Learning by Doing* (DuFour et al., 2024). This chapter, "Establishing a Focus on Learning," offers additional recommendations that can help readers further polish their understanding of—and process for—identifying essential and nonessential standards.

- **Chapter 1 of *Simplifying the Journey: Six Steps to Schoolwide Collaboration, Consistency, and Clarity in a PLC at Work* (Sonju et al., 2024):** An additional reference that you might want to consider while building your knowledge about the roles that essentials and nonessentials play in the work of highly effective teacher teams is the book *Simplifying the Journey*. The first chapter of this text, "Identifying Essential Standards and Skills," explores critical question one of a PLC—"What knowledge, skills, and dispositions should every student acquire as a result of this unit, this course, or this grade level?" (DuFour et al., 2024, p. 44).

Tool: Identifying Essential Learning Outcomes for a Unit of Study Checklist

Instructions: As a team, consult state and district curriculum guides for potential essential outcomes for an upcoming unit of study. Compile the outcomes that your team members think might be essential, and then complete one checklist for each of the outcomes to determine if it should be added to your team's list of essentials for your next unit of study.

Name of Unit:		
Required Content and Skill Objective Under Consideration		
Does this essential learning outcome directly support the mission of our school and our shared vision of quality instruction?	Yes	No
Does this essential learning outcome cover knowledge or skills that will be new to our students, valuable to their continued studies, or important long after they have left school?	Yes	No
Is there any evidence in school curriculum guides that our students have *been exposed to* this essential learning outcome in previous years?	Yes	No
Is there any evidence in recent assessments that our students have *mastered* this essential learning outcome in previous years?	Yes	No
Is there any evidence in recent assessments that our students have *struggled to master* this essential learning outcome in previous years?	Yes	No
Will mastering this essential learning outcome help our students *excel in* other content areas or grade levels? If so, which ones?	Yes	No
Would you recommend that we include this learning outcome on our list of essential learning outcomes for this unit?	Yes	No
Final Thoughts on This Learning Outcome		

Source: Ferriter, W. M. (2020). The big book of tools for collaborative teams in a PLC at Work. *Solution Tree Press.*

Tool: Using REAL to Identify Essential Standards

Instructions: As one of their first steps, teacher teams identify a few essential outcomes to study together. Use the following process to determine whether a standard you are considering is truly essential.

1. Work as a team to generate a list of standards you believe should be considered for your list of grade-level essentials.

2. Provide each team member with one copy of this tool for each standard you evaluate.

3. One standard at a time, ask team members to independently rate each standard using the REAL criteria and rating scale detailed in this tool.

4. Share your ratings; look for standards that earned universally high ratings. Add those to your list of essentials for this unit of study.

5. Share your ratings; look for standards that earned universally low ratings. Remove those from your list of essentials for this unit of study.

6. If you find areas of disagreement in your ratings, turn to outside evidence or experts to resolve those disagreements. Examples: What do your principals or instructional coaches think about this standard? Is this standard considered necessary by national curriculum experts or organizations?

Standard for Consideration:

Rate the standard we are considering against the following criteria using a scale from 1 to 5, where 1 represents not important *and 5 represents* very important.

Criteria		Description	Your Rating
R	Readiness	How important is this standard for student success in the **same subject** in the **next grade level**?	
E	Endurance	How important is this standard for student success **long after they have left school**?	
A	Assessed	How important is this standard for student success on **end-of-grade exams**?	
L	Leverage	How important is this standard for student success in **multiple subject areas**?	
Total Points for This Standard:			

Will this standard go on your list of essentials for this unit?	Yes	No

Reference

Many, T. W., & Horrell, T. (2014). Prioritizing the standards using R.E.A.L. criteria. *TEPSA News, 71*(1), 1–2.

Source: Ferriter, W. M., Mattos, M., & Meyer, R. J. (2025). The big book of tools for RTI at Work. Solution Tree Press.

Tool: A Record of Our Essential Standards and Skills

As your team begins to plan for an upcoming unit of instruction, consider each of the standards that you are expected to cover. Create a record of your shared decisions about what is essential and what is nonessential by sorting those standards into one of the three categories you see here.

Essential standards and skills that all students **must know** to be successful in the course or grade level, which will be the focus of our team's common assessments and intervention efforts	Standards and skills **we will teach well** and could use to extend the learning of students who have mastered the essentials	Standards and skills that are **nice to know** that we may briefly address given our limited instructional time

PART TWO
Focus on Learning

2

We Agree on How to Sequence Content and Pace Our Course

*If teachers have not agreed on the meaning and significance of
what they are being asked to teach, they will not be able to establish
common pacing in their courses and grade levels.*

**—RICHARD DUFOUR, REBECCA DUFOUR, ROBERT EAKER, THOMAS W. MANY,
MIKE MATTOS, AND ANTHONY MUHAMMAD**

One final decision highly effective teams make when establishing clarity and consistency is how to sequence content and pace instruction throughout the school year. Highly effective teams recognize that the order in which they introduce concepts directly impacts student understanding. Certain skills and ideas act as building blocks for others, creating a logical learning progression that supports mastery. A well-sequenced curriculum ensures that students receive instruction in a way that makes sense, scaffolding concepts and reinforcing prior knowledge before introducing more complex ideas.

Beyond supporting student learning, common pacing also provides a foundation for meaningful collaboration. If teachers on the same team are teaching different concepts at different times, opportunities to work together disappear. Highly effective teams enter a whole new level of *operational clarity* when they come to a consensus on sequencing and pacing. Establishing shared pacing means that teams can analyze student learning in real time, compare instructional strategies, and provide targeted interventions together. It also allows students to receive support from multiple teachers, as every educator on the team is focused on the same essential content at roughly the same time.

However, many teachers are initially resistant to the idea of common pacing. In traditional school settings, teachers have made instructional decisions in isolation, determining what to teach, when to teach it, and how much time to spend on each concept. These decisions are often deeply personal, shaped by a teacher's philosophy, experience, and favorite lessons. Some teachers have signature projects they are reluctant to give up, even when those projects take up a lot of instructional time. Others feel strongly about spending more time on certain concepts they see as particularly valuable. And still others worry that shared pacing will lead to scripted lessons, where every teacher must be on the same page, on the same day, and teaching in exactly the same way. This kind of rigid standardization stifles creativity and shifts the focus of our work from ensuring students learn to covering lessons in a predetermined amount of time.

But highly effective teams know that agreeing on pacing does not mean giving up professional autonomy. Instead, it means making collective decisions about how to logically sequence learning while still allowing flexibility in how they deliver instruction. A strong pacing guide provides structure for a collaborative team's work, not rigidity.

Why Highly Effective Teams Do This

That final point may be the most important point to remember. Common pacing isn't about restricting teachers; instead, it is about helping teams be more intentional. Highly effective teams commit to common pacing because they know the following.

- **Concepts build on one another:** Most learning happens in a progression. Students must master certain foundational skills before teachers can introduce more advanced concepts. A shared pacing guide ensures that these relationships are respected and that students receive instruction in a way that supports understanding.

- **Collaboration requires alignment:** If team members are teaching different content at different times, collaboration becomes meaningless. It is difficult, if not impossible, to collaborate with one another if every teacher is at a different place in the curriculum.

- **Common pacing makes interventions more effective:** When teachers agree on common pacing for grade-level essentials, they can work together to provide extra support for students who are not yet meeting grade-level expectations. They can group struggling students across classrooms, taking advantage of the expertise of individual team members to reteach concepts.

- **Common pacing ensures equity for students:** Without common pacing, students in different classrooms can have vastly different learning experiences. Some may get days of instruction on key concepts, while others receive only a basic overview of the exact same topics. Want to know if this is happening on your team? Listen for families and students making comparisons across teachers. If you hear phrases like, "Mrs. Jensen's class is way easier than Mr. Banerjee's," you will know that inconsistency is creating inequity. Common pacing makes sure that all students, no matter whose roster they are on, have access to the same essentials at the same level of instructional depth.

While the first step that teams should take is to work with their own curriculum, highly effective teams also consider vertical alignment when sequencing content and pacing their course. Here's why: Aligning with the previous grade level provides insight into the concepts and skills students have already covered, allowing teams to make informed decisions about where to begin. Similarly, understanding the expectations of the next grade level ensures that teams are effectively preparing students for what comes next in their learning.

This prevents the wasted instructional time that occurs when teachers assume students have mastered skills or concepts that were never explicitly taught in the previous grade level or course. It also ensures that key concepts don't fall through the cracks due to differences in emphasis between grade levels and courses. When teams examine pacing across grade levels, they can create a logical sequence of instruction that builds on student learning year after year, ensuring that knowledge and skills are reinforced rather than repeated unnecessarily. Figure 2.4.1 offers a comparison of language between ineffective groups and highly effective teams around this topic.

The Language of Ineffective Groups	The Language of Highly Effective Teams
"We hope our students learned this skill last year because we don't have time to teach it."	"Let's spend a little time looking at what students learned last year. That way, we will have a better idea of what they are ready to learn this year."
"We've identified our essential standards, and we are committed to teaching the standards, but each teacher can choose their pacing."	"We agree on pacing to help ensure consistency and facilitate collaboration."
"We will have our own opinions of when to teach standards, so we will let teachers decide."	"If we aren't in roughly the same place at roughly the same time, there's nothing to collaborate about! Common pacing just makes everything easier."
"Teaching is already hard. It will take too much time to get on the same page."	"Being efficient is crucial to the success of our students and our team. We can't afford not to commit to common pacing."
"I'm not interested in teaching the exact same way that you do. I'm a different person with my own professional skills and interests."	"We are agreeing on when we'll teach our essentials and how long we'll spend on each one, but we still get to make our own decisions about the best way to teach each lesson. That's where our professional autonomy comes in."

FIGURE 2.4.1: Language comparison.

Notice that ineffective groups are reactive when it comes to common pacing, hoping students have learned prerequisite skills and resisting alignment because it feels like extra work. In contrast, highly effective teams are proactive. They recognize that common pacing is not about control but about the creation of consistency. Instead of assuming students are prepared, they examine prior learning to make informed instructional decisions. Rather than seeing pacing as an individual preference, they see it as a shared commitment that makes working together easier. Ultimately, highly effective teams understand that getting on the same page isn't just about logistics—it's about maximization of learning.

How Highly Effective Teams Do This

Learning by Doing, Fourth Edition (DuFour et al., 2024), details a series of *dangerous detours and seductive shortcuts* that schools sometimes take when sequencing content and pacing courses:

- Distributing state or provincial district guidelines to individual teachers as a substitute for team dialogue
- Assigning a committee of teachers to establish the curriculum and present it to their colleagues
- Purchasing the curriculum
- Allowing the textbook to determine the curriculum (p. 165)

Can you see what all those dangerous detours and seductive shortcuts have in common? First, they strip professional autonomy away from collaborative teams and cheapen educators' expertise. Teacher teams that play an active role in sequencing their content and pacing their course have a greater commitment to the instructional plans they are creating, as well as a greater sense of responsibility for the results of their decisions. That matters because teams with a greater commitment to the plans they create are more likely to course-correct when things go wrong. When teams are given a pacing guide created by someone else and are expected to implement it without question, they stop reflecting and start complying.

And while the detailed dangerous detours and seductive shortcuts will certainly accelerate a group's work—after all, making decisions about sequencing and pacing requires an investment of already limited planning minutes—they strip meaningful learning opportunities away from collaborative teams. We have to remember that when teams engage in deep conversations about the logical progression of key concepts, they aren't just making a pacing guide; they are building a shared understanding of their curriculum that strengthens instruction far beyond a single school year. Stated more simply, this process isn't just about *planning*. It's about *professional learning*, and that learning is dependent on the conversations that highly effective teams engage in when sequencing their content and pacing their course.

Here are some additional tips for teams ready to sequence their content and pace their course.

- **Start with the essentials:** Keep in mind that whether talking about instruction, assessment, or intervention, highly effective teams stay focused on essentials in their work with one another. That focus should also guide discussions about pacing. This ensures that every instructional minute is spent where it has the greatest impact.

- **Determine logical progressions:** Pacing isn't just about deciding unit order. It is about understanding the logical progression of skills and concepts. A well-sequenced curriculum acknowledges that each new concept builds on what came before it, creating a natural flow that makes learning easier for students and more effective for teachers.

- **Allow for flexibility:** Pacing guides provide a clear timeline for when to introduce key concepts and how much time to teach them in, but they shouldn't dictate what someone must teach on specific days. Flexibility is key. Teachers need the ability to adjust based on their students' needs. Rigid, day-by-day pacing ignores the reality that learning doesn't happen on a fixed schedule. Effective pacing allows teams to stay aligned while remaining responsive to what's happening in their classrooms.

- **Use common assessments to guide adjustments:** Regular formative assessments should inform team pacing decisions. (See action 3.1, page 119, for assessment information.) If those assessments show that students are struggling with a concept, slow down and reteach before moving on. Your pacing guide should serve your students, not the other way around, and if students haven't learned an essential yet, moving forward to stay on pace just leaves them further behind.

- **Review and adjust as needed:** Highly effective teams treat their pacing guides as living documents that evolve as they learn more about their students and their course. Teams should revisit them regularly, updating their shared decisions to better reflect their shared knowledge of the best way to teach their content to their students.

- **Keep student learning at the center:** Highly effective teams recognize that they should not base pacing decisions on personal preference. Instead, they base them on what's most essential for student success. That means potentially letting go of enjoyable activities if they aren't as important as we thought they were. When teams prioritize what students need to learn over what teachers like to teach, they create pacing guides that are not only aligned and intentional but also truly impactful.

Finally, remember that establishing common pacing isn't just about keeping teams on the same page. It is about deepening their understanding of what they teach and how students learn best. The real value is not in the document you create but in the conversations that shape it.

Tools and Resources for Highly Effective Teams

The following tools and resources will help you accomplish the work for this essential action.

- **"Tool: Team Pacing Guide Protocol" (page 107):** This protocol can help teams create a pacing guide by identifying essential standards, sequencing learning logically, and aligning instruction. By engaging in these conversations, teams not only clarify what to teach and when but also strengthen their ability to adapt and respond to student needs throughout the year.

- **"Tool: Team Pacing Guide Template" (page 109):** This template is designed to be used alongside "Tool: Team Pacing Guide Protocol." Use it to record your thinking as you begin to make sequencing and pacing decisions for your course or grade level. Remember that the decisions made here can always be revisited. Pacing guides should always be informed by our professional judgment and expertise.

- **"Tool: Pacing Guide for a Cycle of Instruction" (page 110):** While the "Tool: Team Pacing Guide Protocol" and "Tool: Team Pacing Guide Template" help teams sequence an entire course or grade level, this tool—and its corresponding **"Sample: Pacing Guide for a Cycle of Instruction" (page 112)**—is designed for short-term instructional planning. It allows teams to break a unit into manageable learning cycles, aligning essential outcomes, pacing, instructional strategies, and assessments over a two-to-three-week period. By structuring instruction around a handful of key concepts and ensuring each cycle ends with a common formative assessment, this tool helps teams stay focused throughout a school year.

- **"Tool: Critical Issues for Team Consideration—Highly Effective Team Actions" (page 114):** This tool provides teams an opportunity to reflect on their progress, celebrate strengths, and identify next steps worth taking. At the conclusion of each set of actions, teams use a portion of this tool to dialogue about their current practices, to identify strengths and areas of focus, and to identify next steps on their pathway to becoming a highly effective collaborative team.

Tool: Team Pacing Guide Protocol

This activity will help your team develop a common pacing plan for your grade level or course. The goal is not to dictate exact daily lessons but to create a shared plan for teaching your curriculum that ensures consistency, supports collaboration, and allows professional flexibility.

Before You Begin:

- Consider using electronic collaboration tools (Google Docs, shared spreadsheets, digital whiteboards, and so on) to create a pacing guide that is easily accessible and editable by all team members.

- If using a digital format, enable a notes or comments section where team members can document ideas, questions, and suggested revisions throughout the process.

- Set a timer for each step to keep the discussion focused and productive.

Materials Needed:

- Copies of essential standards for your course and grade level

- Blank pacing guide templates (printed or digital)

- Markers, sticky notes, or other annotation tools

- A whiteboard or digital collaboration space

Steps to Create Your Pacing Guide

Step 1: Establish a Purpose and Review Essentials (Five minutes)

1. Ensure all team members have a copy of the essential standards for your course.

2. Have a brief discussion on why common pacing matters and how it benefits both student learning and teacher collaboration.

Step 2: Identify and Prioritize Key Standards (Fifteen minutes)

1. Divide the team into pairs or small groups. Assign each pair or group a portion of the essential standards to analyze. Each group should do the following.

   a. Identify the most critical standards that must be prioritized.

   b. Determine logical progressions, ensuring foundational skills come before more advanced concepts.

   c. Consider real-world constraints, such as state or provincial testing windows, major assessments, or interdisciplinary alignment.

2. Rotate pairs or groups to share their selected standards and priorities with the larger team. Adjust and refine based on team feedback.

Step 3: Draft the Initial Pacing Guide (Thirty minutes)

1. Distribute blank pacing guide templates if members don't already have them.

2. Assign each team member or small group a portion of the pacing guide to develop (such as one quarter, one unit, or one grading period per team member).

page 1 of 2

The Handbook for Highly Effective Teams in a PLC at Work © 2025 Solution Tree Press • SolutionTree.com
Visit **go.SolutionTree.com/PLCbooks** to download this free reproducible.

PART TWO
Focus on Learning

3. As team members draft their assigned sections, they should include the following.

   * Standards' numbers and descriptions
   * Learning objectives tied to each standard
   * Suggested instructional strategies to support student mastery
   * Assessment ideas (both formative and summative)
   * Proficiency scales or success criteria
   * Allocated time frames for each standard or unit

4. Team members should leave comments or sticky notes for any questions or suggested modifications.

Step 4: Review and Refine as a Team (Twenty minutes)

1. Gather as a full team to review each section of the pacing guide.
2. Discuss alignment across units. Does the sequence make sense? Are you balancing depth with coverage?
3. Use sticky notes or digital comment boxes to suggest refinements.
4. Address major concerns and make collaborative adjustments as needed.

Step 5: Do Final Revisions and Determine Next Steps

1. Decide on a process for ongoing review and refinement. When will the team revisit pacing decisions to make necessary adjustments?
2. Document areas where you require flexibility (such as buffer time for reteaching or review weeks).
3. If needed, assign a team lead to consolidate notes and finalize the pacing guide.

Tool: Team Pacing Guide Template

Use this template to record the shared decisions your team makes while working through the "Tool: Team Pacing Guide Protocol" (page 107).

1. **Divide into pairs or small groups**, and assign each group a portion of the essential standards.

2. **Brainstorm and sequence** the standards within your assigned section, considering logical progressions and instructional priorities. All ideas are welcome at this stage.

3. **Share and refine.** Each group presents their suggested sequence to the full team for discussion and feedback.

4. **Organize final pacing decisions** in the following table, ensuring alignment across the course.

Remember that this template is a **living document** that can be revisited and adjusted as needed.

Brainstorm	
Group 1 standards:	Group 2 standards:
Group 3 standards:	Group 4 standards:

Organize	
Quarter 1 standards:	Quarter 2 standards:
Quarter 3 standards:	Quarter 4 standards:

The Handbook for Highly Effective Teams in a PLC at Work® © 2025 Solution Tree Press • SolutionTree.com
Visit **go.SolutionTree.com/PLCbooks** to download this free reproducible.

Tool: Pacing Guide for a Cycle of Instruction

Instructions: In the first column, list sequentially three to five essential outcomes you will cover in this cycle of instruction and use Webb's (1997) Depth of Knowledge (DOK) matrix to identify the level of rigor that each one requires. Then, in the second column, estimate the number of lessons it will take to teach each outcome to mastery. Remember that cycles of instruction should happen quickly in a professional learning community, taking roughly fifteen to twenty instructional days to complete. For the third column, answer these questions: What should every student know and be able to do when we are finished teaching this outcome? What skills should they be able to demonstrate? What vocabulary should they know? In the last column, record the instructional activities you are going to use to teach these concepts to the students in your classes. Finally, fill in the date and requirements for the common formative assessment that will cover this unit.

Name of Unit: _____

Number of Weeks Necessary for Teaching the Outcomes in This Cycle of Instruction: _____

Dates for This Cycle of Instruction:			
Essential Outcomes	**Estimated Pacing**	**Knowledge, Skills, and Vocabulary to Cover**	**Core Instructional Activities**
DOK Level of Target: ☐ Recall and Reproduction ☐ Skills and Concepts ☐ Strategic Thinking ☐ Extended Thinking			
DOK Level of Target: ☐ Recall and Reproduction ☐ Skills and Concepts ☐ Strategic Thinking ☐ Extended Thinking			
DOK Level of Target: ☐ Recall and Reproduction ☐ Skills and Concepts ☐ Strategic Thinking ☐ Extended Thinking			

PART TWO
Focus on Learning

DOK Level of Target: ☐ Recall and Reproduction ☐ Skills and Concepts ☐ Strategic Thinking ☐ Extended Thinking		
DOK Level of Target: ☐ Recall and Reproduction ☐ Skills and Concepts ☐ Strategic Thinking ☐ Extended Thinking		

Date of Common Formative Assessment:

Requirements for Common Formative Assessments:

List assessments here, including where they are stored and any materials necessary to administer them. Remember that a good common formative assessment only covers three to five concepts. Also, remember that it is important to ask three to five questions per concept on your common formative assessment in order to gather enough data to take action.

Reference

Webb, N. L. (1997). *Research monograph number 6: Criteria for alignment of expectations and assessments in mathematics and science education.* Washington, DC: Council of Chief State School Officers.

Source: Ferriter, W. M. (2020). The big book of tools for collaborative teams in a PLC at Work. *Solution Tree Press.*

PART TWO
Focus on Learning

Sample: Pacing Guide for a Cycle of Instruction

Instructions: In the first column, list sequentially three to five essential outcomes you will cover in this cycle of instruction and use Webb's (1997) Depth of Knowledge (DOK) matrix to identify the level of rigor that each one requires. Then, in the second column, estimate the number of lessons it will take to teach each outcome to mastery. Remember that cycles of instruction should happen quickly in a professional learning community, taking roughly fifteen to twenty instructional days to complete. For the third column, answer these questions: What should every student know and be able to do when we are finished teaching this outcome? What skills should they be able to demonstrate? What vocabulary should they know? In the last column, record the instructional activities you are going to use to teach these concepts to the students in your classes. Finally, fill in the date and requirements for the common formative assessment that will cover this unit.

Name of Unit: Matter

Number of Weeks Necessary for Teaching the Outcomes in This Cycle of Instruction: Four Weeks

Dates for This Cycle of Instruction: Monday, October 29, to Friday, November 2			
Essential Outcomes	**Estimated Pacing**	**Knowledge, Skills, and Vocabulary to Cover**	**Core Instructional Activities**
Measuring Matter **DOK Level of Target:** ☐ Recall and Reproduction ☑ Skills and Concepts ☐ Strategic Thinking ☐ Extended Thinking	Two class periods	Students should understand the difference between *mass* and *volume*. Students should understand how mass and volume work together to determine the *density* of a substance. Students will learn to use a *triple beam balance* to measure the mass of an object. Students should understand how to calculate the volume of an *irregular solid* using a *graduated cylinder* and the *displacement of water*.	Activity: What *Is* the Density of Your Silent Reading Book? Activity: Archimedes and the Golden Crown
Density's Role in Floating and Sinking **DOK Level of Target:** ☐ Recall and Reproduction ☐ Skills and Concepts ☑ Strategic Thinking ☐ Extended Thinking	Two class periods	Students should understand that dense materials will always *push through* less dense materials. Students should understand that you can't determine the density of an object just by the size of an object. Instead, density of an object is a function of the relationship between the size of an object and the mass inside of it.	Activity: Get in the Game With Team Density

| Density as a Characteristic Property of Matter

DOK Level of Target:
☑ Recall and Reproduction
☐ Skills and Concepts
☐ Strategic Thinking
☐ Extended Thinking | One class period | Students should understand that *characteristic properties of matter* don't change no matter how much of a substance you have. That makes those properties useful for identifying unknown substances.

Students should understand that density is a characteristic property of matter.

Students should understand that mass and volume are not characteristic properties of matter. They are both dependent on the amount of a substance that you have. | Activity: How Dense *Is* That Modeling Clay? |

Date of Common Formative Assessment:

Monday, November 5

Requirements for Common Formative Assessments:

List assessments here, including where they are stored and any materials necessary to administer them. Remember that a good common formative assessment only covers three to five concepts. Also, remember that it is important to ask three to five questions per concept on your common formative assessment in order to gather enough data to take action.

- **Selected-Response Assessment: Measuring Matter and Understanding Density**—*The assessment is written and stored in our team drive. Mastery = 70 percent or higher*

- **Performance Assessment: Calculating the Density of a Marble**—*Hand each group of two students a marble and ask them to calculate its density. Students should be able to use a triple beam balance to calculate the mass and apply the displacement of water method to determine its volume. A checklist for scoring this performance is stored in our team drive.*

Reference

Webb, N. L. (1997). *Research monograph number 6: Criteria for alignment of expectations and assessments in mathematics and science education.* Washington, DC: Council of Chief State School Officers.

Source: Ferriter, W. M. (2020). The big book of tools for collaborative teams in a PLC at Work. *Solution Tree Press.*

Tool: Critical Issues for Team Consideration— Highly Effective Team Actions

Your honest evaluation is critical!

Please thoughtfully discuss your team's reality in each of the highly effective team indicators. Use the scale to rate your team in each area. At the conclusion of each section, identify areas to celebrate and areas for your team to intensify efforts.

+   This is very true of our team. This belief or action is embedded in our beliefs and actions.

✓   This is sometimes true of our team. We are not consistent about this belief or action.

−   This is rarely or never true of our team. We need to work on implementing this belief or action.

Rating	Part 1: Highly Effective Teams Have a Common Foundation
	Action 1.1: We identify team roles, norms, and protocols to guide us in working together.
	Action 1.2: We have a process for addressing moments when personalities interfere with the team's work.
	Action 1.3: We use SMART goals to drive our work.
	Action 1.4: We regularly evaluate our team's effectiveness.

Celebrations:

Next steps:

Rating	Part 2: Highly Effective Teams Focus on Learning for All Students
	Action 2.1: We collectively identify essential learnings and define what success looks like in student work.
	Action 2.2: We identify the prerequisite knowledge and skills needed to master our essentials.
	Action 2.3: We identify course content and topics we can minimize or eliminate to devote more time to our essentials.
	Action 2.4: We agree on how to sequence content and pace our course.

Celebrations:

Next steps:

Rating	Part 3: Highly Effective Teams Effectively Use Assessments and Data
	Action 3.1: We develop and deliver frequent common formative assessments throughout our units of instruction.
	Action 3.2: We use team assessment data to identify high-impact instructional strategies.
	Action 3.3: We teach students the criteria we will use to judge their work.
	Action 3.4: We create exemplars students can examine to evaluate their own progress toward mastery.

Celebrations:

Next steps:

Rating	Part 4: Highly Effective Teams Provide Extra Time and Support for Learning
	Action 4.1: We create flexible time during our units of instruction to provide extra time and support to learners.
	Action 4.2: We deliver targeted interventions to support students who have not yet reached grade-level expectations.
	Action 4.3: We deliver targeted extensions to students working beyond grade-level expectations.

Celebrations:

Next steps:

PART TWO
Focus on Learning

2

Source: Adapted from DuFour, R., DuFour, R., Eaker, R., Many, T. W., Mattos, M., & Muhammad, A. (2024). Learning by doing: A handbook for Professional Learning Communities at Work (4th ed.). Solution Tree Press.

PART 3

Highly Effective Teams Effectively Use Assessments and Data

Assessments and data are powerful tools for driving improvement for students and teacher teams alike. The third part of *The Handbook for Highly Effective Teams in a PLC at Work* outlines how highly effective teams create and use assessments to monitor student learning, study instruction, and identify areas for intervention or extension. With a focus on both formative and standardized data, teams can ensure their efforts lead to measurable progress.

- **Action 3.1:** We Develop and Deliver Frequent Common Formative Assessments Throughout Our Units of Instruction (page 119)
- **Action 3.2:** We Use Team Assessment Data to Identify High-Impact Instructional Strategies (page 133)
- **Action 3.3:** We Teach Students the Criteria We Will Use to Judge Their Work (page 143)
- **Action 3.4:** We Create Exemplars Students Can Examine to Evaluate Their Own Progress Toward Mastery (page 155)

We Develop and Deliver Frequent Common Formative Assessments Throughout Our Units of Instruction

Teachers and teacher teams don't want to wait until the end of the unit to see where students are in achieving the grade-level standard or learning target. . . . Teacher teams use the common formative assessment data to identify the essential learning students need more support on or time to learn, and plan new lessons or instruction before the end of the unit.

—NICOLE DIMICH

As was described in earlier chapters, the work of highly effective teams begins by identifying the essential standards and skills all students must learn to succeed at grade level or higher. Teams then engage in collaborative discussions about what each identified essential means and what mastery of those essentials would look like in student work. These conversations ensure continuity within the team and provide a shared focus for their instructional decisions. Once teams have a shared understanding of mastery for each essential outcome, they can more effectively design common formative assessments that identify students in need of additional time and support for learning.

It is important to note that teams develop or agree on common formative assessments only *after* they have developed a shared understanding of the essential that they are trying to teach. Without building this knowledge first, it is impossible for a team to ensure that the assessments they write accurately measure the concepts and skills outlined in the standard. Teams that begin their assessment work with a shared understanding of the essential they are trying to teach, on the other hand, can better align their assessments with the intended rigor and focus of the standard, avoiding misaligned tasks that fail to provide reliable insights into student progress.

It is also important to note that the act of giving a common formative assessment does little to improve student learning. Instead, it's *what the team does with the results they collect* that impacts student learning and increases the team's efficacy. To be clear, collaborative teams can identify essentials, administer frequent assessments, and even build in extra time and support for those students who require it, but if they don't use common formative assessment data to learn together and increase their instructional effectiveness, they will never function as a true community of professionals (Sonju et al., 2024).

Finally, it is important to note that if the assessments we write are going to inform our next professional actions, we must do more than identify who passed and who failed when analyzing data. Instead, teams must determine the exact skills and standards that each student has mastered and where gaps in their learning remain. This detailed analysis ensures that our instructional responses align with individual student needs. Education author Robert Eaker (2020) reaffirms this work when he says, "Improved student learning only occurs to the degree that teacher teams collaboratively analyze the results of each formative assessment, using a predetermined protocol to *assess the learning of each student*" (p. 191, emphasis added). Our goal when assessing learning is not to simply sort students into groups for intervention but to guarantee learning for all.

Why Highly Effective Teams Do This

One of our favorite ways to explain why highly effective teams use frequent common formative assessments to track progress by student, by standard, and by skill is to have you think of your last physical. When you went in to see your doctor, they evaluated you in many different categories. They almost certainly took your blood pressure, your temperature, and your heart rate. They almost certainly checked your weight and height, looked closely at your skin for moles or rashes, and listened to your heart and lungs to detect abnormal sounds, murmurs, or breathing issues. Finally, they almost certainly ordered blood work to screen for diabetes, high cholesterol, or other signs of internal diseases. Each of these observations was documented individually in your patient chart, contributing to the ongoing record your doctor maintains to guide your care.

What your doctor *didn't* do was give you a single score at the end of your physical—"You earned a 73 this year, Amy!"—to describe your overall health. And that makes sense, doesn't it? General scores bundling together a wide range of indicators of your health would do little to help your doctor identify actionable next steps to move your care forward. Need an example? Imagine that you went to your doctor complaining of fatigue and weight gain. Without tracking your specific health indicators over time, she might simply recommend general lifestyle changes like improving your diet and exercise, which may not address the root cause of the issue. On the other hand, if she has been tracking your iron levels, she might identify a specific condition like anemia, which often causes fatigue and weight gain in patients. Detailed information helps doctors make more accurate diagnoses and offer patients more targeted treatments.

In the same way, highly effective teams understand that detailed, specific data on student progress—rather than a single, general score representing mastery—are essential for ensuring every student learns at high levels. Knowing that a group of fifth-grade students, for example, has failed an assessment of their ability to multiply fractions is not nearly as important as being able to identify the reasons that they struggled. Instead, it is critical to determine whether the issue lies in their conceptual understanding of multiplication, in their understanding of the individual steps necessary to multiply fractions, or in their understanding of foundational skills like basic multiplication facts. Without pinpointing the exact cause of student struggles, interventions may miss the mark, leaving the students without the support they need to learn at high levels. Figure 3.1.1 offers a comparison of language between ineffective groups and highly effective teams around this topic.

The Language of Ineffective Groups	The Language of Highly Effective Teams
"The end-of-unit assessment will give us all the information we need."	"Common formative assessments provide us valuable information we can use to make our interventions more effective."
"We only need to know who passed or failed the assessment."	"For intervention, let's focus on strategies that align with the specific needs we spot in the data."
"Our common formative assessments are mainly for adding grades to the gradebook."	"Collaborating to examine assessment results ensures our instruction meets student needs."
"It's too time-consuming to figure out exactly why students are struggling."	"We need to know the specific skills or concepts our students are struggling with to make sure our interventions make a difference."

FIGURE 3.1.1: Language comparison.

Notice that ineffective groups often prioritize convenience over meaningful analysis when assessing learning. They treat common formative assessments as tools for the gradebook instead of tools for guidance of student growth. On the other hand, highly effective teams use language that reflects a commitment to ensuring all students learn at high levels. They see common formative assessments as opportunities to identify specific skill gaps and tailor interventions to meet individual needs.

How Highly Effective Teams Do This

One of our favorite definitions of the term *common formative assessment* comes from our colleague and friend Kim Bailey, who writes, "Common formative assessments are team-designed, intentional measures leading to the production of a permanent product that can be examined by teachers and students for the purpose of monitoring attainment of essential learning targets throughout a unit of instruction" (K. Bailey, personal communication, March 10, 2016). Bailey's definition has five parts. Can you spot them? Here's what we see.

1. **Common formative assessments are team designed:** One of the most common mistakes schools make with common formative assessments is overlooking the importance of having teacher team members design them together. When teams

collaborate to create common assessments, they are not just building tests—they are having critical conversations about what mastery looks like in student work.

2. **Common formative assessments are intentional measures:** Every question on a common formative assessment should directly tie to a specific essential standard or learning target that students are expected to learn. This connection allows teams to use the results to provide learners targeted support. When questions aren't intentionally linked to essential standards or learning targets, the information gathered can't be used to identify meaningful next steps worth taking.

3. **Common formative assessments should lead to the production of a permanent product that can be examined:** The purpose of giving a common formative assessment is to gather information that a collaborative team can learn from and act on. That learning and action only happens when teams have an artifact to examine. Whether that artifact involves item analyses from multiple-choice tests, samples of responses to open-ended questions, or performance recordings, teams need something tangible to study together if they are going to learn from an assessment.

4. **Common formative assessments are used by both teachers and students:** Notice that Bailey's definition of common formative assessments highlights two audiences for the results of common formative assessments: (1) teachers and (2) students. You probably weren't surprised by the suggestion that teachers should use common formative assessments to inform their next instructional actions. That has been a cornerstone of collaborative team practices for years. But highly effective teams take it a step further. They turn their students into partners in the learning process, helping them monitor their own progress and make meaningful adjustments along the way.

5. **Common formative assessments are given throughout a unit of instruction:** Unlike summative assessments, which serve as a final certification of student performance *at the end* of a learning cycle, common formative assessments are designed to generate information that moves learning forward *during* the cycle. That's why there are no hard-and-fast rules about when common assessments should be given; teams should administer them whenever they need insight into student mastery during a unit. The key is to give these assessments early enough for teachers and students to make meaningful changes before students fall so far behind that more intensive interventions are required.

There are also no firm rules about what teams should use as a common formative assessment. Instead, ask yourself, "What evidence would we want to collect to know if a student has met success in the essential that we are studying?" You can use anything from simple exit tickets and multiple-choice questions written with your peers or chosen from district curriculum materials to rubrics, graphic organizers, and student performances for common formative assessments. As long as the task you create is an accurate measure of the agreed-on proficiency level for the essential standard, learning target, or skill that you are currently teaching, it works as a common formative assessment. Again, what a team does with the results of their common formative assessments is what makes this practice so powerful.

While there are no firm rules about how long common formative assessments should be or how frequently you should give them, we share the following recommendations.

- **Keep your common formative assessments intentionally short:** How short? Aim for no more than five questions, and focus on no more than two key concepts, ideas, targets, or skills. Why? Shorter assessments are quicker to develop, deliver, grade, and analyze, which makes it far more likely that you will actually use the results to drive your next instructional actions.

- **Give your common assessments more frequently:** How frequently? Think about giving a common assessment roughly once every five to eight instructional days. Why? Shorter, more frequent assessments prevent students from falling so far behind that catching up feels impossible. They also make assessing learning feel like a natural part of the classroom rhythm, rather than an interruption to instruction.

- **Be clear about how you will administer a common formative assessment:** How clear? Exceptionally clear. Agree in advance on details like how much time students will have to complete the assessment, what directions and support you will provide while students are taking the assessment, and the best point during a unit to give the assessment. By standardizing these elements, teams can ensure the collected results are valid, comparable, and useful for guiding instruction.

After giving a common formative assessment designed to generate specific data on progress, highly effective teams use the results to identify which students have met the team's agreed-on expectation of proficiency. More importantly, highly effective teams decide how they will collectively respond to the students who are not yet proficient with the assessed standard or skill. To guide their thinking when analyzing the assessment results, highly effective teams answer the following questions.

- **According to our team's agreed-on definition of success, which students have mastered the skill or standard?** This is where the time spent building shared clarity about the meaning of a standard and defining what proficiency looks like in student work pays off. That collective understanding becomes the basis for analyzing student responses to common formative assessments and identifying which have mastered grade-level essentials after initial instruction.

- **According to our team's agreed-on definition of success, which students need extra time and support?** Teams also use their shared understanding of the essentials covered on an assessment to identify students who are not yet proficient. More specifically, they analyze the common misunderstandings and errors that they see in student responses to identify the specific reasons for their struggles. Team discussions about students who are not yet proficient center on when to provide additional support and which reengagement strategies are most likely to help struggling students succeed. These strategies might include small-group instruction, reteaching by another team member, or a different instructional approach than was used during the initial lesson.

- **Which instructional strategies and practices proved most effective?** To improve interventions, teams use assessment results to identify which instructional strategies were most effective for students. By analyzing this information—understanding who benefited from the initial teaching methods and why those strategies were successful—teams deepen their shared knowledge about the most effective ways to teach grade-level essentials. Teams apply these insights as they design and deliver targeted reteaching to struggling students.

- **Are there individual questions or skills that our students tend to struggle with?** Finally, highly effective teams look for patterns in student performance on specific tasks or skills when analyzing assessment data. By identifying trends (such as consistent struggles with certain types of questions or recurring challenges in applying specific skills), teams can better plan interventions for struggling students. More importantly, recognizing these patterns over time allows teams to refine their initial instruction. By addressing common areas of difficulty before students are ever assessed, teams can reduce the number of students who need supplemental interventions on future assessments.

Figure 3.1.2 is a graphic version of those questions.

Data Question One	Data Question Two	Data Question Three	Data Question Four
Mastery	Extra Time and Support	Teaching Strategies	Question Analysis
According to our team's agreed-on definition of mastery, which students have mastered the skill or standard?	According to our team's agreed-on definition of mastery, which students need extra time and support?	Which teaching practices or strategies proved most effective?	Are there individual questions or skills that *our* students tend to struggle with?

Source: Sonju et al., 2024, p. 118.

FIGURE 3.1.2: Four data questions for teams.

*Visit **go.SolutionTree.com/PLCbooks** for a free reproducible version of this figure.*

Notice how the first two questions help teams focus on identifying which students have met grade-level expectations and which students require additional time and support. Questions 3 and 4, on the other hand, encourage teams to analyze learning trends, evaluate effective strategies, and collaborate on decisions about interventions. By efficiently analyzing the results of their common formative assessments, teams gain the insights they need to provide timely support to ensure all students master grade-level essentials.

Tools and Resources for Highly Effective Teams

The following tools and resources will help you accomplish the work for this essential action.

- **"Tool: Building a Common Formative Assessment" (page 126):** This tool is designed to guide teams as they work together to create short common assessments. It includes opportunities to reflect on the level of rigor required by the standard being assessed and prompts teams to record both the expected answers and the common mistakes they anticipate in student responses. With just the right amount of structure, this tool ensures that teams create assessments that accurately measure student mastery.

- **"Tool: Using the ACID Test to Evaluate a Common Formative Assessment" (page 127):** In *Simplifying Common Assessment: A Guide for Professional Learning Communities at Work*, Kim Bailey and Chris Jakicic (2017) introduce a set of questions—the ACID (aligned, clearly written, informative, designed) test—teams can use to evaluate the quality of a common formative assessment: Is it aligned to the complexity of the standard? Are the questions clearly written? Will the assessment provide meaningful information for teachers and students about mastery? Does the assessment design support the demands of the standard? This tool helps your team use these questions to evaluate an assessment you are planning to use.

- **"Tool: Actionable Data Tool" (page 129):** This tool is designed to help teams systematically analyze the results of their common formative assessments and plan targeted interventions for students who need additional time and support. By documenting their responses to the four key questions shared earlier in this chapter, teams can act more efficiently when identifying and addressing specific student needs. Additionally, maintaining a written record of these discussions allows teams to reflect on their practices and track patterns over time, informing future instructional planning and intervention efforts.

- **"Tool: Team Protocol for Analyzing Assessment Results" (page 130):** It is important for readers of this text to understand that there isn't a single "right" tool for using assessments to identify students who need additional time and support. The key is to choose a tool that guides you through a careful analysis of your assessment results, helps you identify patterns in student responses, and allows you to maintain a clear record of students requiring additional support. The previous tool, centered on the four key questions outlined in this chapter, might be an ideal fit for your team. However, you may also find this tool's structure better suited to your needs.

Tool: Building a Common Formative Assessment

Instructions: This template is designed to help you write a short common formative assessment for one essential standard. Start by writing down the learning target you will assess and then checking one box in each column. Fill in your potential assessment questions, expected answers, and common mistakes. Three reminders about the characteristics of high-quality common formative assessments can be found at the bottom of this template.

Essential Learning Target to Be Assessed:

Depth of Knowledge Level of Target	Best Strategy for Assessing This Target	Percentage of Questions on District Benchmarks and Standardized Tests That Cover This Target	How Important This Target Is for Future Success in and Beyond School
☐ Recall and Reproduction ☐ Skills and Concepts ☐ Strategic Thinking ☐ Extended Thinking	☐ Selected response ☐ Constructed response ☐ Performance task ☐ Other:	☐ 0–5 percent ☐ 6–10 percent ☐ 11–15 percent ☐ More than 15 percent	☐ Not important ☐ Somewhat important ☐ Very important ☐ Essential

Potential Assessment Questions

Question	Expected Answer	Common Mistakes We Might See

Three Important Common Formative Assessment Reminders

1. A good common formative assessment will cover no more than three essential learning targets. Limiting the length of a common formative assessment makes it possible for teachers to analyze and then act on collected data in a timely manner.

2. A good common formative assessment should include at least three questions for each learning target that is being tested. That protects data sets against the impact of poorly written questions.

3. The complexity of a question should align with the complexity of the learning target it is designed to measure. That means performance tasks are unnecessary for lower-order learning targets that require recall and reproduction but essential for higher-order learning targets that require strategic or extended thinking.

Source: Ferriter, W. M. (2020). The big book of tools for collaborative teams in a PLC at Work. *Solution Tree Press.*

Tool: Using the ACID Test to Evaluate a Common Formative Assessment

Instructions: Use the following questions to evaluate the overall quality of a common formative assessment written by your learning team.

A	Is the assessment **aligned** to the context, content, and rigor or complexity of the standards? Look at the language of the standard and the learning targets (from the unwrapped standard) in comparison to the task. Are the thinking types on the assessment aligned to those targets? Do the various items target the various levels of rigor or application (for example, Depth of Knowledge; Webb, 1997) represented in the learning targets? For example, is the difficulty of the task or questions at the same level as the target? Examine any exemplars related to your targeted level of complexity. Is the level of scaffolding or cueing appropriate? Is the designated level of mastery or proficiency appropriate and aligned?	**Your Response:**
C	Are the items on the assessment **clearly written**? Read the prompt and any distractors provided. By completing this task as written, will students be demonstrating the skills and concepts you are targeting? Will students understand what you want them to do?	**Your Response:**
I	Will this assessment be **informative** about student learning and produce meaningful data? Will teams benefit from gathering data on these learning targets in this fashion? Will specific information on learning targets steer teams toward meaningful interventions and support? Will this assessment be an opportunity to provide feedback to students?	**Your Response:**

PART THREE
Using Assessments and Data

3

page 1 of 2

D	Is the assessment **designed** to reflect and support the demands of the standards? Will the items ask students to show what they know in a way similar to high-stakes assessments? Are students asked to provide reasoning for their answers? Are students looking for evidence? Are students digging into information in a variety of texts and sources?	**Your Response:**

Questions for Reflection

What are the strengths of this assessment?

What are the weaknesses of this assessment?

What changes, if any, do you need to make to this assessment?

What strategies from this assessment can be easily integrated into future assessments?

Reference

Webb, N. L. (1997). *Research monograph number 6: Criteria for alignment of expectations and assessments in mathematics and science education.* Washington, DC: Council of Chief State School Officers.

Source: Ferriter, W. M. (2020). The big book of tools for collaborative teams in a PLC at Work. *Solution Tree Press. Adapted from Bailey, K., & Jakicic, C. (2017).* Simplifying common assessment: A guide for Professional Learning Communities at Work. *Solution Tree Press.*

PART THREE Using Assessments and Data

Tool: Actionable Data Tool

Highly effective teams recognize that learning collaboratively from the results of their common formative assessments and taking collective action based on those results is essential for leveraging student learning and increasing team efficacy. They also understand the importance of efficiently analyzing assessment results in the limited time they may have. The following data questions offer a practical framework to guide teams in acting on shared data and making informed instructional decisions.

Data Question	Team Action	Team Information
According to our team's agreed-on definition of proficiency, which students have met proficiency in the skill or standard?	Use common formative assessment data to identify students who have met proficiency in the essential learning. These are the students for whom the team will provide extensions during their in-unit flexible time.	Student names:
According to our team's agreed-on definition of proficiency, which students need extra time and support?	Use common formative assessment data to identify students who have not yet met proficiency in the essential learning. These are the students for whom the team will provide targeted intervention on the skill that needs more work.	Student names:
Which teaching practices or strategies proved most effective?	Use common formative assessment data to identify which instructional strategies have proven most effective. These are the strategies the team will use for students who didn't meet proficiency in the essential learning during the initial instruction.	High-impact strategies: 1. 2. 3.
Are there individual questions or skills that our students tend to struggle with?	Use common formative assessment data to identify trends in student learning, such as which questions or skills students demonstrated success in, which they collectively struggled with, and so on.	Trends in the data: 1. 2. 3.

PART THREE Using Assessments and Data

Tool: Team Protocol for Analyzing Assessment Results

Team Data Analysis Protocol

Use results from common formative or end-of-unit assessments.

Note: Enter data prior to the meeting and have access to student work for the discussion. Designate a timekeeper and a notetaker for the conversation.

Question One: What? (Ten minutes)

- What targets seem to have been well established? Not well established?
- Are we seeing some common errors or misunderstandings?
- Is there a common group of students who are not scoring well?
- Do we see significantly different results among our classes?
- Are there any "fuzzy" areas in the scoring of student work? Do we need to calibrate and clarify?
- What student groupings emerge from the data (such as not proficient, close, and beyond proficient)?
- Which students have not achieved proficiency? On what targets do they need support?
- Which students have gone beyond proficiency and may benefit from extended learning opportunities?

Question Two: So What? (Seven minutes)

- What is our hypothesis for these results?
- Did we actually teach what we intended?
- What might be the obstacle for students who are struggling?
- Are our resource materials actually aligned to our targeted learning outcomes?
- What instructional strategies appeared to be highly effective when we were examining our different results?
- Are there any practices we need to research or learn about in order to better support student learning?

Question Three: Now What? (Intervention and extension plan; twenty minutes)

- What concepts or skills need to be retaught to the whole class (based on our data)?
- What short-term interventions and reteaching will we provide to help students reach proficiency?
- Given the errors or misconceptions we see, what strategies will we use? How will these interventions be delivered? Who will deliver them?
- What evidence will we gather throughout the interventions to monitor student learning?
- How might we provide reinforcement or extend student learning for those who demonstrate proficiency (for example, what may we implement within the class or during Tier 2 support)?
- How will we provide students feedback on a timely basis? How are they expected to engage with this feedback?

PART THREE
Using Assessments and Data

Sample Organizer

Students Needing Intervention (They may be subdivided into more than one group.)	Support Plan
Students Needing Additional Practice	**Support Plan**
Students Needing Extension	**Support Plan**

Question Four: What Have We Learned? (Five minutes)

- Are there any changes we would make to our assessments, pacing, or instructional strategies the next time we teach this unit?

Source: Bailey, K., & Jakicic, C. (2023). Common formative assessment: A toolkit for Professional Learning Communities at Work (2nd ed.). Bloomington, IN: Solution Tree Press, pp. 149–150.

ACTION 3.2

We Use Team Assessment Data to Identify High-Impact Instructional Strategies

Individual team members use common assessment data to gain a point of comparison for their teaching practices, identifying the specific instructional practices that had the greatest impact on student learning.

—RICHARD DUFOUR, REBECCA DUFOUR, ROBERT EAKER, MIKE MATTOS, AND ANTHONY MUHAMMAD

If you ask any teacher why their school or district has invested in collaboration as a change strategy, they are likely to say something like "to ensure that all students learn at high levels." While that answer is technically correct—the ultimate goal of teacher collaboration *is* to improve student learning—it also leaves out important context. A more complete answer would be "to ensure that all students learn at high levels *by giving every teacher someone to study their professional practice with*." Notice the distinction between those two responses: The first identifies the goal, while the second outlines the strategy for achieving it. Highly effective teams ensure all students learn at high levels by engaging in rich conversations about the *effectiveness of their teaching strategies*.

So, what does this shared study of practice look like? It begins before instruction even starts, with teachers sharing how they have previously taught the essentials covered in an upcoming unit and reflecting on what worked well and what didn't. Teams also examine the recommendations in curriculum guides or other instructional resources, identifying strategies they'd like to try. Rather than standardizing their approaches from the start, teachers intentionally use different strategies for teaching the same essential outcomes. This variety provides valuable points of comparison, allowing the team to study which approaches are most effective for their students.

Then, teams choose times to bring student work samples, formative assessment data, and reflections on their instruction back to their collaborative meetings. These regularly scheduled conversations focus on uncovering patterns in the evidence that the team is collecting.

By comparing student outcomes across the different strategies, teams can identify specific practices that lead to higher levels of learning. This evidence-based approach to the shared study of practice allows teachers to make informed decisions about which methods to keep, adapt, or abandon, ensuring their instructional choices are always improving.

Why Highly Effective Teams Do This

The importance of rich, evidence-based conversations between teachers about the effectiveness of their practices has been validated by educational researchers for over sixty years. From John Holt (1964), who argued that the core work of highly effective teams was to "flunk unsuccessful methods" (p. 8), to John Hattie (2018), who suggested that teacher teams become "dramatically powerful" when they have evidence of the efficacy of their professional choices, these insights highlight the impact of collaboration centered on the study of instruction. As education researcher Jon Saphier (2005) explains, "The reason professional learning communities increase student learning is that they produce more good teaching by more teachers more of the time" (p. 23). Robert Eaker (2020), one of the original architects of the PLC at Work process, echoes the importance of the shared study of practice when he writes, "I've come to believe that the impact of virtually every research finding related to *effective instructional practices* can be enhanced when teachers are organized and collaboratively engaged in planning, sharing, learning, and *analyzing the impact of their instructional efforts*" (p. 63, emphasis added).

In many ways, highly effective teams see collaboration as an opportunity to experiment with instruction together—and that experimentation with instruction can become one of the most rewarding aspects of working in a PLC. Instead of simply following a scripted curriculum, teachers try new approaches for teaching essential outcomes, polishing their professional expertise over time. This process makes teaching both more effective and more efficient, allowing teams to build a collection of well-developed strategies that lead to better results for students.

More importantly, this process keeps our shared focus on factors that we can control, and that focus makes all the difference. Too often, teams use the results of common formative assessments solely to separate students into two groups: (1) those who have mastered the essentials and (2) those who need additional time and support for learning. While this approach is essential for identifying where interventions are needed, it risks shifting the responsibility for assessment results entirely onto the students and preventing teams from asking more reflective questions like, "What aspects of our instruction were effective?" and "What could we adjust to improve outcomes for all students?" Figure 3.2.1 offers a comparison of language between ineffective groups and highly effective teams around this topic.

In this example, the differences between the language used by ineffective groups and the language used by highly effective teams highlight a fundamental shift in how teachers interpret the purpose of common formative assessments. Ineffective groups see assessments as opportunities to generate information *about their students*, often attributing poor results to factors like student ability, effort, or choices. Highly effective teams see assessments as opportunities to generate information *about their instruction*. Their language reflects a shared belief that teaching practices—not student limitations—are the key to ensuring success for every learner.

The Language of Ineffective Groups	The Language of Highly Effective Teams
"Some students just aren't going to get it, no matter what we do."	"Let's dig into what worked well for the students who mastered this essential and see how we can adapt those practices for the students who are still struggling."
"Our job is to identify the kids who need interventions, provide some reteaching, and move on to the next lesson."	"Our job is to use the data to identify what we can improve in our instruction."
"My scores were the highest, so I must be the best teacher on our team."	"My scores were the highest, so I must have found a strategy that works really well at teaching this essential to our students."
"I taught it, and they didn't get it. That's on them."	"What can we change or refine in our teaching to better meet students' needs?"

FIGURE 3.2.1: Language comparison.

How Highly Effective Teams Do This

To make the most of common formative assessments, teams need to do more than just identify which students need interventions. The real power lies in using the results of common formative assessments to improve instruction. That requires a deliberate shift in how teams approach their data. Teams can take the following practical steps to ensure their work with common formative assessment data leads to deliberate reflection on the efficacy of their instructional choices: select data analysis tools that prompt you to reflect on practices; remember that you are using data to evaluate practices, not people; use peer observations to build your team's instructional capacity; use the most effective practices to plan for and deliver interventions; and recognize that no single practice works for all students.

Select Data Analysis Tools That Prompt You to Reflect on Practices

One of the most effective ways to ensure that teams focus on instructional practices when analyzing common assessment results is to use a structured data analysis protocol. Many of the protocols that we see in schools where we work center primarily on identifying which students need interventions, often to create groups for reteaching. While this is an important outcome, teams also need tools that promote reflection on instruction.

For example, a data analysis tool could include questions like the following.

- Which instructional strategies or practices seemed to have the greatest impact on student learning?
- Are there patterns in the data that suggest some strategies were more effective than others?
- What did students who mastered the concept do differently than those who struggled?
- How can we replicate our most effective strategies to reach more students?

By asking these types of questions, teams can move beyond simply grouping students for interventions and begin identifying instructional strategies that are worth amplifying. When used consistently, such tools can change how teams approach data analysis, ensuring that their collaborative time is spent on what matters most: improving instruction.

Remember That You Are Using Data to Evaluate Practices, Not People

Teams must remember that we aren't using assessment data to evaluate the effectiveness of *our peers*; we are using assessment data to evaluate the effectiveness of *our practices*. This shift in thinking is essential for creating the trust necessary to study instruction with one another. When teams mistakenly frame data as a measure of teacher performance, conversations can become defensive and emotional, undermining the trust needed for collaboration. By focusing on practices instead of people, teams can approach data with curiosity and openness, asking critical questions like, "What worked?" and "How can we replicate this success?"

Use Peer Observations to Build Your Team's Instructional Capacity

Peer observations are a powerful way for teams to learn from one another and improve their practice. When a teacher has the strongest results on a common formative assessment, the team should want to know more about the strategies that teacher is using. Observing peers in action—whether in person or through recorded video lessons—provides valuable insights into how effective practices are implemented in real time.

To make the most of peer observations, teams should establish clear protocols that focus attention on the impact of instructional strategies on student learning. Observers might track how students engage with the lesson, the types of questions the teacher asks, or how the teacher provides feedback to students. The goal is not to critique the teacher but to learn from their practice. By seeing effective strategies in action, team members can bring new tools and ideas back to their own classrooms, building the entire team's instructional capacity.

Use the Most Effective Practices to Plan for and Deliver Interventions

Once teams have identified effective instructional practices, the next step is to use that knowledge to plan interventions for students who are still struggling. Teachers with the strongest assessment results should lead reteaching efforts because they have already identified strategies that work. Having these teachers work directly with students who need extra time and support during schoolwide intervention periods ensures that struggling learners benefit from the team's most effective instructional practices.

Recognize That No Single Practice Works for All Students

One of the most important realizations for highly effective teams is that no single strategy will work for every student. For example, an approach that supports students with strong language skills might not be as effective for students who are still developing their academic vocabulary or language proficiency. By identifying these patterns, teams can better differentiate their instruction and provide all students with access to strategies that meet their unique needs. This kind of targeted analysis enables teams to make more informed instructional decisions and fosters collaboration that leads to equitable learning for all students.

Richard DuFour and Douglas Reeves (2016) once argued that "any school that is not using the results of team-developed common formative assessments to improve professional practice is not yet fully engaged in the PLC process." By applying these five recommendations when analyzing common formative assessment data, teams can increase their instructional capacity and build a tool kit of effective strategies that maximize student learning.

Tools and Resources for Highly Effective Teams

The following tools and resources will help you accomplish the work for this essential action.

- **"Tool: Evidence of Practice in Action—Teacher Self-Reflection" (page 138):** One of the most powerful ways teams can grow together is by focusing their collective energy on studying one instructional practice at a time. By narrowing their focus, teams can develop a deeper understanding of what makes that practice effective and how it can be refined to meet the needs of all students. Teachers can use this template to reflect on their comfort level with an instructional practice their team is studying and document their experiences attempting to implement that practice in their classrooms.

- **"Tool: Practice-Centered Peer Observation" (page 140):** As mentioned, peer observations are a powerful way for teachers to learn from one another and deepen their understanding of key instructional practices. This tool is designed to guide teachers as they observe a colleague using an instructional practice their team is studying. The questions included are designed to help observers stay focused on the most important aspect of the observation: the impact of the instructional practice on student learning.

- **Chapter 5 of *Simplifying the Journey: Six Steps to Schoolwide Collaboration, Consistency, and Clarity in a PLC at Work* by Bob Sonju and colleagues (2024):** Titled "Learning From Formative Data," this chapter from *Simplifying the Journey* features short scenarios that illustrate common challenges and opportunities teams encounter when analyzing assessment results. Each scenario is paired with coaching tips and actionable tools designed to help teams focus their efforts on improving instruction. By exploring this chapter, you can gain valuable strategies for turning data into a driver of professional growth.

- **Global PD Teams video "Formative Assessments Create a Change in Instructional Practices":** In this video, available with a subscription at www.globalpdteams.com, Richard DuFour shares a humorous and relatable story that highlights the power in identifying and utilizing effective practices. It is an excellent resource for educators looking for practical insights into why using formative assessments to study instruction is a collaborative practice worth embracing.

Tool: Evidence of Practice in Action—Teacher Self-Reflection

Step 1: Determine Your Current Self-Rating

Instructions: Circle a rating to show your current comfort level with the key instructional practice your team is studying. Remember to update this rating by erasing and recircling as you continue to use the key practice in your classroom.

Name of Key Instructional Practice: _____

Beginning	Mastering	Excelling
I understand the rationale for this instructional practice and have a basic idea of how to implement it in my classroom, but I'm not confident when using it in lessons with my students yet.	I am comfortable with this instructional practice and use it with regularity in my classroom. I think of it often while planning and can easily adapt it to new lessons. I've gotten great results when using this strategy with my students.	Not only do I use this instructional practice with regularity, but also I am experimenting with revisions that might make it even more effective. I have tried my revisions a few times and am collecting data to see if they are worth sharing with the entire team.

Step 2: Record Your Attempts With This Key Instructional Practice

Instructions: Add a new reflection each time that you use this key instructional practice in your classroom with your students. Then use the reflection questions at the end of this table to help you determine how to move forward.

Date of Attempt and Name of Lesson	What Went Well	What Could Be Improved
When did you use this key practice in your classroom? What concept were you teaching? What lesson were you delivering?	Did you prepare materials in a way that was particularly effective? Did you give directions differently than usual? Did you ask a good question? How did you monitor student learning?	Were there moments where students struggled with the key practice? Were there moments where you struggled? What caused those struggles? How would you change your approach next time?

The Handbook for Highly Effective Teams in a PLC at Work® © 2025 Solution Tree Press • SolutionTree.com
Visit **go.SolutionTree.com/PLCbooks** to download this free reproducible.

Date of Attempt and Name of Lesson	What Went Well	What Could Be Improved

Questions for Reflection

Are you getting better at using this key instructional practice in your classroom? How do you know? Was there a moment when you knew that you were beginning to use this practice effectively in your classroom? What was that moment?

How are other teachers on your learning team doing with this key instructional practice? Is anyone struggling to use it with his or her students? What help can you offer? Is anyone using it more effectively than you are? What can you learn from that person?

Have you gathered feedback from students about this key instructional practice yet? How do they feel about it? What suggestions have they made for improving the practice?

Source: Ferriter, W. M. (2020). The big book of tools for collaborative teams in a PLC at Work. Solution Tree Press.

PART THREE
Using Assessments and Data

Tool: Practice-Centered Peer Observation

Instructions: Arrange to observe a peer teaching a lesson using one of your learning team's key instructional practices. Then, use the following tool—which includes questions that you should answer before your observation, during your observation, and after your observation—to document what you are learning about the key practice that you are observing. Remember, the focus of this observation is to improve your own understanding of how this key instructional practice can be implemented in classrooms.

Observer Name: _____
Peer to Observe: _____

Questions	Your Response
Questions to Answer *Before* Your Scheduled Observation	
What instructional practice are you planning to observe in your upcoming peer observation? • How do you implement this practice in your classroom? • Is there anything about your implementation that is unique or quirky? • Have you made any modifications to this instructional practice to fit your teaching style? Do you think those modifications have been successful?	
How would you rate the effectiveness of the instructional practice that you are planning to observe on a scale of 1 to 5, where 1 represents *very ineffective* and 5 represents *very effective*? • Is there anything about this instructional practice that you love? That you hate? • How do your students respond to this instructional practice? What do you think explains their response?	
Questions to Answer *During* Your Scheduled Observation	
How does your peer implement the instructional practice that you are observing? • Are there any unique phrases or directions that your peer uses to structure the activity for students that you hadn't considered? • Does your peer use body positioning or inflection in order to enhance the instructional practice in any way? • What about your peer's approach to this instructional practice will you try in your classroom?	

PART THREE
Using Assessments and Data

How do your peer's students respond to the instructional practice that you are observing?	
• Do they appear to be engaged and motivated? Do they appear to be struggling with the instructional practice in any way? • Does the instructional practice appear to be more effective for some students or student groups than others? How do you know? • Is the response of your peer's students to this instructional practice different from the response that you get from your own students? In what ways?	
Questions to Answer *After* Your Scheduled Observation	
Have you learned anything new about this instructional practice, or about the needs of your students, during your observation?	
• What logical next steps can you and your team take in the development of this instructional practice? • Can you think of ways to tailor this instructional practice for students in need of remediation or enrichment? • Are there ways that this instructional practice can be used with different content or in different contexts? • Are there other learning teams that might benefit from what you have learned about this instructional practice?	
Final Thoughts and Next Steps	

Source: Ferriter, W. M. (2020). The big book of tools for collaborative teams in a PLC at Work. Solution Tree Press. Adapted from Ferriter, W. M., Graham, P., & Wight, M. (2013). Making teamwork meaningful: Leading progress-driven collaboration in a PLC at Work. Solution Tree Press.

PART THREE
Using Assessments and Data

3

We Teach Students the Criteria We Will Use to Judge Their Work

A summative assessment gives the student the opportunity to prove what they have learned by a certain deadline, and it results in a dichotomy—pass or fail, proficient or not proficient. A formative assessment gives the student the opportunity to improve their learning because it informs both the teacher and the student as to appropriate next steps in the learning process.

—RICHARD DUFOUR, REBECCA DUFOUR, ROBERT EAKER, THOMAS W. MANY, MIKE MATTOS, AND ANTHONY MUHAMMAD

Odds are readers of this text know that assessment is a critical element of the process we use to ensure students learn at high levels. Short, frequently administered common formative assessments inform our next instructional steps and allow us to provide immediate support to students struggling to learn the standards or skills we want them to learn. Summative assessments given at the end of our instruction are used as a final certification of student mastery. Regardless of which type of assessment we use, we analyze results together—sorting students by name and need, comparing results across teachers to spot instructional practices with promise, and identifying appropriate responses based on the data we have collected. This evidence-based examination of teaching and learning (detailed more thoroughly in actions 3.1, page 119, and 3.2, page 133) is a defining characteristic of highly effective teams (DuFour et al., 2024).

However, something is often missing in the assessment work of even the highest-performing collaborative teams. Can you spot it in the epigraph for this essential action? While information from assessments should certainly guide the instructional decisions of collaborative teams, teachers are not the only stakeholders who should use evidence to evaluate learning. Instead, teachers should consistently and intentionally *build the assessment capacity of their students.* Doing so turns students into powerful partners in the learning process who are capable of better understanding our expectations, monitoring their own progress, and seeking help when they need it.

Building students' assessment capacity starts by explicitly introducing the evidence learners can collect to identify next steps worth taking (Fisher, Frey, Ortega, & Hattie, 2023). Highly effective teams accomplish this by sharing clear learning intentions and success criteria at the beginning of critical instructional sequences. Learning intentions help students answer the question, "What should I know and be able to do by the end of these lessons?" (Brown & Ferriter, 2021). They build engagement by helping students see the connections between the activities we use in class, the work products we ask them to create, and the overall purpose of learning (Fisher et al., 2023). Success criteria help students answer the question, "How will I know if I am making progress?" (Brown & Ferriter, 2021), and allow students to accurately assess their current proficiency levels and set individual goals to move themselves forward (Fisher et al., 2023).

Why Highly Effective Teams Do This

You aren't surprised by the argument that turning students into powerful partners in the learning process starts by sharing learning intentions and success criteria, are you? Like so many instructional moves that have a positive impact on learning, sharing learning intentions and success criteria with students feels like a commonsense strategy. As education authors Douglas Fisher and Nancy Frey (2022) explain, "When a person can see a target well, they are much more likely to meet that target successfully and confidently."

For Hattie, sharing learning intentions and success criteria with students is a part of the influence on learning called *teacher clarity*—and it has an effect size of 0.85, indicating a strategy with the "potential to considerably accelerate student achievement" (Visible Learning Meta[X], 2023). Building clarity by sharing learning intentions and success criteria with students is impactful because "when teachers and students know what needs to be learned and what successful learning looks like, organized experiences can be designed to ensure that students develop increased proficiency" (Fisher et al., 2023, p. 46). When they communicate learning intentions and success criteria transparently, teachers and students can quickly identify opportunities for intervention or extension.

Sharing learning intentions and success criteria with students also directly impacts engagement. Few people—including classroom teachers in professional development sessions—are willing to invest in new learning without having a clear sense of what they are expected to learn and why that learning is essential to them (Anderman, Sheng, & Cha, 2024). Need proof? Look around during your next faculty meeting and see how many of your colleagues are fully engaged and how many are answering emails, grading papers, or ordering groceries.

When teachers share learning intentions and success criteria, they are making a bid for student attention—and if you know anything about how the human brain works, you know just how vital that bid for attention really is. Here's why: Our senses absorb 11 million bits of information every second, but our brains can only process 120 bits of information per second (Goodwin & Rouleau, 2022). The result: "To avoid information overload, our brains . . . pay attention only to what we deem the most important bits of information" (Goodwin & Rouleau, 2022, p. 11). As surprising as it may seem, interest and motivation—factors we can influence by intentionally sharing learning intentions and success criteria with students at the beginning of critical instructional sequences—account for more of the variance in student performance than teacher quality or socioeconomic status (Goodwin & Rouleau, 2022).

Equally surprising, however, is how infrequently teachers make this bid for student attention. In their research on the impact that choice and relevance have on student interest and engagement, researchers Joan Dabrowski and Tanji Reed Marshall (2018) examined 6,800 middle school assignments. They found that only 12 percent of English language arts, science, and social studies assignments—and only 2 percent of mathematics assignments—included any intentional attempts to help students understand the purpose behind the work they were completing (Dabrowski & Marshall, 2018). That is a point echoed by Douglas Fisher, Nancy Frey, and Alejandro Gonzalez (2023), who write, "We know why the content we're teaching is important, but do students?"

Sharing learning intentions and success criteria with students also accelerates achievement by ensuring that teachers and students have a shared vision of what proficiency looks like. Doing so allows students to self-monitor and advocate for the interventions or extensions they need. In a world where it sometimes feels like we are drowning in change recommendations, sharing learning intentions and success criteria is a simple strategy for focusing your collaborative team's effort on what matters most. The research overwhelmingly endorses it as good teaching. Figure 3.3.1 offers a comparison of language between ineffective groups and highly effective teams around this topic.

The Language of Ineffective Groups	The Language of Highly Effective Teams
"If the students are paying attention, they will know exactly what the learning target is for each day's lesson. It's obvious."	"What if we started every lesson by clearly sharing the learning target and success criteria with students? What impact would that have on their interest in the lesson?"
"It's not our job to spoon-feed students what they need to do."	"Providing clear learning intentions and success criteria for each lesson isn't spoon-feeding students. It's scaffolding to support understanding, and students who understand expectations are more likely to meet them."
"We don't have time to create success criteria for every lesson; it's just busywork."	"Providing students with success criteria will save us time in the long run because students are more likely to produce products that meet our expectations to begin with."
"Why do we all have to give kids the same learning intentions and success criteria? What if I see things differently than you do? Can't we make our own choices?"	"Developing learning intentions and success criteria together is a great learning opportunity. It allows us to really dig into what we believe mastery looks like for each essential."

FIGURE 3.3.1: Language comparison.

The biggest difference between the language of ineffective groups and the language of highly effective teams when it comes to sharing learning intentions and success criteria with students rests in where responsibility lies for building clarity around expectations. Ineffective groups believe that if students need more clarity, it is their responsibility to either pay closer attention or ask for clarification. Highly effective teams understand that being clear about expectations is the teacher's responsibility and that expecting students to meet expectations that haven't been fully articulated is irresponsible and unrealistic. What's more, by using learning intentions and success criteria to clarify expectations, effective teams save themselves time and effort. After all, students are more likely to meet our expectations during initial instruction when they fully understand just what those expectations are at the beginning of each lesson.

How Highly Effective Teams Do This

The good news is that developing learning intentions and success criteria to share with students is a natural extension of the work that a highly effective team does to study essential standards—a process detailed in action 2.1 (page 67). If you have finished that process, the decisions that you made together are great starting points for creating learning intentions and success criteria for your lessons.

Develop Learning Intentions

Sometimes, the greatest challenge of developing learning intentions and success criteria is confusion around how they differ from other terms used in the process of unpacking a standard, such as *learning targets*, *learning progressions*, and *learning ladders*. To clarify, remember that all your collaborative work begins by identifying *essential standards* every student must master. Those standards are often broad statements of what students are expected to know and be able to do set by states, provinces, districts, or curriculum providers. *Learning targets* deconstruct broader standards into smaller, measurable objectives. Learning targets are more specific than standards; once identified, you can arrange them into logical instructional sequences known as *learning progressions* to guide daily lesson planning. Those instructional sequences often begin with the simplest learning targets and progressively increase in complexity. Because each new target is a step up in complexity, the term *learning ladder* is often used as a metaphor describing the sequential steps necessary to master an essential.

Learning intentions are modified versions of *learning targets* designed to focus students' attention during a specific lesson. They focus on what the student will learn and frame the learning target or standard in the tasks that students will complete during instruction. Figure 3.3.2 is an example of an essential standard broken into learning targets and intentions.

Notice the following.

- Because most standards describe complex concepts that require mastery of several discrete skills or concepts, there will almost always be more than one learning target unpacked from an essential standard.

- While *learning targets* and *intentions* are extensions of the same ideas, learning intentions are intentionally designed to give a specific purpose to the day's lesson.

Essential Standard: 5.NBT.B.5—Fluently multiply multi-digit whole numbers using the standard algorithm.

Learning Targets	Possible Learning Intentions
Multiply multi-digit whole numbers by single-digit whole numbers.	• Today, we are learning to multiply larger whole numbers by single-digit numbers using the standard algorithm. • Today, we are practicing the step-by-step process for multiplying three-digit by single-digit numbers using the standard algorithm. • Today, we are solving word problems where we need to multiply larger numbers by single digits to find totals in real-world contexts.
Multiply multi-digit whole numbers by multi-digit whole numbers.	• Today, we are learning to multiply multi-digit numbers using the standard algorithm to find accurate products. • Today, we are extending our multiplication skills to multiply up to four-digit numbers by two-digit numbers using the standard algorithm.
Use the standard algorithm to multiply.	• Today, we are practicing multiplication to build fluency with the standard algorithm. • Today, we are using the standard multiplication algorithm to solve multi-step word problems with larger numbers in real-world contexts.

Source for standard: NGA & CCSSO, 2010b.

FIGURE 3.3.2: Essential standard breakdown.

- There is no right way to write a learning intention. Some learning intentions focus on acquiring core concepts and content knowledge. Other learning intentions focus on the procedures or skills that students must practice and apply proficiently. If the statements you create help students answer the question, "What am I supposed to know or be able to do?", you have written your learning intentions correctly.

Develop Success Criteria

Once your team has written a learning intention for a specific lesson or series of lessons, you develop success criteria for the intention. *Success criteria* are often a series of bulleted statements designed to help students answer the question, "How will I know if I'm making progress?" by "describing what learners must know and be able to do that would demonstrate that they have met the learning intentions for the day" (Almarode, Fisher, Thunder, & Frey, 2021, p. 16). While classroom teachers can use success criteria to monitor student progress and to provide differentiated support as needed, the primary purpose of developing and sharing success criteria with students is to turn students into partners in the assessment process. When teachers use success criteria to articulate the steps that students must take to master a learning intention, students can identify their own academic strengths and areas for improvement. Figure 3.3.3 (page 148) includes a set of success criteria for one of the learning intentions found in figure 3.3.2.

Look carefully at the differences between this example's learning intention and its success criteria. The learning intention explains *what* students are expected to learn, and the success criteria explain *how* students will engage in their learning (Goodwin & Rouleau, 2022).

Learning Intention	Success Criteria
Today, we are using the standard multiplication algorithm to solve multi-step word problems with larger numbers in real-world contexts.	I can identify the information necessary to set up the multiplication. I can use the standard algorithm to multiply accurately. I can check if my answer is reasonable using estimation.

FIGURE 3.3.3: Success criteria.

Sharing this level of clarity with students can provide "a clear pathway and motivation for learning" (Goodwin & Rouleau, 2022, p. 35). Teams should also use student-centered phrasing when writing success criteria. Starting each success criterion with a phrase like *I can explain*, *I can use*, and *I can check* turns the success criteria in the right column into action items students can use to monitor their progress. Consider introducing success criteria to students as *doing tasks*: steps they can take to move their learning forward.

Instructional experts Douglas Fisher and Nancy Frey suggest another way to share learning intentions and success criteria with students—using the following sentence frame to communicate learning intentions and success criteria to students at the beginning of every lesson: *Today, we're learning [learning intention] so that [statement of relevance]. You'll know you've learned it when [success criteria]* (as cited in Ferlazzo, 2022). Can you see how this is a logical next step for teachers who post their objectives for daily lessons? If you already share *what* students will learn in each lesson, take that a step further by also communicating *why* those outcomes matter and *how* students can measure their progress toward mastery.

Another way to share learning intentions and success criteria with students is to develop simple outcome trackers like the one in figure 3.3.4. There are several things to notice about this outcome tracker. First, the bold text in the top-left corner is the learning intention for this instructional sequence. It communicates what students should know and be able to do by the end of the lessons. The checkboxes underneath the bold text indicate the success criteria (doing tasks) for this learning intention. These describe how students will demonstrate mastery during this instructional sequence. Students can use the My Proof column to complete the doing tasks for this learning intention and check off each task as they gather evidence of learning. Finally, students can use the Rate Your Level of Understanding bar at the bottom left of the tracker to track their progress and, under Grades Earned, record the grades they earn on classroom assignments tied to the learning intention. By bundling the learning intention and success criteria onto a tracker with built-in self-assessment features and space for students to gather evidence, teachers can use one tool to promote metacognition, self-regulation, and a sense of ownership over learning in students.

Finally, teacher teams can create and use success checklists to communicate learning intentions and success criteria to students (Brown & Ferriter, 2021). Figure 3.3.5 includes a sample of a success checklist.

Learning Target	Can you complete the work detailed in the bulleted doing tasks for this learning target? Prove it here.
(1) I can describe the different invisible pieces that substances are made of. ☐ This means that I can detail the basic components of an atom and the basic differences between how atoms act in solids, liquids, and gases. ☐ This also means that I can create models to show the difference between atoms, molecules, elements, compounds, and mixtures. **Rate your level of understanding:** 1 2 3 4 5 **Grades earned:**	

Source: Adapted from Ferriter, 2020; Ferriter & Cancellieri, 2017.

FIGURE 3.3.4: Learning intention and doing tasks.

I can describe the plot of a story.	I can evaluate the characters of a story.	I can determine the theme of a story.
☐ This means I can answer who, what, where, when, why, and how questions about a story. ☐ This also means I can use specific events and details from the text to answer questions about the story. ☐ Finally, this means I can use specific events and details from the text to draw inferences about the story. **Ready for a challenge?** Try making a claim about the story you have read—and then using quotes from the story to support your claim.	☐ This means I can describe how characters respond to the major events in a story. ☐ This also means I can describe the motivations of characters in a story and explain how their actions impact the sequence of events in a story. ☐ Finally, this means I can use a character's thoughts, words, and actions to describe their personality. **Ready for a challenge?** Try using specific details in the text to compare and contrast two different characters.	☐ This means I know the difference between the theme of a story and the topic of a story. ☐ This also means I can name five themes commonly found in stories—and I can name the themes of several popular fairy tales. ☐ Finally, this means I can write a simple sentence describing the message the author of the story is trying to share with readers—and I can name specific events and actions from the story to support my claim. **Ready for a challenge?** Try finding two different stories that have similar themes to one another.

Source for standard: NGA & CCSSO, 2010a.

FIGURE 3.3.5: Success checklist.

Can you spot the two primary differences between outcome trackers and success checklists? Success checklists include multiple learning intentions and success criteria, whereas outcome trackers detail only one learning intention and its corresponding success criteria. Bundling multiple learning intentions onto one success checklist can make sharing expectations with students throughout an entire unit of study logistically easier for classroom teachers. However, that ease of use comes with a compromise: Unlike outcome trackers—which have proof boxes and rating bars for self-assessment—success checklists do not include room for students to gather evidence of their mastery or to track their progress over time.

However you decide to share learning intentions and success criteria with your students, remember that sharing learning intentions and success criteria has to go beyond simply posting objectives for students to see at the beginning of each lesson. The goal is not just to *communicate your learning outcomes* to students. Instead, the goal is to create opportunities for students to *interact with the learning outcomes* you expect them to master. If your strategy doesn't include time for students to use success criteria to evaluate their own progress, your efforts will not have a positive impact on student achievement.

Finally, remember not to overwhelm your students. As James A. Nottingham (2024) explains in *Teach Brilliantly*:

> The erroneous ideas that every single lesson needs to have a learning intention displayed on the board, every learning standard has to be translated into *I can* statements, all curriculum documents have to be supported by multiple learning intentions, and success criteria are best served up with a rubric for every occasion make a lot of people tire of them before their value is realized. (p. 166)

The key is using your learning intentions and success criteria to promote metacognition in your students. To make that work more manageable for everyone, start by developing and sharing learning intentions and success criteria for a small handful of essential standards and then creating opportunities for students to use those intentions and criteria for self-assessment.

Tools and Resources for Highly Effective Teams

The following tools and resources will help you accomplish the work for this essential action.

- **"Tool: Developing an Outcome Tracker" (https://b.link/outcometracker):** To help you quickly get started with outcome trackers, we have created this template collection in Google Slides. Follow the link, and you receive your own copy of the template collection in your Google Drive, which you can edit in any way that you like. The collection includes an overview of what outcome trackers are, a review of the individual elements of an outcome tracker, a sample of an outcome tracker created by a middle school science student, and a blank slide that you can use to begin creating your own outcome trackers.

- **"Tool: Developing a Success Checklist for a Learning Intention" (page 152):** Remember that if your team has already unpacked essential standards into learning targets or written proficiency scales together, you have all that you need to write learning intentions and success criteria. Simply rewrite your learning intentions in student-friendly language and simplify your proficiency scales by choosing a few action steps for your students to focus on. However, if you would like additional support in developing a success checklist, you can use **"Tool: Template for Developing a Success Checklist" (page 154)** to start a conversation with your colleagues.

Tool: Developing a Success Checklist for a Learning Intention

To engage students as full partners in the learning process, highly effective teams explicitly define the steps that students need to take to demonstrate mastery of a learning intention and then share those steps with students on success checklists that they can refer to during the course of instruction. Answer the questions that follow with your collaborative team to begin developing a success checklist for an upcoming learning intention.

Learning Intention:	
Questions to Consider	**Your Team's Response**
What kinds of things should students know by the time that they are done with this learning intention?	
What kinds of things should students be able to do by the time that they are done with this learning intention?	
Is there a logical progression that students should follow when working with this learning intention? What should they do first? What should they do second? What should they do third?	
What are the common mistakes that we see students making when working on this learning intention? Why do they make those mistakes?	

Now, use this page of the tool to craft a success checklist that you can share with students at the beginning of your assignment. Remember that a good success checklist might include more than one learning intention. Good success checklists should also meet the following criteria.

- Be written in student-friendly language
- Include both a description of what students should know by the end of an assignment and a specific set of success criteria detailing things that students should be able to do to meet their teacher's expectations

PART THREE
Using Assessments and Data

PART THREE
Using Assessments and Data

Tool: Template for Developing a Success Checklist

Use the template to develop a success checklist for an upcoming unit of study.

Learning Intention 1:	Learning Intention 2:	Learning Intention 3:
Doing Tasks:	Doing Tasks:	Doing Tasks:
Extend Your Learning:	Extend Your Learning:	Extend Your Learning:

ACTION 3.4

We Create Exemplars Students Can Examine to Evaluate Their Own Progress Toward Mastery

When done well, formative assessment advances and motivates, rather than merely reports on, student learning. The clearly defined goals and descriptive feedback provide students with specific insights regarding how to improve, and the growth that students experience helps build their confidence as learners.

—RICHARD DUFOUR, REBECCA DUFOUR, ROBERT EAKER, THOMAS W. MANY, MIKE MATTOS, AND ANTHONY MUHAMMAD

Teams interested in building their students' assessment capacity start by developing and sharing clear learning intentions and success criteria at the beginning of each new sequence of instruction—a process introduced in action 3.3 (page 143). These efforts are crucial first steps at helping students answer two critical questions about their learning: (1) "What should I know and be able to do by the end of these lessons?" and (2) "How will I know if I am making progress?" (Brown & Ferriter, 2021). To extend this work, highly effective teams develop sets of exemplars that clarify and reinforce expectations for students.

Exemplars are "examples of excellence in a task" designed to demonstrate mastery of learning intentions or success criteria at different skill levels (White, 2022, p. 74). There is no rule about what exemplars should look like except for one: They should model the products you expect students to produce. They can be as complex as portfolios of work samples or recorded technique demonstrations highlighting mastery of entire standards or as simple as worked solutions to individual problems, labeled cycle diagrams, or isolated sentences and paragraphs from longer written responses highlighting mastery of individual success criteria.

There is also no rule about when to share exemplar sets with students (Lipnevich, Panadero, & Calistro, 2023). It might make sense to share exemplars for familiar tasks after students have practiced with processes and created first drafts of their products or performances. Doing so provides a point of comparison to help guide revisions, and also helps avoid stifling student creativity (White, 2022). For new or unfamiliar tasks, sharing exemplars at the beginning of instruction might make sense to "allow students to visualize their own efforts in tangible ways and see the path to success more clearly"; the key is to consider your learning goals and where students are "in their own learning journeys" when determining when to share sets of exemplars with learners (White, 2022, p. 76).

Regardless of the format they take or when in the learning cycle you share them, exemplars facilitate effective self-assessment, an essential step in ensuring that learners receive targeted feedback on their current levels of performance in a timely manner (Lipnevich et al., 2023).

Why Highly Effective Teams Do This

Much of what we know about the connection between feedback and learning was first articulated by D. Royce Sadler, who wrote a seminal article in 1989 titled "Formative Assessment and the Design of Instructional Systems." In that text, Sadler (1989) argues that students need "more than summary grades if they are to develop expertise intelligently"—a surprising argument during an era where grades were often the only tool for student feedback (p. 121). Instead, Sadler (1989) argues that three conditions have to be in place for feedback to lead to learning:

> The learner has to (a) possess a concept of the *standard* (or goal, or reference level) being aimed for, (b) compare the *actual (or current) level of performance* with the standard, and (c) engage in appropriate *action* which leads to some closure of the gap. (p. 121)

Fast-forward to 2023, and you find versions of those same ideas echoed in *Visible Learning: The Sequel*, a comprehensive summary of research published by John Hattie (2023b), where he writes, "Feedback is the answer to three questions: Where am I going? How am I going? and Where to next?" (p. 321).

Can you see the similarities in Sadler's and Hattie's arguments about effective feedback? Both emphasize the role that next steps must play in the feedback process. More feedback does not automatically lead to higher levels of learning. Instead, feedback with more information on how students can move forward leads to higher levels of learning (Hattie, 2023b). Specifically, students value feedback that helps them spot what they have done well, what they need to improve, how they can improve, and what they can do differently the next time (Mandouit, 2020). Researchers call this *high-information feedback*, and it is effective because it builds both metacognitive skills and learner efficacy by surfacing actionable steps for improving performance (Wisniewski, Zierer, & Hattie, 2020). Its effect size is 0.99, suggesting it is a strategy with the potential to considerably accelerate student achievement (Wisniewski et al., 2020).

Sadly, while where-to-next feedback is the most valuable, it is also the least common type of feedback learners receive (Brooks, Carroll, Gillies, & Hattie, 2019). What keeps teachers from giving next-step feedback to their learners? Are teachers unaware of the research detailing the importance of next-step feedback? Do they lack the expertise to prioritize next-step feedback in their assessment practices?

We believe that while most teachers understand the value of providing next-step feedback to students and have the professional expertise to make it part of their assessment practices, doing so consistently and intentionally does not always feel doable. Larger class sizes paired with increasingly socially, economically, and academically diverse student populations make giving high-information feedback to every learner a seemingly overwhelming task (Lipnevich et al., 2023)—and instructional strategies recognized as essential but not doable are not readily embraced or sustained by classroom teachers (Ferriter, 2024b).

That's why teaching students to use exemplars to assess their own progress toward mastery is an essential action of highly effective teams. Developing students with the capacity to accurately evaluate their performances against exemplars reduces the assessment demands on classroom teachers, ensuring that the goal of all students having high-information feedback in a timely manner becomes a reality (Lipnevich et al., 2023). Put more clearly, when used correctly, exemplars allow students to *generate their own feedback* instead of having to *wait for feedback* from their teachers, families, or peers.

More importantly, teaching students to use exemplars to generate their own next-step feedback develops "intellectual independence" in students (Ferriter & Cancellieri, 2017, p. 38). That intellectual independence—the ability to understand the criteria for success on a task, recognize that criteria in work samples, compare those samples to your products, and integrate changes based on information gathered through observation—is often recognized as one of the primary outcomes of education (Lipnevich et al., 2023). Finally, creating exemplars for important products and performances "gives teams the chance to build collective clarity around the success criteria for an assignment and to share professional knowledge about the common mistakes that students are likely to make" (Brown & Ferriter, 2021, p. 38). This collective clarity helps individual teachers become more efficient and effective assessors of student learning. Figure 3.4.1 offers a comparison of language between ineffective groups and highly effective teams around this topic.

The Language of Ineffective Groups	The Language of Highly Effective Teams
"Exemplars just give students the answers. They need to figure it out themselves."	"Exemplars guide students by showing what quality work looks like and helping them self-assess against our expectations."
"Students don't need to see examples. They should use the rubric to figure it out."	"Exemplars are designed to provide students with information about expectations. Rubrics are designed to evaluate student performances against those expectations. They are both important tools, but we use them at different times."
"If we give students examples, they'll just copy them."	"If we teach students to analyze exemplars, it will help them apply the criteria for success to their own work."
"Students will get feedback after they turn in their assignment. Why show them an exemplar first?"	"Exemplars provide students with important information before they turn anything in, which helps them make improvements in real time."

FIGURE 3.4.1: Language comparison.

Look through the language of ineffective groups, and you will see a common misconception held by many teachers: Giving students exemplars means *giving them the answers*. Highly effective teams recognize that giving students exemplars means *giving them information* they can use to evaluate their own performance. Ineffective groups also see assessment as something that teachers do after a student has turned in an assignment, while highly effective teams see students as partners in the assessment process. As simple as that distinction seems, it marks a real turning point in our belief about the roles students should play in our classrooms. Providing students with regular opportunities to assess themselves against expectations—a practice supported by using exemplars—reinforces the notion that learners are always assessing themselves, rather than just waiting to be assessed by others.

How Highly Effective Teams Do This

Before teams develop exemplars to facilitate self-assessment, they must understand that self-assessment will be a new academic behavior for most students, who are often given "permission to be passive" in classrooms (White, 2022, p. 80). While schools may give lip service to the notion of developing learners who can accurately assess themselves, students in most classrooms remain "teacher-dependent" (Fisher & Frey, 2012, p. 73), waiting for teachers to tell them what to learn, how they are doing, and what steps to take next. Creating students capable of generating self-feedback from exemplars takes patience and carefully structured learning opportunities. Students *can* learn to assess their progress. However, they need support during their early experiences with exemplars simply because it is not a practice they will automatically be familiar with (Lipnevich et al., 2023).

You can make learning visible through exemplars three ways: (1) developing sets of answers to simple, knowledge-driven questions; (2) providing worked-out examples; and (3) creating high/low comparison tasks.

Develop Sets of Answers to Simple, Knowledge-Driven Questions

One strategy that you can use to develop students capable of generating self-feedback is creating sets of answers to simple, knowledge-driven questions for students to explore (Cancellieri, 2020a). Each exemplar set should include three sample responses: one that meets all expectations for mastery and two that are intentionally missing elements required for a strong final product. Then, set aside time for students to work in groups with exemplar sets *just after* they have created a first draft and *just before* turning in their final copy (Cancellieri, 2020a). Doing so can build your students' understanding of how learners use exemplars as points of comparison when assessing their own performance.

Here's an example: Imagine you are teaching world history and want your high school students to craft an answer to the question, *How was the Magna Carta created?* You could use the set of exemplars in figure 3.4.2 to encourage self-assessment in your classroom.

After you have developed your exemplar set, give student groups in your classroom several different challenge tasks that force them to examine and discuss the sample responses. For

The Magna Carta was created because King John was abusing his power, like raising taxes too much. The barons were angry and rebelled. They forced the king to accept limits on his power and recognize their rights.	The Magna Carta was created in 1215 because King John of England was abusing his power. He raised taxes and failed in wars, which made the barons very angry. The barons rebelled, captured London, and forced King John to meet with them. They met at Runnymede, where the king agreed to sign the Magna Carta.	The barons captured London and forced King John to sign the Magna Carta in 1215. They met at Runnymede, where King John agreed to limit his power. The Magna Carta made sure the king couldn't just do whatever he wanted and had to follow certain rules.

Source: OpenAI, 2024.

FIGURE 3.4.2: Exemplar set.

instance, you might ask them to rank the provided exemplars from most to least accurate or to sort exemplars into groups based on the success criteria that they are missing. Give them sample feedback comments, and ask them to match each comment with the exemplar that it is designed to support (Cancellieri, 2020a). During this work, circulate throughout the room, asking groups to defend their decisions. Doing so can help you determine whether students can effectively identify the characteristics of strong and weak responses to the assignment they are currently working on (Cancellieri, 2020a).

After your groups have had plenty of time to rank and sort exemplars, engage your students in the shared development of a single-point rubric for the task (Cancellieri, 2020a). Single-point rubrics describe only what *meeting* grade-level expectations looks like, making sure that students new to self-assessment are not overwhelmed by the amount of information they are using to evaluate their own performances (Cancellieri, 2020b). Figure 3.4.3 is an example of a single-point rubric that a class studying the exemplar set in figure 3.4.2 might develop together.

What Needs to Improve to Meet Expectations?	Mastery	What Went Beyond Expectations?
	☐ Addresses the reasons for the tension between King John and his barons ☐ Addresses the actions the barons took to pressure King John to negotiate an agreement with them ☐ Addresses when and where the Magna Carta was signed	

FIGURE 3.4.3: Generic single-point rubric example.

Involving students in developing a shared rubric for a task after exploring exemplars provides students with the information and language necessary to more effectively evaluate their own performance on the same task (Cancellieri, 2020a). As John Hattie and Shirley Clarke (2019) explain, "When the success criteria are co-constructed with the students, rather than simply given to them, students have a still greater chance of understanding and internalizing their meanings and possessing a concept of a goal" (pp. 57–58).

After students work together to examine exemplars and create a single-point rubric, allow them to work individually to improve their original drafts based on their new understandings of proficiency. Doing so encourages students to apply their "error-detection skills," an essential trait for independently closing the gap between where one is and where they need to be (Hattie & Clarke, 2019, p. 9). Doing so also ensures that feedback leads to action, which is essential since teaching students "to receive, interpret and use the feedback provided is probably much more important than focusing on how much feedback is provided by the teacher, as feedback given but not heard is of little use" (Hattie & Clarke, 2019, p. 5).

Consider two final thoughts. First, while creating exemplar sets for simple, knowledge-driven questions may seem like a lot of work for a task that is not cognitively rigorous, it is the right starting point for students who are new to generating self-feedback. Remember that the rigor in the task doesn't come from the questions you are asking students to answer. Instead, the rigor comes from evaluating sample responses and cocreating success criteria for the task. Asking students to do the same work with more complex tasks will overwhelm your learners and prevent them from experiencing early successes with self-assessment.

Second, the exemplars that you share should always be original work products based on your team's shared understanding of the common mistakes students make. This turns exemplar creation into an opportunity for your team to engage in meaningful conversations about what mastery looks like (Cancellieri, 2020a). Generating original work products also ensures that your team's exemplars are anonymous, which is an important step for protecting students' academic confidence (Chappuis, 2015). No matter how hard teachers work to create safe and supportive classroom cultures, seeing their work highlighted as examples of what not to do can cause students to doubt their academic ability. In addition, generating original work products to use as exemplars addresses the "friendship bias" found in classrooms where students assess products created by their peers (Ruiz-Primo & Brookhart, 2018, p. 106). Students are far more likely to identify weaknesses in original exemplars generated by teachers because there are no social risks tied to giving negative feedback.

If your team struggles to generate original work products to use in exemplar sets, consider using an AI chatbot like ChatGPT (https://chatgpt.com), Claude (https://claude.ai), or Gemini (https://gemini.google.com) as a thought partner. In fact, we used the following prompt sequence to generate the Magna Carta exemplars highlighted earlier in this chapter.

- What are the three most important points you would expect to see in a response to this question: How was the Magna Carta created?
- Can you create a set of three exemplars highlighting different answers to that question? Pretend that you are a ninth-grade student while creating your responses. Include one exemplar that includes all three of the points you would expect to see in a complete response. Then, include two additional exemplars that are missing key points.
- Can you tell me which key points are missing from each of the exemplars that you have created?

Notice that, like the prompt suggestions found throughout this book, the more detail that you share when prompting an AI chatbot, the more likely that you will get content that you can use the first time. For example, by asking the chatbot to pretend that it was a ninth-grade student while generating exemplars for this chapter, we received responses that aligned nicely with the kinds of responses you would likely see in a high school world history class. If we had left that part of the prompt out, we may have gotten responses more in line with the content generated by students in college-level classes.

At the time of publication of this text, AI chatbots are most effective at generating exemplars for responses to text-based questions: asking fourth graders to identify equivalent fractions, sixth graders to write poetry with figurative language, or eighth graders to balance chemical equations, for instance. If you are asking art students to create batik paintings, physical education students to make a layup, or band students to play with vibrato, your team must work together to come up with your own exemplar sets until AI tools that generate audio, video, and images get better at developing visual responses.

Provide Worked-Out Examples

Another way to allow students to generate self-feedback from exemplars is to provide worked-out examples to follow when learning new skills and procedures (Goodwin & Rouleau, 2022). Worked-out examples are exactly what they sound like: samples of final products demonstrating the same skills and procedures as the tasks students are being asked to complete. Figure 3.4.4 includes a worked-out example for a seventh-grade mathematics lesson on solving percentage problems.

Instructions: In class, we have been learning how to solve percentage problems. There are three problems here for you to solve. There is also one worked-out problem for you to refer to as a sample. Be prepared to share your solutions with a shoulder partner when finished.

Worked-Out Problem: 150 is 25% of what number?

Solution 1:

$$25\% x = 150$$
$$.25x = 150$$
$$\frac{.25x}{.25} = \frac{150}{.25}$$
$$x = 600$$

Solution 2:

$$\frac{150}{x} \times \frac{25}{100}$$
$$25x = 150 \cdot 100$$
$$\frac{25x}{25} = \frac{150 \cdot 100}{25}$$
$$x = 600$$

Question 1:	**Question 2:**	**Question 3:**
75 is 60% of what value?	120 is 20% of what value?	If 45 is 15% of a number, what is that number?

FIGURE 3.4.4: Studying worked-out problems.

There are two things to notice about the sample in figure 3.4.4. Most importantly, the worked-out examples are shared alongside the task students are expected to complete. To many teachers, this seems counterintuitive. Why would we share worked-out examples students can follow while they are practicing the processes we want them to master? Doesn't that automatically reduce the rigor of the task? The answer is simple: Students can use worked-out examples to generate self-feedback when they struggle by returning to the example and determining where they went wrong (Goodwin & Rouleau, 2022). By providing students with "examples of correct procedures . . . in a side-by-side format," worked-out examples decrease the mental effort required to make sense of new information for students who are still learning complex procedures (Goodwin & Rouleau, 2022, p. 57). Reducing that initial cognitive load can make it easier for students to understand unfamiliar ideas and to connect them to their prior knowledge, both of which are key steps in cementing new learning into long-term memory (Simms, 2024).

It is also important to note that the worked-out examples in figure 3.4.4 are similar to—but not the same as—the problems students are asked to solve. The goal is not to show students solutions. The goal is to provide students with a reference point they can return to when evaluating the process they use to generate their own solutions. For the mathematics teachers who created figure 3.4.4, that was as simple as using different integers for the part and the whole in percentage problems.

The key to turning worked-out examples into effective feedback for learning is choosing samples that effectively illustrate the steps necessary to create high-quality responses to content-specific prompts. Examples follow.

- Language arts teachers can use writing samples on unrelated topics as worked-out examples for students learning to use different types of evidence to support arguments.
- Art teachers can use paintings from different genres as worked-out examples for students learning to use overlap, shadow, and color intensity to create perspective.
- Elementary teachers can use videos of readers reading different texts as worked-out examples for students learning to use segmenting, blending, and finger tapping to sound out words.

Create High/Low Comparison Tasks

A third way to allow students to generate self-feedback from exemplars is to create high/low comparison tasks. The best high/low comparison tasks share three essential traits (Ferriter & Cancellieri, 2017).

1. They list between three and five success criteria written in short, approachable phrases that students should be able to find in work products generated for a classroom assignment (Ferriter & Cancellieri, 2017).

2. They present two exemplars: one modeling a performance that meets all expectations of mastery and one modeling a performance that is missing one or two of the criteria necessary for demonstrating mastery (Ferriter & Cancellieri, 2017).

3. They include a feedback grid where students can keep track of the success criteria they can find in each exemplar. Figure 3.4.5 is an example.

High/Low Comparison—Paper Towel Lab Conclusions

A good conclusion to a science lab does four different things.

1. *Summarize* your findings.
2. *Reflect* on any surprising results.
3. *Share lessons* that people can learn from your findings.
4. *Design* a follow-up experiment answering a new and interesting question related to your topic.

Knowing that, explain why conclusion 1 is better than conclusion 2.

Conclusion 1	Conclusion 2
The paper towel that held the least amount of water was the paper towel that was folded into eighths. It held 34.3 mL of water. The paper towel that held the most water was the regular paper towel that had nothing done to it. It held 41 mL of water. I thought this was very interesting because I thought, at first, that the original paper towel would hold the least amount of water because it wasn't modified. I always thought that the more you modify something, the better it gets—but not in this case. One lesson I learned from this lab is that if you are cleaning up at home, don't modify your paper towel because the regular paper towel holds the most water. If you don't use a regular paper towel, you are wasting paper, and wasting paper hurts the environment. If I did another lab, I would want to find out which brand of paper towel holds the most water because I have already found out what the best way is to soak up water. If I find out which is the best brand, I can tell my mom to only buy that brand and to use that brand without modifying it. That way, we'll use less paper and help the environment.	One of the things that we learned in our paper towel lab trials was that the paper towel that is folded doesn't absorb as much water as a paper towel that is used in one flat sheet. This was surprising to me because I thought that anytime you use more layers of paper towel, you could absorb more water. I know that when I am using paper towels at home, I often have to lay more than one sheet down on top of one another in order to clean up a spill. I was pretty sure that folding a paper towel would work just like laying more than one sheet down on top of one another, but that's just not true. We tried folding our paper towels in a bunch of different ways. We folded the paper towel horizontally and vertically. We also folded the paper towel over multiple times. The greatest number of folds in any one paper towel was eight. That surprised me simply because I didn't think that we could get eight folds in a paper towel. We could, though, even though folding the paper towel and keeping it folded while it was in the water got harder every single time.

Feedback Grid:

Use the following feedback grid to rate the two sample conclusions and your own conclusion. If a trait appears in the conclusion you are studying, place an X in the appropriate box. If a trait doesn't appear, leave the box blank. If you aren't sure whether the trait appears, place a ? in the box. Then, check your ratings with a partner. Do your ratings for each category match? If not, why not? More importantly, if not, come to consensus on your ratings.

Conclusion You Are Studying	Summarize Your Findings	Reflect on Surprising Results	Record Lessons Learned From Findings	Design a Follow-Up Experiment
Conclusion 1				
Conclusion 2				
My Conclusion				

Source: Adapted from Ferriter & Cancellieri, 2017; Wiliam, 2017.

FIGURE 3.4.5: Conclusion comparison.

Working individually, students can use the feedback grid to track the success criteria they spot in both exemplars. Then, they can compare their individual ratings of each exemplar with their peers', looking for areas of agreement and supporting their decisions with specific evidence from the exemplars. Finally, students can return to their own work and use the information gathered while exploring both exemplars to evaluate and improve their final products (Ferriter & Cancellieri, 2017).

Regardless of the strategy you use to generate exemplars for students, there are three important points to keep in mind.

1. Your students should be working with exemplars *while* practicing with new processes and completing new assignments. By offering students high-quality examples to refer to while they generate their own demonstrations of mastery, educators create opportunities for each learner to assess and adjust in the moment.

2. The first exemplars you share with students should be simple. Remember that your students are likely to need more experience with generating self-feedback. To ensure that early attempts to use exemplars are positive, avoid overwhelming students with information. The right amount of feedback to ask students to gather from your first exemplars is the amount of feedback they have the capacity to act on.

3. You must build time into your instructional sequence for students to work with the exemplars that you create. It's not the information in the exemplars that matters—it's the opportunity for students to engage with that information that makes the difference.

Tools and Resources for Highly Effective Teams

The following tools and resources will help you accomplish the work for this essential action.

- **"Tool: Developing Exemplars to Make Learning Intentions Explicit" (page 166):** Providing students with exemplars of final products is a valuable practice because it allows students to see what learning intentions and success criteria for assignments look like in action. When students can spot success criteria—or a lack thereof— in exemplars, they are better prepared to spot those criteria in their work. Answer the questions included in this tool with your learning team to develop a set of exemplars for an upcoming task you will ask students to complete. There is also an example completed exemplar set, **"Sample: Developing Exemplars to Make Learning Intentions Explicit—Middle School Science" (page 168)**.

- **"Tool: Developing a Single-Point Rubric With Your Students" (page 169):** One of the best instructional moves that teachers introducing exemplars to students can make is to follow up their work with exemplars by cocreating single-point rubrics with their students (Cancellieri, 2020a). Doing so allows students to articulate the success criteria for the assignment that they are working on before submitting final drafts. This practice provides students with valuable knowledge and expertise they can apply when reviewing their work. Consider using this tool to create a single-point rubric with your students.

- **"Tool: Sample Video-Based High/Low Comparison Task" (page 171):** It is important to remember that the exemplars you create for your students should mirror the tasks you are asking them to complete. That means teachers of primary students or subjects where performances serve as the primary demonstrations of mastery will rely on video-based exemplars when creating high/low comparison tasks. To help you imagine what that can look like, explore this high/low comparison task created to help elementary mathematics students understand how to use the area method of multiplication. Notice that while the task remains the same—students are asked to use success criteria to evaluate two different solutions to the problems they are working on in class—QR codes in the document point users to video-based exemplars of a student completing a multiplication problem while working on a whiteboard.

- **"Tool: Critical Issues for Team Consideration—Highly Effective Team Actions" (page 172):** This tool provides teams an opportunity to reflect on their progress, celebrate strengths, and identify next steps worth taking. At the conclusion of each set of actions, teams use a portion of this tool to dialogue about their current practices, to identify strengths and areas of focus, and to identify next steps on their pathway to becoming a highly effective collaborative team.

Tool: Developing Exemplars to Make Learning Intentions Explicit

On this page, describe the task that all students will be asked to complete as a demonstration of mastery in the first row. Then, in the second row, describe the learning target you are assessing with this task. In the left column, fill in the exemplar that your team has generated to spotlight common patterns present in student responses at this level of performance. In the right column, add teacher comments: reasons that this exemplar accurately represents responses at this level of performance. Finally, in the last row, write a one- to two-sentence summary of the characteristics of responses that demonstrate this level of performance. Remember to use student-friendly language throughout your exemplars. Doing so will make your final products more useful to your learners.

Task Students Will Complete or Question Students Will Answer to Demonstrate Mastery:

Learning Target This Task Is Designed to Assess:

Level of Performance Demonstrated by This Exemplar
(Circle one.)

Beginning	Developing	Mastering	Exceeding
Exemplar		**Teacher Comments**	

Defining Characteristics of Responses Demonstrating This Level of Performance

PART THREE
Using Assessments and Data

On this page, use the questions in the first column of the following table to clarify your expectations for an upcoming classroom activity. Then, use the template for this tool and its corresponding sample to develop an exemplar for this assignment that students can examine while creating their own final products.

Name of Assignment:	
Essential Concepts and Skills Covered During This Assignment:	

Questions to Consider	Your Team's Response
Name three elements you would expect to find in a final product that **met your team's expectations** for proficiency on this assignment.	
Name three elements you would expect to find in a final product that **went beyond your team's expectations** for proficiency on this assignment.	
What **mistakes** do students struggling to demonstrate proficiency typically make on this assignment?	

Now, use the template for this tool to develop an exemplar for this assignment. Remember that a good exemplar should fulfill the following three criteria.

1. Be a teacher-created example designed to illustrate both the success criteria and common mistakes found in student work.

2. Include teacher comments explaining the overall rating for the exemplar.

3. Include an opportunity for students to compare their work to the exemplar.

Source: Ferriter, W. M. (2020). The big book of tools for collaborative teams in a PLC at Work. Solution Tree Press; Ferriter, W. M., Mattos, M., & Meyer, R. J. (2025). The big book of tools for RTI at Work. Solution Tree Press.

The Handbook for Highly Effective Teams in a PLC at Work® © 2025 Solution Tree Press • SolutionTree.com
Visit **go.SolutionTree.com/PLCbooks** to download this free reproducible.

PART THREE
Using Assessments and Data

3

Sample: Developing Exemplars to Make Learning Intentions Explicit—Middle School Science

---

Task Students Will Complete or Question Students Will Answer to Demonstrate Mastery:

Gap Thinking: *MythBusters*—"Archimedes Death Ray"

In this task, students are asked to predict the outcomes of the experiments conducted in a *MythBusters* episode titled "Archimedes Death Ray." Then, students are asked to identify additional information that they would need to know before they could determine whether their predictions were correct. We call this work "identifying gaps in your thinking."

Learning Target This Task Is Designed to Assess:
(Written in student-friendly language)

I can explain the role that questioning my own thinking can play in thinking critically. This means I can make a prediction and identify gaps in my thinking that make it difficult to ensure that my prediction is accurate.

Level of Performance Demonstrated by This Exemplar
(Circle one.)

Beginning	Developing	Mastering	Exceeding

Exemplar *(Sample generated by the team to spotlight commonalities seen in student responses at this performance level)*	**Teacher Comments** *(Detailed reasons this exemplar is an accurate representation of responses at this performance level)*
I think the MythBusters *will* be able to light a ship on fire using mirrors because I know that the mirrors in solar farms can generate temperatures over 1,000 degrees Celsius. That means the MythBusters should be able to harness a lot of the sun's energy. **But I'm not sure because:** • I don't know how far heat rays can travel. • I don't know if light loses energy as it travels from one place to another. • I don't know if the boat will absorb all of the light. • I don't know what materials ancient boats were made of.	• The student response is on topic and shows evidence of attempts to apply the content we have been studying in class to the prediction and the gaps in thinking. • The student includes at least two gaps in thinking connected to the question under study and the student's original prediction. • Gaps in thinking show extensive reflection about the topic being studied. • There is no question that if this student had more detail about the gaps in his thinking, he would definitely be able to make a more accurate prediction.

Defining Characteristics of Responses Demonstrating This Level of Performance
(One- or two-sentence summary written in student-friendly language)

The defining characteristic of a student response that exceeds expectations is a very clear connection between the prediction that you originally made and the gaps in thinking that you have identified. You cannot exceed expectations if the gaps in thinking that you identify are not related to your original prediction.

Source: Adapted from Ferriter, W. M. (2020). The big book of tools for collaborative teams in a PLC at Work. *Solution Tree Press.*

Tool: Developing a Single-Point Rubric With Your Students

Remember that single-point rubrics should be developed together with your students after they have had the chance to grapple with a set of exemplars designed to highlight both the success criteria and common mistakes found in student responses to classroom tasks (Cancellieri, 2020a). To develop a single-point rubric with your students, consider projecting this template onto your classroom whiteboard and then leading a classroom discussion around the following questions.

1. What kinds of things would we see in a successful student response to this question or assignment?

2. If a student were struggling with this question or assignment, what kinds of mistakes would they make?

3. Are there any basics or *fundamentals*—things like proper grammar in writing or accurate calculations in mathematics—that we would expect students to demonstrate consistently when answering questions or completing assignments like this?

As you spot trends in student responses during your classroom discussion, begin crafting the success criteria for the assignment in the center column of the following table. When you think all important success criteria have been identified, ask students to vote on the criteria statements that you have crafted. Allow any student who feels that essential criteria have been left out of your statements to share his or her thinking with the class.

Areas Where You Could Improve Your Work	Criteria for the Assignment	Areas Where You Went Beyond Expectations

PART THREE
Using Assessments and Data

Areas Where You Could Improve Your Work	Criteria for the Assignment	Areas Where You Went Beyond Expectations

PART THREE
Using Assessments and Data

Source: Cancellieri, P. (2020a, June 11). Creating a Culture of Feedback book study: Session two—How am I doing? [Video file]. Accessed at https://solutiontree.wistia.com/medias/ra3371pryg on June 27, 2020.

Tool: Sample Video-Based High/Low Comparison Task

Using the area method of multiplication correctly requires a student to do the following.

1. **Set up** your area lattice correctly.

2. **Multiply and add** all numbers accurately.

3. **Write neatly** so you can read all numbers in each step of solving the problem.

Knowing that, decide how you would rate the quality of the work done by the student in the following samples.

Solution 1	Solution 2

Feedback Grid:

Use the following feedback grid to rate the two sample solutions *and* your own solution. If a trait appears in the solution you are studying, place an *X* in the appropriate box. If a trait doesn't appear, leave the box blank. If you aren't sure whether the trait appears, place a *?* in the box. Then, check your ratings with a partner. Do your ratings for each criterion agree? If not, why not? If the ratings are not the same, come to an agreement about your ratings.

Solution You Are Studying	Set Up Lattice Correctly	Multiply and Add Accurately	Write Neatly
Solution 1			
Solution 2			
My Solution			

Tool: Critical Issues for Team Consideration— Highly Effective Team Actions

Your honest evaluation is critical!

Please thoughtfully discuss your team's reality in each of the highly effective team indicators. Use the scale to rate your team in each area. At the conclusion of each section, identify areas to celebrate and areas for your team to intensify efforts.

+   This is very true of our team. This belief or action is embedded in our beliefs and actions.

✓   This is sometimes true of our team. We are not consistent about this belief or action.

−   This is rarely or never true of our team. We need to work on implementing this belief or action.

Rating	Part 1: Highly Effective Teams Have a Common Foundation
	Action 1.1: We identify team roles, norms, and protocols to guide us in working together.
	Action 1.2: We have a process for addressing moments when personalities interfere with the team's work.
	Action 1.3: We use SMART goals to drive our work.
	Action 1.4: We regularly evaluate our team's effectiveness.

Celebrations:

Next steps:

Rating	Part 2: Highly Effective Teams Focus on Learning for All Students
	Action 2.1: We collectively identify essential learnings and define what success looks like in student work.
	Action 2.2: We identify the prerequisite knowledge and skills needed to master our essentials.
	Action 2.3: We identify course content and topics we can minimize or eliminate to devote more time to our essentials.
	Action 2.4: We agree on how to sequence content and pace our course.

The Handbook for Highly Effective Teams in a PLC at Work® © 2025 Solution Tree Press • SolutionTree.com
Visit **go.SolutionTree.com/PLCbooks** to download this free reproducible.

Celebrations:	
Next steps:	

Rating	Part 3: Highly Effective Teams Effectively Use Assessments and Data
	Action 3.1: We develop and deliver frequent common formative assessments throughout our units of instruction.
	Action 3.2: We use team assessment data to identify high-impact instructional strategies.
	Action 3.3: We teach students the criteria we will use to judge their work.
	Action 3.4: We create exemplars students can examine to evaluate their own progress toward mastery.

Celebrations:	
Next steps:	

Rating	Part 4: Highly Effective Teams Provide Extra Time and Support for Learning
	Action 4.1: We create flexible time during our units of instruction to provide extra time and support to learners.
	Action 4.2: We deliver targeted interventions to support students who have not yet reached grade-level expectations.
	Action 4.3: We deliver targeted extensions to students working beyond grade-level expectations.

Celebrations:	
Next steps:	

PART THREE
Using Assessments and Data

Source: Adapted from DuFour, R., DuFour, R., Eaker, R., Many, T. W., Mattos, M., & Muhammad, A. (2024). Learning by doing: A handbook for Professional Learning Communities at Work (4th ed.). Solution Tree Press.

PART 4

Highly Effective Teams Provide Extra Time and Support for Learning

Meeting the needs of all students requires intentional planning to provide both initial interventions and extensions around grade-level essentials. The fourth and final part of *The Handbook for Highly Effective Teams in a PLC at Work* addresses how teams provide additional time and targeted assistance to help students master prerequisite skills, accelerate their learning, and reach their full potential. By acting together, highly effective teams ensure all students grow and high achievers are challenged to go further.

- **Action 4.1:** We Create Flexible Time During Our Units of Instruction to Provide Extra Time and Support to Learners (page 177)

- **Action 4.2:** We Deliver Targeted Interventions to Support Students Who Have Not Yet Reached Grade-Level Expectations (page 191)

- **Action 4.3:** We Deliver Targeted Extensions to Students Working Beyond Grade-Level Expectations (page 211)

We Create Flexible Time During Our Units of Instruction to Provide Extra Time and Support to Learners

You can make all the complicated plans you want, but higher levels of learning starts when we pull up a chair next to a student and teach them to do something they don't know how to do.

—ROBERT EAKER

Think about all the time and energy that collaborative teams invest in planning a unit of instruction. They start by identifying a small handful of essentials to prioritize, focusing on the standards that have the greatest leverage for student success. Then, they work together to deconstruct those standards, building a shared understanding of what the standard means and what mastery of the standard looks like in student work. Next, teams discuss instructional strategies that align with these essentials, sharing best practices to ensure every student has access to high-quality instruction. They examine their curriculum together, determining which resources best support the learning targets they are trying to teach. Finally, teams map out their pacing, ensuring they are teaching roughly the same thing at roughly the same time so they can administer common formative assessments at roughly the same points in the unit. Each of these steps requires deep collaboration, thoughtful discussion, and a shared commitment to ensuring that every student learns at high levels.

After investing so much time and energy into planning a unit of instruction, it only makes sense for teams to pause along the way and provide additional time and support to students who are struggling. The purpose of all that collaboration, after all, isn't just to create a great plan—it's to ensure that the plan *leads to real learning for students*. By intentionally building in time to provide extra support during a unit, teams can address gaps in the learning of students who have fallen behind before those gaps become significant. This helps teachers avoid the trap of overteaching—plowing ahead to cover new material while failing to provide the necessary support for learners who have not yet mastered the current essentials.

Pausing to assess, adjust, and intervene isn't just smart—it's what keeps students moving forward and ensures that the team's hard work has its intended impact. Just as importantly, pausing to assess, adjust, and intervene will help teams minimize the number of students who need more intensive supports to master grade-level essentials later during the school year.

Why Highly Effective Teams Do This

In their presentations on the culture changes that schools must make to build multitiered systems of support, Mike Mattos (Mattos et al., 2025) and Luis Cruz (2024), internationally recognized experts on the response to intervention (RTI) process, ask audiences the following five questions.

1. **Can we agree that not all students learn in the same way?**

   Example: Is it possible that some students in a tenth-grade sports medicine class will best process new information about injury prevention techniques by reading in a textbook, while others would benefit more from watching instructional videos or listening to podcasts featuring professionals in the field?

2. **Can we agree that not all students learn at the same speed?**

   Example: Is it possible that one sixth-grade art student might master the steps of creating a batik painting after observing a single demonstration, while another might need additional time and hands-on practice to feel confident independently applying the wax and dye?

3. **Can we agree that some students lack the prior knowledge and skills necessary to succeed?**

   Example: Is it possible that a first-grade student might struggle to read simple sentences fluently because they didn't fully master letter-sound recognition and blending skills in kindergarten?

4. **Can we agree that some students lack the proper academic and social behaviors necessary to succeed?**

   Example: Is it possible that a ninth-grade student in a civics class might struggle to complete a long-term research project because they lack effective time-management skills or organizational strategies?

5. **Can we agree that some students have a home life that is counterproductive to academic success?**

   Example: Is it possible that a third-grade student might struggle to complete homework assignments or other practice tasks designed to reinforce new learning because their parents work multiple jobs and are rarely home to provide guidance or support?

If we can agree that ensuring all students learn at grade level or higher is the constant for collaborative teams—and we should, given that high levels of learning for all students is the ultimate purpose of collaboration in PLCs—then each of these fundamental assumptions highlights a variable. Whether it's the way students learn, the pace at which they progress, or the challenges they face outside of school, these variables make it unlikely that every student will meet grade-level expectations the first time we teach a new concept or skill. In other words, no matter how well planned and thoughtful our initial instruction, some students will need additional time and support to succeed.

To act responsibly, then, collaborative teams must acknowledge this reality and develop a plan to address it. This requires intentionally building opportunities into every unit to respond to students who need additional time, practice, or support to master essential standards. It's this willingness to intervene in real time—rather than waiting until after the unit is complete—that distinguishes highly effective teams from ineffective groups.

Having pitched these concepts to thousands of teachers in hundreds of schools, we can guess what you might be thinking right now: "Are you kidding? I don't have time to stop during a unit and provide interventions for struggling students—I have too much content to cover!" And you are absolutely right: If your goal is to *cover* every standard in the curriculum, then you definitely don't have time to pause, assess, adjust, and intervene.

But let's not forget that our goal *isn't* to teach every standard in the required curriculum. Our goal is to ensure that all students master the most important outcomes in the required curriculum. That means you don't need to carve out extra time to assess, adjust, and intervene for students struggling with the *nonessentials* in your current unit. The focus is on providing that time and support to students who haven't mastered the *essentials*. Does that make this task seem more doable? Figure 4.1.1 offers a comparison of language between ineffective groups and highly effective teams around this topic.

The Language of Ineffective Groups	The Language of Highly Effective Teams
"I can't afford to give up any of my instructional time. I have too much material to cover."	"Pausing to assess, adjust, and intervene is instructional time! It is essential to providing the support that some students need to master our essentials."
"It's my job to teach the material. If students didn't learn it during the initial instruction, they're just not going to learn it."	"We know some students won't master the material on the first try. That's why we build time into our instructional plan for reteaching and targeted support."
"I'm tired of students who come to us without knowing the things they were supposed to learn in last year's class. What are those teachers doing all day?"	"We know that some students are going to come to us with gaps in their understanding of the content we are trying to teach. What if we set aside some intervention time to preteach some important prerequisites to those students?"
"Don't we have special education teachers around here who can provide interventions to struggling students?"	"We know our grade-level curriculum better than anyone else in the building. Why wouldn't we accept responsibility for finding the time and the strategies to reteach our essentials to struggling students?"
"Interventions are just for the struggling students. My job is to keep moving forward with my curriculum."	"Interventions are for everyone who needs them, and we use them to make sure every student masters our essentials."

FIGURE 4.1.1: Language comparison.

Notice that ineffective groups often focus on simply covering all grade-level or course standards, leaving little room for responding to student needs. They also tend to shift the responsibility for interventions to other professionals—special education teachers, interventionists, content specialists—rather than taking ownership for ensuring that all students master their grade-level essentials. In contrast, highly effective teams stand ready to work collaboratively to ensure every student masters the essentials in their current unit of instruction. To do so, they willingly set time aside during their unit plan to provide the additional time and support that some students will need to succeed. If we agree that students learn at different times and in different ways, then we must plan to respond to students who will need extra time and support *during* the unit of instruction.

How Highly Effective Teams Do This

Highly effective teams recognize that even after their best efforts at initial instruction, some students will not have mastered the essentials. To address this, they strategically build time into their instructional calendars for interventions. These interventions can take various forms, depending on the needs of the students and the structure of the team's collaborative plans. Educational consultant Sarah Schuhl (2022) provides the following practical examples of how teams can incorporate flexible time for interventions during a unit.

- **Building in time for support at the end of each day's instruction**
  - *Advantages*—Students get immediate opportunities to receive clarification and reinforcement while the lesson is still fresh. Teachers can quickly address misunderstandings before they snowball into larger gaps in learning.
  - *Disadvantages*—It can be difficult to fit intervention time into an already packed daily schedule, especially in schools with shorter periods. Teachers may feel pressure to rush through instruction just to make time for interventions.
- **Dedicating a specific day during the week to provide extra support**
  - *Advantages*—Having a designated day each week for interventions allows teachers to focus on reteaching without the distraction of new instruction. It provides a predictable routine for students who need additional time and support.
  - *Disadvantages*—Losing a full day of new instruction can feel disruptive to pacing, and it may cause stress if the team falls behind in content coverage. This strategy works best with careful planning and essentials prioritization.
- **Using targeted small-group instruction**
  - *Advantages*—Teachers can tailor instruction to specific student needs, making interventions more effective and personalized. Students often feel more comfortable asking questions in settings with fewer people.
  - *Disadvantages*—Managing the rest of the class during small-group interventions can be challenging, especially if the remaining students need meaningful, independent tasks to remain engaged. It requires strong classroom management and preparation.

- **Adding brief intervention periods on designated days**
  - *Advantages*—Short intervention periods are easier to fit into the schedule and maintain the flow of regular instruction. The periods provide frequent opportunities to address learning gaps without disrupting the overall unit pacing.
  - *Disadvantages*—Brief periods may not provide enough time to fully address deeper learning needs or provide sufficient practice for students struggling with complex concepts.

Figure 4.1.2 offers a visual representation of how a team's weekly schedule might look based on the strategy for providing time for additional support that they choose to implement.

Example: Build in time for support at the end of each day's instruction.

Monday	Tuesday	Wednesday	Thursday	Friday
Tier 1 instruction	Tier 1 instruction	Tier 1 instruction	Tier 1 instruction	Tier 1 instruction
Extra time and support	Extra time and support	Extra time and support	Extra time and support	Extra time and support

Example: Select a specific day to provide extra support for students who require it.

Monday	Tuesday	Wednesday	Thursday	Friday
Tier 1 instruction	Tier 1 instruction	Extra time and support	Tier 1 instruction	Tier 1 instruction

Example: Dedicate specific days for targeted, small-group instruction at the end of instruction.

Monday	Tuesday	Wednesday	Thursday	Friday
Tier 1 instruction	Tier 1 instruction	Tier 1 instruction	Tier 1 instruction	Tier 1 instruction
	Small group	Small group	Small group	

Example: Identify two days and dedicate the last thirty minutes of the instructional period to providing extra time and support.

Monday	Tuesday	Wednesday	Thursday	Friday
Tier 1 instruction	Tier 1 instruction	Tier 1 instruction	Tier 1 instruction	Tier 1 instruction
	Thirty minutes of extra time and support		Thirty minutes of extra time and support	

Source: Schuhl & Kanold, 2024; Schuhl, Toncheff, Deinhart, & Buckhalter, 2024.

FIGURE 4.1.2: Finding time for extra instruction.

It is important to note that there is no one right way for teams to find flexible time for extra instruction. Teams can adapt each of these approaches to fit various school schedules. A secondary school on a block schedule with eighty-five-minute periods might allocate one hour for instruction each period and use the final twenty-five minutes for intervention and extension, while schools with shorter periods might designate a specific day each week for targeted support.

It is also worth noting that teams don't need to wait for their entire school to adopt a specific strategy for providing additional time and support for learning. As long as they have control over their instructional time, a team can create a schedule that allows flexible interventions, even if the rest of the school isn't ready yet. While having a schoolwide period for interventions offers real advantages—shared resources, the ability to group students across teams, and greater consistency for families—teams can begin this work independently. By taking the initiative, they can start addressing their students' needs and serve as a model for how flexible scheduling can support higher levels of learning.

Whenever possible, however, all teachers on a collaborative team should use the same schedule for building flexible time into their instructional plan to provide extra support for learning. Doing so allows the team to share students and group them by specific learning needs. This approach is far more effective than trying to address a wide range of needs within a single class. Additionally, shared scheduling makes it possible for students to receive instruction from the teacher on the team who has identified the most effective strategy for teaching the current grade-level essential—a practice discussed in action 3.2 (page 133). This not only increases the likelihood of student success but also strengthens the collective impact of the team's work.

By committing to building flexible time into their unit plans, highly effective collaborative teams get out in front of the very real challenge of meeting their students' diverse needs. Regardless of the specific strategy, the key for teams is to act intentionally, making sure that every student has access to the support they need to master essential learning.

Tools and Resources for Highly Effective Teams

The following tools and resources will help you accomplish the work for this essential action.

- **"Tool: Team Flexible Time Planning Prompts" (page 184):** Highly effective teams recognize the need to reflect on their shared practices while creating extra time and support as they plan their units of instruction together. This tool provides targeted questions that teams can address as they plan for extra time and support during a unit.

- **"Tool: Building Shared Knowledge About Tier 2 Interventions and Extensions" (page 185):** To make the most of the flexible time built into unit plans for interventions and extensions, teams need a solid understanding of both the work that happens during these periods and the reasons why providing timely support is critical for student success. This tool helps readers deepen their understanding of these essential practices. Featuring a series of true/false questions and a corresponding **"Answer Key: Building Shared Knowledge About Tier 2 Interventions and Extensions" (page 187)**, it can serve as both a knowledge check and a learning resource. Use it with your team to build an understanding of what supplemental interventions around grade-level essentials are all about.

- **"Tool: Team-Based Intervention Plan for Struggling Learners" (page 189):** This tool helps teams create an intentional plan for reteaching an essential standard by identifying the standard, defining the specific student need the intervention is designed to meet, and developing a detailed reteaching plan. It also includes space to record the students in each class who would benefit from the intervention. By using this resource, your team can make sure to use your intervention time effectively.

Tool: Team Flexible Time Planning Prompts

As a team, reflect and discuss the questions for each unit of instruction.

Is there adequate flexible time built into our units of instruction to reteach or extend the essential learnings?
Is the focus during the flexible time on reteaching essential learnings?
During the flexible time, do we divide students according to need?
During the flexible time, what are our plans for students who have already mastered the essential learnings?
Do we have a way to quickly determine whether a student mastered the essential learnings after reteaching?

Tool: Building Shared Knowledge About Tier 2 Interventions and Extensions

Instructions: To surface what you already know about the role teacher teams play in designing and leading supplemental interventions for academic essentials, work with your team to decide whether the following statements are true or false. Then, check your answers against those provided in "Answer Key: Building Shared Knowledge About Tier 2 Interventions and Extensions" (page 187) and correct your answers if necessary.

Statement	Your Answer	Correct Answer	Your Rationale
Teams should provide intervention and extension for every outcome in their required curriculum.	☐ True ☐ False	☐ True ☐ False	
Classroom teachers always provide interventions for struggling students.	☐ True ☐ False	☐ True ☐ False	
Teachers cannot move forward in their curriculum until all students have mastered the standards they are currently studying.	☐ True ☐ False	☐ True ☐ False	
The best intervention strategy is good initial instruction.	☐ True ☐ False	☐ True ☐ False	

Teams with successful interventions always start instruction by administering pretests of grade-level essentials.	☐ True ☐ False	☐ True ☐ False	
Sorting students into targeted intervention groups is the most important action teams take when analyzing common formative assessment results.	☐ True ☐ False	☐ True ☐ False	
Teams should use state testing results early in the school year to identify students who need intervention, extension, or both.	☐ True ☐ False	☐ True ☐ False	
The most important interventions that we provide to students address the outcomes we are required to teach by our state standards.	☐ True ☐ False	☐ True ☐ False	
I can name the four most common strategies for extending learning.	☐ True ☐ False	☐ True ☐ False	
I can name the four most common reasons why students struggle to master grade-level essentials.	☐ True ☐ False	☐ True ☐ False	

Source: Ferriter, W. M., Mattos, M., & Meyer, R. J. (2025). The big book of tools for RTI at Work. Solution Tree Press.

PART FOUR
Providing Extra Time and Support

Answer Key: Building Shared Knowledge About Tier 2 Interventions and Extensions

Instructions: Review the answers and rationale provided in the second and third columns of the following table. Compare them to the answers that your team generated on the previous page. What answers did you get right? What answers did you get wrong? What answers surprised you, had you wondering, or left you relieved? What changes do you need to make to your intervention efforts?

Statement	Correct Answer	Explanation
Teams should provide intervention and extension for every outcome in their required curriculum.	☐ True ☑ False	Because the total number of standards for most courses is overwhelming, it is both unrealistic and unreasonable to expect teachers and teams to provide intervention and extension for every outcome. Instead, teams focus their Tier 2 intervention and extension efforts on the essentials in their required curriculum. If time allows for additional interventions and extensions, teams can begin targeting nonessentials, but ensuring that students receive additional time and support to master essentials is the top priority.
Classroom teachers always provide interventions for struggling students.	☐ True ☑ False	It is true that classroom teachers accept primary responsibility for providing interventions in grade-level academic standards, but students struggle in school for reasons that go beyond academics. In a system of interventions, the school's guiding coalition accepts primary responsibility for interventions in social behaviors, health and home issues that prevent a student from succeeding, and learners' dispositions.
Teachers cannot move forward in their curriculum until all students have mastered the standards they are currently studying.	☐ True ☑ False	While it is true that all students must master grade-level essential standards before the end of the school year, that does not mean teams can't move forward in their instruction until all students have mastered those essentials. Instead, teams should keep a careful record of students who have yet to master current essentials, continue discussions about additional intervention strategies worth trying, and set aside time for continued reteaching of those essentials.
The best intervention strategy is good initial instruction.	☑ True ☐ False	There is not enough time or personnel available to provide intervention to large numbers of students. Instead, teams should invest their time and energy in finding the most effective strategies for teaching their essentials, therefore preventing students from needing intervention.
Teams with successful interventions always start instruction by administering pretests of grade-level essentials.	☐ True ☑ False	Pretests of grade-level essentials *could* be a valuable tool, if teachers and teams are willing to carefully analyze data to identify specific outcomes that individual students have mastered and plan differentiated instruction for those students. The problem is that teachers rarely do this work because it can be incredibly time consuming. Instead, teams should design and deliver *pretests of prerequisite skills*—things students need to know before working with grade-level essentials—and use the information gathered to preteach those prerequisites to students before starting instruction in a grade-level essential.

PART FOUR
Providing Extra Time and Support

page 1 of 2

Sorting students into targeted intervention groups is the most important action teams take when analyzing common formative assessment results.	☐ True ☑ False	While it is true that teams must sort students into targeted intervention groups, that work is rarely difficult for teams. In fact, teachers can probably build those groups without much effort at all. Instead, looking for common patterns in student work samples is most important when analyzing common formative assessment results. What can students in each intervention group already do? What common mistakes are they making? What common misunderstandings do they have? Spotting those patterns can help teams effectively target their Tier 2 intervention efforts.
Teams should use state testing results early in the school year to identify students who need intervention, extension, or both.	☐ True ☑ False	Tier 2 interventions provide students with extra time and support to master the essentials that are currently being taught in class. That information cannot be gleaned from state testing results. Instead, it is gleaned from team-created common formative assessments given during a cycle of instruction.
The most important interventions that we provide to students address the outcomes we are required to teach by state standards.	☐ True ☑ False	The most important interventions are those that address specific reasons why students are struggling in school—and sometimes, students aren't struggling for academic reasons. Instead, they are struggling with essential skills, dispositions, or social behaviors. Providing students who are missing essential skills, dispositions, or behaviors with academic interventions won't address the root causes of their classroom struggles.
I can name the four most common strategies for extending learning.	☑ True ☐ False	Teachers can extend learning by doing the following. • Introduce students to above-grade-level curriculum. • Ask students to work beyond grade-level expectations. • Introduce students to nonessential outcomes in the required grade-level curriculum. • Ask students to explore how grade-level curriculum impacts the world beyond the classroom.
I can name the four most common reasons why students struggle to master grade-level essentials.	☑ True ☐ False	The following are the four most common reasons why students struggle to master essentials. 1. They have gaps in prerequisite knowledge that teachers must address before students can master the grade-level essential. 2. They need additional practice opportunities with the grade-level essential. 3. They need an alternative way to demonstrate mastery of the grade-level essential. 4. Their work behaviors—participation, work completion, and effort—are preventing them from mastering the grade-level essential.

Source: Ferriter, W. M., Mattos, M., & Meyer, R. J. (2025). The big book of tools for RTI at Work. *Solution Tree Press.*

Tool: Team-Based Intervention Plan for Struggling Learners

Instructions: Record the essential outcomes that you are currently teaching. Then, indicate the type of intervention that you are planning and outline your intervention plan in the provided space. Finally, list the students in each classroom who need this intervention. Remember that students struggle to master essential outcomes for different reasons. You will need to create a separate intervention plan for each of the reasons that the students of your learning team are struggling.

Essential Outcomes We Are Currently Teaching:

Type of Intervention We Are Planning

☐ **Support with prerequisite learning** for students with gaps in foundational knowledge and skills that are preventing them from mastering the essential outcomes that we are currently teaching

☐ **Additional practice** for students who are making common mistakes that are likely to be easily corrected with a few opportunities to work with the essential outcomes again

☐ **Alternative demonstrations of mastery** for students who are struggling with a specific task and who might be able to demonstrate mastery of an essential outcome in a different way

☐ **Support for work behaviors** for students who are struggling to master an essential outcome because they haven't yet developed the habits demonstrated by successful learners (for example, coming to class prepared, participating in classroom discussions, or completing homework)

Our Intervention Plan:

List the students in each class who are currently in need of this intervention.

Teacher:	Teacher:	Teacher:	Teacher:

Source: Ferriter, W. M. (2020). The big book of tools for collaborative teams in a PLC at Work. *Solution Tree Press.*

PART FOUR Providing Extra Time and Support

We Deliver Targeted Interventions to Support Students Who Have Not Yet Reached Grade-Level Expectations

We cannot make this point emphatically enough: it is disingenuous for any school to claim its purpose is to help all students learn at high levels and then fail to create a system of interventions to give struggling learners additional time and support for learning. If time and support remain constant in schools, learning will always be the variable.

—RICHARD DUFOUR, REBECCA DUFOUR, ROBERT EAKER, THOMAS W. MANY, MIKE MATTOS, AND ANTHONY MUHAMMAD

For many collaborative teams, creating flexible time for intervention during units of instruction—a process detailed in action 4.1 (page 177)—marks a turning point in their work to ensure that every student learns at the highest levels. And that makes sense. After all, making room for extra time and support requires an intentional investment of instructional minutes, the most valuable currency that we have in schools. This investment, whether it is made at the team or the school level, serves as concrete proof of our shared commitment to learning.

How will we create flexible time to give students extra time and support for learning? isn't the only question that teams have to answer if they are going to deliver on the promise of higher levels of learning for all, however. The next logical question is, *What do we do with the time we have created?* It's not enough to simply carve out space in the schedule for interventions. Teams must ensure that they use intervention time effectively.

To ensure this time is truly effective, teams must invest in their own professional learning about interventions. They must study research-backed reengagement strategies, understanding that some approaches are far more effective than others. They must deepen their knowledge of how learning happens and recognize that understanding how the brain processes new information can mean the difference between mastery and continued struggle for some students. They must analyze their content, identifying the common misconceptions that often trip students up; they must explore alternative ways for students to demonstrate mastery; and they must create a shared playbook of high-impact intervention strategies to use when students need extra support. Learning together is the key to building the professional capacity necessary to make every minute of intervention time count.

Why Highly Effective Teams Do This

In the previous essential action, we detailed five fundamental assumptions that all teachers need to hold about their students (Cruz, 2024; Mattos et al., 2025).

1. Not all students learn in the same way.
2. Not all students learn at the same speed.
3. Some students lack the prior knowledge and skills necessary to succeed.
4. Some students lack the proper academic and social behaviors necessary to succeed.
5. Some students have a home life that is counterproductive to academic success.

Similarly, we believe there are five core truths that describe teachers on highly effective teams.

1. **They want every student to learn at the highest levels.**

   Teachers enter the profession with a deep commitment to student success, driven by a belief that all children deserve the opportunity to thrive academically.

2. **They are using the best strategies that they know to deliver initial instruction to students.**

   Instructional decisions are drawn from teachers' current knowledge, experience, and expertise, meaning they are always applying what they believe to be the most effective approaches to help students understand new content.

3. **They understand that reteaching when students struggle is a professional responsibility.**

   Effective educators recognize that teaching isn't just about delivering content—it's about making sure students learn it. When students struggle, teachers don't just move on; they adjust, reteach, and keep working the problem.

4. **Sometimes, however, they aren't sure how to teach an essential differently to students who didn't master it the first time.**

   The challenge isn't knowing that some students will need a second opportunity to learn essential outcomes. It's figuring out how to give them that second opportunity in a way that actually works. Doing the same thing again isn't reteaching; it's just repeating.

5. **No matter how skilled they currently are, there will always be new instructional strategies worth learning.**

The field of education is constantly evolving with new research and insights, making continuous professional growth an essential part of improving our effectiveness. Stated more simply, the more we learn, the better we get, and the better we get, the more we can do for our students.

Can you see how these core truths shape the way we approach intervention in schools? If teachers are already using the best strategies they know during initial instruction, chances are they will lean on those same strategies when reteaching. And that's where things get tricky. If a strategy didn't work the first time, it's unlikely to work the second time either; "louder and slower," after all, is not an intervention (Williams, 2016). The real danger, however, is that when students don't respond, teachers start to lose confidence—not just in interventions, but in their students. Think about it this way: If you invest valuable instructional minutes into reteaching and get no results, it is easy to start wondering if interventions are even worth the effort. Worse yet, if you've already used your best approach twice and students still don't get it, you may start questioning whether they ever will.

In fact, while the term *reteaching* has become a common way to describe what we do during the flexible time we create for interventions, it may actually do more harm than good. Why? Because it implies that the original instructional approach was effective and simply needs to be repeated for better results. This mindset prioritizes delivering content rather than ensuring learning, overlooking the reality that since some students learn in different ways and at different speeds, effective instruction of any essential is going to require more than just one strategy. Highly effective teams recognize that reteaching is really facilitating *relearning* and that students who struggle to master essentials don't just need *another chance*—they need *a different approach*.

The impact of this simple shift in thinking on struggling learners is also significant. In schools that focus on reteaching rather than relearning during flexible time for interventions, struggling students are repeatedly exposed to the same ineffective instructional approach, and they repeatedly fail. Over time, those failures take a toll. Instead of recognizing that they just haven't been taught in a way that makes sense to them yet, struggling students start to believe they *can't* learn at all. The result? Disengagement—not just during interventions, but also during initial instruction. To teachers, that disengagement looks like a lack of motivation. "Why won't that kid just try?" we wonder, or worse yet, "That kid just doesn't care." But research is clear: People won't invest in learning unless they believe they have a real chance of success (Simms, 2024). And for struggling students stuck in a cycle of ineffective reteaching, there is little reason to believe that effort will pay off.

Highly effective teams, then, commit to continuously studying instruction, understanding that deepening their collective knowledge of how learning happens, identifying the concepts that commonly cause students to struggle, and exploring new ways to explain those concepts all strengthen their ability to help every student succeed. As their expertise with facilitating relearning grows, so does their collective efficacy—the confidence that they really can find solutions to help all students learn at high levels. Figure 4.2.1 (page 194) offers a comparison of language between ineffective groups and highly effective teams around this topic.

The Language of Ineffective Groups	The Language of Highly Effective Teams
"Sometimes, I get tired of interventions. It's always the same kids who need them. If those kids paid attention the first time, they just might learn something!"	"There's something about my instructional strategies that isn't working for a group of students in my class. I want to see if I can figure out what that is so I can better reach them, in both my initial instruction and my interventions."
"I know my teaching works. After all, most kids learn what they are supposed to learn the first time around."	"I know my teaching works for most of my kids, and that's a relief! I'm doing a great job. But I've got to do some research to figure out a few new things to try for the kids I'm still not reaching yet."
"If these kids in intervention don't learn this time, we'll just have to move on. Why teach the same thing again and again?"	"There's got to be a strategy that can help our students learn this essential. We just haven't found it yet. But let's keep looking!"
"I'm going to give my kids a bunch of practice problems to work on during interventions today. That's got to be why they are struggling. They just need more practice."	"I wonder if the reason kids are struggling with the practice problems that I gave them in class is because they misunderstood something during my direct instruction. I'll have to figure out what that is and try to explain it a different way."

FIGURE 4.2.1: Language comparison.

Can you spot the differences in how ineffective groups and highly effective teams see the work done to improve interventions for struggling students? Ineffective groups place the responsibility for relearning squarely on the students' shoulders, assuming that their struggles stem from a lack of attention or effort. To them, intervention is a frustrating, repetitive process rather than an opportunity to refine instruction. Highly effective teams, on the other hand, take ownership of student learning, recognizing that student struggles signal a need to adjust instruction. They view interventions not as a last-ditch effort to teach a concept, but as a chance to experiment with new strategies and to add to their professional skill set. More simply put, ineffective groups see interventions as an obligation, while highly effective teams see them as an opportunity to learn more about good teaching.

How Highly Effective Teams Do This

While there are lots of reasons students struggle to master grade-level essentials, teachers are likely to see five factors again and again: (1) misconceptions that lead to predictable mistakes; (2) struggles with the task, not the standard; (3) challenges accessing learning through text; (4) work habits that interfere with learning; and (5) lack of confidence as a learner. By anticipating these challenges, collaborative teams can proactively design targeted interventions to meet the specific needs of struggling students. Each of these factors is detailed in the following sections.

Misconceptions That Lead to Predictable Mistakes

Experienced teachers can predict many student mistakes with grade-level essentials before instruction even begins. Why? Because students often share common misconceptions about the core concepts they are learning. Here's an example: Lots of middle school science students assume that heavier objects always sink in water. Given their experiences, this belief makes sense. They've seen forks sink in dishwater, macaroni settle at the bottom of a pot, and rocks drop to the bottom of a pond. But this misconception can make it difficult for students to grasp the concept of density, which depends on both mass and volume.

Highly effective teams identify these kinds of common misconceptions in advance and design targeted instructional strategies to address them. Not sure of the common misconceptions that students might have about the concept you are trying to teach? Consider asking an AI chatbot like ChatGPT (https://chatgpt.com) for help. Prompts like those that follow can give you valuable information that you can use to target interventions around a grade-level essential.

- Can you list the three most common mistakes that [*grade-level*] students make when learning this standard: [*Standard*]?
- Can you tell me the most common misconceptions that [*grade-level*] students have about this standard: [*Standard*]?

Struggles With the Task, Not the Standard

Experienced teachers also know that sometimes struggling students aren't having trouble with the standard itself. Instead, they are struggling with the task we have assigned as a demonstration of mastery. For example, if fourth graders are asked to identify a story's theme by reading a passage and writing a paragraph that explains the theme with supporting details, some students may struggle because they haven't yet developed the writing skills to fully express their thinking, not because they can't identify the theme.

When this happens, highly effective teams offer alternative ways for students to demonstrate mastery. In this case, teachers might ask students who find writing challenging to instead record their thinking using a digital platform like Seesaw (https://seesaw.com) or Padlet (https://padlet.com), allowing them to share their understanding in a way that better reflects what they know.

Not sure how to develop an alternative demonstration of mastery that maintains the rigor of the original standard? Try partnering with an AI chatbot again. Prompts like the following can help you find new ways to determine what students know.

- What would be a reasonable way to ask students to demonstrate mastery of this standard: [*Standard*]?
- Can you give me five different ways that students who [*learning needs you are trying to address*] can show me mastery of this standard: [*Standard*]? Your suggestions should maintain the rigor of the original standard.

Challenges Accessing Learning Through Text

Many students have the cognitive and metacognitive skills needed to learn new concepts but struggle when those concepts are presented through text. Since many classrooms, especially in subjects like English language arts, science, and social studies, still rely heavily on text-based learning, these students will need intentional support to access and engage with new ideas.

Highly effective teams create opportunities for students to engage with text content before introducing it in class, and they explore alternative ways to present key ideas. This might involve using intervention periods to preteach essential vocabulary for an upcoming unit or allowing students to preview complex texts in advance, ensuring they have the foundational knowledge needed to access new learning more confidently during initial instruction. This could also include incorporating podcasts or video essays that explore class concepts, or leveraging digital tools like NotebookLM (https://notebooklm.google.com) to generate AI-powered audio versions of text-based content, making the material more accessible to students who struggle to access ideas through text. Finally, this could include using AI tools like Diffit (https://app.diffit.me) to create differentiated reading passages for students who aren't yet reading on grade level.

Work Habits That Interfere With Learning

Sometimes, a student's difficulty mastering grade-level essentials isn't due to a gap in understanding; it's a result of their work behaviors. Some students struggle because they haven't practiced enough. Others disengage because they don't see the value in what they are learning. Many lack effective note-taking or organizational skills, making it difficult to retain and apply new information over time.

A common mistake teams make is responding to these challenges with academic interventions instead of addressing the root issue: the student's work habits. When students receive academic reteaching they don't actually need, they see intervention as a waste of time. Meanwhile, the real barrier to their success remains unaddressed, leading to continued struggles.

Highly effective teams recognize that not every student who needs additional support requires an academic intervention. Instead, they design targeted interventions that help students develop productive work behaviors—such as structured practice routines, strategies for organizing their thinking, and explicit instruction in how to engage with learning tasks—so that students have the skills they need to succeed independently.

You're probably wondering how to teach work behaviors to students. That's fair. Many teachers haven't received specific training in designing interventions for work habits. But by now, you can probably guess our recommendation: Leverage an AI chatbot as a thought partner. Thoughtfully crafted prompts can help you explore research-backed strategies for teaching work behaviors. Try asking the following prompts.

- According to experts in education, what are the most effective ways to teach [*work behavior*] to [*grade-level*] students? Please cite supporting sources.
- Can you create six detailed scenarios showing how teachers can teach [*work behavior*] to [*grade-level*] students? Each scenario should describe a specific strategy in action from a third-person perspective.

By using AI to jump-start your professional learning, you can quickly gather practical insights on helping students build the work behaviors they need to succeed.

Lack of Confidence as a Learner

Even the best instruction and intervention plans won't work if students don't see themselves as capable learners. When students lack confidence in their ability to succeed, they disengage from learning experiences, often before they've even given themselves a chance to grow.

This is a more common issue than many schools realize. We often assume that academic struggles are caused by gaps in understanding when, in reality, some students could master the concepts we are teaching if they were fully invested in learning. But for students who have faced repeated failure, doubt can take over. They stop trying—not because they aren't capable, but because they don't believe success is possible.

For these students, interventions must focus on building their confidence as learners. Highly effective teams prioritize strategies that strengthen self-efficacy, such as helping students set and achieve short-term goals, tracking their progress toward mastery, and providing frequent, meaningful feedback that highlights growth. When students see tangible proof of their own ability, learning feels possible, and when learning feels possible, they are far more likely to persist, even when the work is challenging.

Students struggle to master grade-level essentials for all kinds of reasons, but highly effective teams don't wait for those struggles to surface before taking action. They anticipate the most common challenges—whether rooted in misconceptions, task design, access to text, work habits, or self-confidence—and develop targeted interventions that tackle the real barriers holding students back. With the right mindset and the right tools, teams can create learning experiences that keep every student engaged, build persistence, and lead to academic success.

Tools and Resources for Highly Effective Teams

The following tools and resources will help you accomplish the work for this essential action.

- **"Tool: List of Common Misconceptions for an Essential Outcome" (page 199):** Maintaining a record of common misconceptions and mistakes helps teams focus interventions on the exact gaps preventing student mastery. This tool provides a simple framework for documenting misconceptions. By using it consistently, teams can move beyond reteaching entire lessons and deliver more targeted support.

- **"Tool: Targeting Tier 2 Interventions for an Individual Student" (page 200):** When a student continues to struggle with an essential standard despite repeated interventions, it's a sign that the support provided may not be addressing the real reason behind their difficulties. This tool uses a series of reflection questions to help teams diagnose the actual cause of a student's struggles—whether it's a lack of prerequisite skills, ineffective instructional approaches, or disengagement—and then develop an intervention plan designed to address those struggles.

- **"Tool: Strategies for Modifying Assignments" (page 202):** Differentiation often involves modifying assignments to better meet student needs, but what does that look like in practice? This tool and its corresponding **"Sample: Strategies for Modifying Assignments" (page 203)** outline five key areas where teachers can adjust their original tasks—altering student response methods, adapting instructional materials, providing additional supports, changing the learning environment, and adjusting scheduling. By considering these types of modifications, educators can create alternative demonstrations of mastery that align with standards while accommodating the unique learning needs of struggling students.

- **"Tool: Instructional Strategies to Consider" (page 204):** Teachers looking for evidence-based strategies to use during flexible time for interventions can turn to *The New Classroom Instruction That Works: The Best Research-Based Strategies for Increasing Student Achievement* (Goodwin & Rouleau, 2022), which shares the science behind dozens of teaching practices that are proven to increase student achievement. This tool highlights six of the highest-leverage strategies from the text and, where applicable, connects them to earlier versions from the *Classroom Instruction That Works* series. These strategies can be used to support students who need additional time and support to master grade-level essentials. Consider also integrating these practices into your initial instruction. When teachers use high-impact strategies in their daily lessons, they reduce the number of students who need intervention in the first place.

- **"Tool: Tier 2 AI Prompts for Classroom Teachers" (page 209):** Designing effective interventions can be challenging, especially when students need customized support. AI tools like ChatGPT (https://chatgpt.com), Claude (https://claude.ai), and Gemini (https://gemini.google.com) can help by generating alternative demonstrations of mastery, identifying common mistakes, and offering creative reteaching strategies. This tool provides practical AI prompts to help teams design targeted interventions that better meet student needs.

Tool: List of Common Misconceptions for an Essential Outcome

Instructions: Complete one common mistake or misconception template for each of the essential outcomes that you will cover in your upcoming unit of study. In the first column, describe up to three misconceptions that prevent students from mastering this essential learning outcome, or mistakes that you see students making frequently when working with this essential learning outcome. In the second column, provide an example of what each misconception or mistake looks like to help your team spot it easily in work samples. Copy your sample from a student work product or create one together with your learning team. In the last column, record your planned strategy, answering the following questions.

- *What steps will you take when you see this misconception or mistake in student work samples?*

- *Do you have follow-up assignments or question sets for addressing this misconception or mistake? Different instructional language worth trying? Reminders worth sharing with students?*

Essential Learning Outcome We Are Monitoring:		
Common Misconception or Mistake	**Example of This Misconception or Mistake**	**Planned Strategy**

Source: Ferriter, W. M. (2020). The big book of tools for collaborative teams in a PLC at Work. *Solution Tree Press.*

Tool: Targeting Tier 2 Interventions for an Individual Student

Instructions: Use the following template to develop a targeted intervention plan for a student who is not responding to your supplemental interventions.

Name of Student:
Essential Standard or Standards Student Is Struggling to Master:

Questions for Reflection	Your Responses
Why do you think this student is struggling to master this essential standard?	**This student:** ☐ Needs more time to master the standard ☐ Isn't motivated to work on the standard ☐ Doesn't understand how the standard was taught ☐ Doesn't have the foundational prerequisite skills from prior years related to mastery of the standard ☐ Doesn't have the immediate prerequisite skills to master the standard ☐ Other:
What evidence supports your conclusions about why this student struggles to master this essential standard? • What specific evidence from assessments (pretests, universal screeners, and common formative assessments) can you use to support your conclusions? • What specific evidence from classroom observations can you use to support your conclusions? • What specific evidence from previous performances can you use to support your conclusions?	

The Handbook for Highly Effective Teams in a PLC at Work® © 2025 Solution Tree Press • SolutionTree.com
Visit **go.SolutionTree.com/PLCbooks** to download this free reproducible.

PART FOUR
Providing Extra Time and Support

What next steps will you take to support this student? • Will you reteach this concept to this student using a different instructional practice? • Will you assign this student to a specific intervention group and provide additional support during a schoolwide intervention period? • Will you reteach prerequisite skills to this student and then reassess, looking for mastery on the grade-level essential you are teaching? • Will you modify how this student can demonstrate mastery, considering their struggles with foundational skills in reading, written expression, basic numeracy, or the primary language of instruction?	
Which other students are struggling to master this essential standard for the same reasons? • Would they benefit from the same interventions?	
When will you take action? • Does this intervention have to occur before you move forward in your instructional sequence? • Do you need to coordinate with your collaborative team before you can deliver an intervention to this student? • Do you need to do additional research before you can provide effective interventions to this student?	

Source: Ferriter, W. M., Mattos, M., & Meyer, R. J. (2025). The big book of tools for RTI at Work. Solution Tree Press.

PART FOUR
Providing Extra Time and Support

Tool: Strategies for Modifying Assignments

Most teachers know that differentiation can include modifying assignments. But what does "modifying assignments" mean? Review the table and determine the best ways to create alternative demonstrations of mastery for your students.

When reviewing standards to develop alternative demonstrations of mastery, teachers can consider five types of changes to their original tasks.	Modifying Student Responses: How can we change the ways students respond to the task we are asking them to complete? Can they give oral answers instead of creating written products? Can they create graphic organizers instead of paragraphs? Can they communicate in their home language, or must they respond in English?	Modifying Instructional Materials: What changes can we make to the instructional materials that students use to demonstrate mastery? Can we simplify assignments by removing questions? Can we lower the reading level of passages? Can we shorten passages? Can we change the passage's format (bulleted lists, nonfiction, fiction, poems, and so on)?
Modifying Supporting Materials: Can we provide students with supporting materials (text-to-speech tools, audiobooks, or copies of teacher notes) while demonstrating mastery?	Modifying the Setting: How can we change the settings (working independently, working with the whole class, working in small groups, or working one-to-one with the teacher) that students use when demonstrating mastery?	Modifying the Scheduling: Does the standard require a demonstration of mastery to occur in a certain time period, or can students complete parts of the tasks one at a time?

Questions to Consider	Your Response
What is the standard that you are trying to assess? What does it explicitly require students to do to demonstrate mastery?	
What task do you plan to use with most students?	
What challenges will struggling students have with your current demonstration of mastery?	
Refer to the other table. What changes can you make to the demonstration of mastery? *Remember: You must refer to the standard to determine what types of modifications you can make to your demonstration of mastery.*	

Source: Adapted from Center for Parent Information and Resources. (2020, March). Supports, modifications, and accommodations for students. Accessed at www.parentcenterhub.org/accommodations on February 3, 2025.

PART FOUR Providing Extra Time and Support

Sample: Strategies for Modifying Assignments

Most teachers know that differentiation can include modifying assignments. But what does "modifying assignments" mean? Review the table and determine the best ways to create alternative demonstrations of mastery for your students.

When reviewing standards to develop alternative demonstrations of mastery, teachers can consider five types of changes to their original tasks.	Modifying Student Responses: How can we change the ways students respond to the task we are asking them to complete? Can they give oral answers instead of creating written products? Can they create graphic organizers instead of paragraphs? Can they communicate in their home language, or must they respond in English?	Modifying Instructional Materials: What changes can we make to the instructional materials that students use to demonstrate mastery? Can we simplify assignments by removing questions? Can we lower the reading level of passages? Can we shorten passages? Can we change the passage's format (bulleted lists, nonfiction, fiction, poems, and so on)?
Modifying Supporting Materials: Can we provide students with supporting materials (text-to-speech tools, audiobooks, or copies of teacher notes) while demonstrating mastery?	Modifying the Setting: How can we change the settings (working independently, working with the whole class, working in small groups, or working one-to-one with the teacher) that students use when demonstrating mastery?	Modifying the Scheduling: Does the standard require a demonstration of mastery to occur in a certain time period, or can students complete parts of the tasks one at a time?

Questions to Consider	Your Response
What is the standard that you are trying to assess? What does it explicitly require students to do to demonstrate mastery?	4.RC.9.RL: "Determine the theme of a story." (p. 25) The only thing explicitly stated in this standard is that students must determine the theme of a story.
What task do you plan to use with most students?	Students will be given a piece of grade-level text to read independently. Students will write a short paragraph identifying the story theme and providing a piece of evidence to support their answer.
What challenges will struggling students have with your current demonstration of mastery?	Some students will struggle with reading grade-level text independently. Some students will struggle with writing a short paragraph as a demonstration of mastery.
Refer to the other table. What changes can you make to the demonstration of mastery? *Remember: You must refer to the standard to determine what types of modifications you can make to your demonstration of mastery.*	We can allow students to use text-to-speech when reading the story. We can allow students to read a shorter passage. We can allow students to read a passage in their home language.

Source for standard: Arkansas Department of Education. (2023a). Arkansas English language arts standards: Grades K–12. Accessed at https://dese.ade.arkansas.gov/Files/AR_2023_K-12_ELA_Standards_LS_7.2023_LS.docx on February 3, 2025.

Source: Adapted from Center for Parent Information and Resources. (2020, March). Supports, modifications, and accommodations for students. Accessed at www.parentcenterhub.org/accommodations on February 3, 2025.

PART FOUR Providing Extra Time and Support

PART FOUR
Providing Extra Time and Support
④

Tool: Instructional Strategies to Consider

This document outlines six of the most impactful strategies from *The New Classroom Instruction That Works: The Best Research-Based Strategies for Increasing Student Achievement* (Goodwin & Rouleau, 2022) and, where applicable, connects them to strategies from earlier editions of the series (Marzano, Pickering, & Pollock, 2001). As a team, review these strategies and identify those that could be seamlessly integrated into your initial instruction or used to support students who need intervention.

Strategy to Consider	Reason the Strategy Matters	Implementation Considerations	Your Reflections *How are you already using this strategy in your work? How hard would it be to implement this strategy into your work? How motivated are you to try this strategy?*
Cognitive Interest Cues: "Cognitive interest cues motivate learning by framing units and lessons in ways that make learning stimulating and relevant to students." (Goodwin & Rouleau, 2022, p. 14) **Improvement Index:** Across 14 studies, cognitive interest cues had improvement indexes ranging from 8 to 49 percentile points. **Alignment With Earlier Editions:** None	• Our brains absorb 11 million bits of information per second but can only process 120 bits of information per second. • Our brains have evolved to ignore any information that they don't deem important. • Building student interest, then, is an essential part of effective instruction. • It is hard to learn something if you aren't paying attention to it. • Building interest and motivation also leads to additional effort that translates to learning.	• Simply being engaging isn't enough. Efforts to build interest and motivation must be carefully designed to draw attention to the content we want students to learn. • Thought-provoking questions or meaningful challenges related to the topic are effective tools for building interest. • Pointing out gaps in student knowledge about the topic is another effective strategy. • Making personal connections between students and the topic is another way to build interest and motivation.	

Student Goal Setting and Monitoring:

"When you help students set and achieve personal goals for learning, you are helping them train their brains to expect dopamine rewards from effortful thinking and, thus, remain committed to learning." (Goodwin & Rouleau, 2022, p. 29)

Improvement Index:
Across 16 studies, student goal setting and monitoring had improvement indexes ranging from 14 to 47 percentile points.

Alignment With Earlier Editions:
Reinforce effort and provide recognition

- The human brain tends to resist engaging in demanding cognitive processes needed for effective learning.
- One way to counter this tendency is to show students how to set and attain goals.
- Students who learn to set and attain goals also learn that effort is the key to success.
- Students who work harder are more likely to learn the outcomes we are teaching.

- To increase motivation in learners, the goals that students set, monitor, and attain don't have to be overambitious.
- Consider starting goal-setting efforts by asking students to set goals that are concrete, easy to monitor, and attainable.
- To be effective, pair setting goals with tracking progress toward mastery and self-evaluation.
- The goal is to convince students that they can move their learning forward.

Strategy Instruction and Modeling:

"Strategy instruction and modeling means demonstrating for students how to perform specific skills or tasks, such as solving word problems, writing extended essays, reading for comprehension, and reflecting on their learning." (Goodwin & Rouleau, 2022, p. 50)

Improvement Index:
Across 23 studies, strategy instruction and modeling had improvement indexes ranging from 8 to 47 percentile points.

Alignment With Earlier Editions:
Setting objectives and providing feedback

- Students learn best when we offer clear guidance and demonstrate new skills step by step.
- That is because as we learn new skills, our brains are turning the steps in mastering those skills into automated scripts that we will use later to repeat the same tasks.
- Once our brains have learned to apply those automated scripts for new skills, mental energy is freed to engage in higher-order thinking.
- We can help students develop those automated scripts by providing direct instruction in, and repeated practice with, the expectations that we have for completing any task.

- Consider providing your students with step-by-step demonstrations of what you expect them to do.
- Students need step-by-step demonstrations of thinking strategies, too.
- Behaviors like summarizing, questioning, and self-monitoring are skills students can learn, but they are not intuitive. They must be taught through direct instruction.
- The first step to providing direct instruction is to fully understand your standards. Unpacking a standard and then developing a proficiency scale can help you identify the strategies that you need to teach students.

PART FOUR
Providing Extra Time and Support

The Handbook for Highly Effective Teams in a PLC at Work® © 2025 Solution Tree Press • SolutionTree.com
Visit go.SolutionTree.com/PLCbooks to download this free reproducible.

Strategy to Consider	Reason the Strategy Matters	Implementation Considerations	Your Reflections
Visualizations and Concrete Examples: "Visual representations and examples—diagrams, graphic organizers, manipulatives, worked examples, videos, and simulations—support visual and verbal (dual-coding) comprehension of new ideas." (Goodwin & Rouleau, 2022, p. 56) **Improvement Index:** Across 23 studies, visualizations and concrete examples had improvement indexes ranging from 11 to 45 percentile points. **Alignment With Earlier Editions:** Encourage nonlinguistic representations	• Our short-term memory is restricted, allowing us to juggle a finite amount of information simultaneously. • Studies indicate that we can manage merely four bits of information in our short-term memory at any given moment. • Interestingly, our minds have the capability to handle both verbal and visual data simultaneously, essentially doubling our information-processing capacity. • This phenomenon is referred to as *dual coding*.	• Visualizations are most helpful when students are focusing on new learning. • Provide students with concrete examples and exemplars of the work products you are asking them to create so they can monitor their mastery while generating their own work products. • Visualizations and concrete examples enhance learning only when students can refer to them while working. Providing examples and exemplars after students complete their work is ineffective. • Consider using metaphors to help students understand abstract concepts. Relating abstract concepts to a more familiar, concrete example is an anchoring routine for students learning new information.	

High-Level Questions and Student Explanations:

"High-level questions and student explanations support consolidation of learning through cognitive and metacognitive processing of new knowledge and skills." (Goodwin & Rouleau, 2022, p. 64)

Improvement Index:

Across 17 studies, high-level questions and student explanations had improvement indexes ranging from 14 to 47 percentile points.

Alignment With Earlier Editions:

Use questions, cues, and advance organizers

- When the brain learns something new, it converts sensory inputs into memories in a process called *encoding*.
- New learning starts as memory traces that are scattered in our brains.
- Arranging memory traces in our brains happens in a process called *consolidation*.
- Until memory traces are consolidated, it is impossible for a learner to access them easily or to use them fluently.
- The best way to consolidate (arrange) memory traces is to actively think about them while learning.
- We can encourage students to actively think about new learning by asking high-level questions or asking students to explain what they are learning.

- Asking students to connect new learning to prior knowledge is an effective strategy for encouraging consolidation.
- Asking students to cluster or categorize new learning is another effective strategy for encouraging consolidation.
- Giving students chances to pause and process is a third strategy for encouraging consolidation.
- Questioning and student explanations are not primarily about assessing students. Instead, they're about encouraging students to reflect on their learning, link it to their previous knowledge, and organize it into broader concepts.
- Low-level questions do little to help students move new learning into their long-term memory (consolidate).

PART FOUR
Providing Extra Time and Support

Strategy to Consider	Reason the Strategy Matters	Implementation Considerations	Your Reflections
Peer-Assisted Consolidation of Learning: "Peer-assisted consolidation of learning engages groups or pairs of students in processing, discussing, and practicing new learning." (Goodwin & Rouleau, 2022, p. 77) **Improvement Index:** Across 9 studies, peer-assisted consolidation of learning had improvement indexes ranging from 8 to 42 percentile points. **Alignment With Earlier Editions:** Cooperative learning	• Humans are drawn to social connection, always seeking chances to share our stories, experiences, and challenges with one another. • These interactions push us to think about what we know, what we don't know, and how our understandings compare to those of others. • More importantly, these interactions force us to slow down and think about what we have learned—an essential step in consolidating new memory traces into long-term understanding. • Peer-assisted consolidation of learning is not the same thing as cooperative learning. • Cooperative learning has long been used to introduce students to new ideas as part of initial instruction. • There is no research to support this practice. Cooperative learning as an introduction to new ideas does not lead to new learning. • Instead, cooperative learning that *follows* direct instruction of new ideas leads to new learning because it allows students to reflect on and test what they know. • That reflection and testing leads to consolidation of learning.	• Students need structure when engaging in processing, discussing, and practicing new learning. • One way to provide this structure is to generate specific questions for groups to consider. • Teachers should integrate individual accountability with positive interdependence in their peer-assisted consolidation of learning experiences. • For example, groups of three can generate answers to comprehension check questions over a period of several lessons (positive interdependence). • After those lessons, students can engage in a peer-evaluation process, taking time to reflect on how each member contributed to the group's success (individual accountability). • Because students' attention spans tend to time out after five to ten minutes of concentrated effort, the most effective peer-assisted consolidation of learning occurs when it's integrated throughout a lesson. • Teachers can amplify the impact of this teaching strategy by pairing it with high-level questions and student explanations.	

Source: Adapted from Goodwin, B., & Rouleau, K. (2022). The new classroom instruction that works: The best research-based strategies for increasing student achievement. ASCD; Marzano, R. J., Pickering, D. J., & Pollock, J. E. (2001). Classroom instruction that works: The best research-based strategies for increasing student achievement. ASCD.

Tool: Tier 2 AI Prompts for Classroom Teachers

Instructions: Collaborative teacher teams should ensure that all students master grade-level academic essentials. That means you must design and lead supplemental interventions whenever students are struggling. Use the following prompts with an AI chatbot like ChatGPT (https://chat.openai.com) or Gemini (https://gemini.google .com) to help you with this work.

AI chatbots can help you identify common mistakes students might be making.	AI chatbots can generate alternative demonstrations of mastery.
• I am a *[grade level and subject area]* teacher. I have students struggling to *[grade-level concept or skill]*. Can you tell me the most common mistakes they will make? **Sample:** *I am a middle school pottery teacher. I have students struggling to glaze pottery. Can you tell me the most common mistakes they will make?*	• Can you give me ten different ways *[grade level and subject area]* students can demonstrate mastery of *[grade-level concept or skill]* without making a written product or summary? **Sample:** *Can you give me ten different ways third-grade students can demonstrate mastery of rounding three-digit numbers without making a written product or summary?*
AI chatbots can offer unique strategies for reteaching a concept.	**AI chatbots can generate, level, and translate reading passages.**
• I am a *[grade level and subject area]* teacher. I need to teach my students *[grade-level concept or skill]*. Can you give me five original ideas for teaching this concept to my students? **Sample:** *I am a third-grade teacher. I need to teach my students to multiply. Can you give me five original ideas for teaching this concept to my students?*	• Can you write a high-interest, five-paragraph reading passage for *[grade level and subject area]* students on *[grade-level concept or skill]*? • Can you rewrite that passage on the *[grade level]* reading level? • Can you translate this passage into *[language]*? • Can you summarize the most important points of this passage in five bullets written at the *[grade level]* reading level?
AI chatbots can provide new ways to explain ideas to struggling students.	**AI chatbots can create mnemonic devices.**
• I am a *[grade level and subject area]* student. Can you explain *[grade-level concept or skill]* to me like a beginner? **Sample:** *I am a third-grade student learning science. Can you explain implosion to me like I am a beginner?* **Note:** Pretending to be a student in this prompt will ensure that ChatGPT returns an explanation in language your students are likely to understand.	• Can you create a mnemonic device that *[grade level and subject area]* students can use to remember *[grade-level concept or skill]*? **Sample:** *Can you create a mnemonic device that civics students can use to remember the steps that a bill must take to become a law?*

PART FOUR
Providing Extra Time and Support

page 1 of 2

AI chatbots work for behaviors too.	**AI chatbots can write songs.**
• Can you give me three activities for teaching *[behavioral expectation]* like *[examples of behavioral expectation]* to *[grade level]* students?	• Can you create a song that *[grade level and subject area]* students can use to remember *[grade-level concept or skill]*?
Sample: *Can you give me three activities for teaching proper work behaviors like organization, coming to class prepared, and participating in class to middle school students?*	**Sample:** *Can you create a song that high school students can use to remember what happened at the Potsdam Conference?*
AI chatbots can create review games for students to play.	**AI chatbots can create body movements.**
• Can you create a game that *[grade level and subject area]* students can play to review *[grade-level concept or skill]*?	• Can you create a body movement that *[grade level and subject area]* students can use to remember *[grade-level concept or skill]*?
Sample: *Can you create a game that kindergarten students can play to review their letter sounds?*	**Sample:** *Can you create a body movement that seventh-grade students can use to remember the rules of the caste system?*

Source: Ferriter, W. M., Mattos, M., & Meyer, R. J. (2025). The big book of tools for RTI at Work. *Solution Tree Press.*

We Deliver Targeted Extensions to Students Working Beyond Grade-Level Expectations

*If a school is going to embed flexible time into its master schedule
so it can provide targeted students with additional time and support in learning
essential grade-level standards, then there is no reason why it could not also use
this time to extend students who have already learned these outcomes.*

**—RICHARD DUFOUR, REBECCA DUFOUR, ROBERT EAKER, THOMAS W. MANY,
MIKE MATTOS, AND ANTHONY MUHAMMAD**

As we work collaboratively to improve our schools, our focus is often on helping students meet or exceed grade-level essentials. But let's not forget about another group of learners who deserve our attention—those students who are consistently working beyond grade-level expectations. These learners present both a challenge and an opportunity for collaborative teams dedicated to creating an environment where every student, regardless of their starting point, learns at high levels. The challenge is that our communities are under increased pressure to "produce results," which often means "increasing the number of students who are passing end-of-grade standardized tests." This pressure makes it difficult for teams to see value in committing already limited planning, instruction, and intervention minutes to students who we know are going to pass those same high-stakes tests. But the opportunity is equally powerful: When we follow through on our commitment to ensuring that all students learn at the highest levels—including those who are working beyond grade-level expectations—we more fully deliver on our promise of promoting equity in our instruction.

That's an interesting argument, isn't it? We don't usually think about our highest-performing students in discussions about equity in education—but we should. Equity in education is not just about lifting those at the bottom; it is also about pushing the ceiling higher for those who can reach it. As differentiation expert Carol Ann Tomlinson (2017) argues, "It is every bit as damaging in the long term to 'under challenge' advanced learners as it is to overlook the frustrations and mounting academic gaps in struggling ones" (p. 35).

And are you ready for an even more interesting argument from Tomlinson? Highly effective teams should *begin* their planning by developing lessons for students working beyond grade-level expectations (Tomlinson, 2015). She calls this *teaching up*, and it leads to more cognitively rigorous instruction for all students (Tomlinson, 2015). While planning first for extensions may initially seem counterintuitive to teams that feel a very real sense of urgency for students working below grade-level expectations, it makes sense. Here's why: The types of tasks we design for high-achieving students—which often require students to think creatively or analytically, to pursue their curiosity, or to examine how content impacts the world beyond the schoolhouse walls—are the same kinds of tasks we should design for *all students*. Teams that plan extension tasks first are more likely to scaffold "instruction to enable less advanced students to access those rich learning experiences" (Tomlinson, 2015), while teams that leave extension planning until the end may never develop those experiences at all.

Highly effective teams think of extension as an opportunity to broaden their definition of success. By dedicating time to challenging their highest achievers, they send a clear message: Learning isn't just about reaching minimum expectations. It's about growth for everyone. More importantly, they create a learning space where *every student*, not just those who need support to catch up, is encouraged to reach further.

Why Highly Effective Teams Do This

Extending learning for students working beyond grade-level expectations isn't just another task on the to-do list for highly effective teams—it's a moral responsibility. It requires a commitment to recognizing the potential in each student, ensuring that our classrooms are spaces where *everyone is challenged*. Sadly, it is a moral imperative that we too frequently fall short of meeting in schools—and the consequences for high-achieving students are many.

Perhaps the greatest consequence of failing to systematically provide extensions for students working beyond grade-level expectations is the underachievement of an entire subgroup of students. Studies show that initially high-achieving students display a slower growth rate during the school year but maintain a consistent pace of growth over the summer, as opposed to average students, who show steep growth during the school year but little to no growth during the summer (Hurst, 2022; Rambo-Hernandez & McCoach, 2015). This pattern suggests that the learning of high-achieving students is less influenced by the school environment than the learning of their average-achieving peers. The pattern is so pronounced that Karen E. Rambo-Hernandez and D. Betsy McCoach (2015), researchers who conducted a three-year longitudinal study of the academic performance of 118,000 third-grade students in 2,000 schools, argue that "having 12 months of vacation would be as effective as attending school" for high-achieving students (p. 127).

Just as important are the direct effects that failing to extend learning has on individual students. Some students become "mentally lazy, even though they do well in school"

(Tomlinson, 2017, p. 35). After all, school is where students are most often asked to think deeply, and yet high achievers are rarely challenged. Others fail to develop essential life skills like determination, perseverance, and grit because they move through school without ever being challenged. Then, when faced with more rigorous learning experiences later in life, they begin to doubt their abilities (Tomlinson, 2017). Finally, high-achieving students can "become hooked on the trappings of success," intentionally avoiding rigorous work because they want to earn the highest marks possible (Tomlinson, 2017, p. 35). When chasing points and praise from families and teachers becomes more important to learners than tackling new academic challenges, we have failed to create a space that ensures the highest levels of learning for all.

And it is important to recognize that *high achieving* isn't a permanent label given to some students and kept from others. Stated more simply, students formally identified as gifted are not the only ones who will need extensions in your classroom. Instead, *all students* are likely to work beyond grade-level expectations at different points during the school year. As a result, highly effective teams don't use labels to identify students who need access to additional challenges. Instead, they look for any student who has demonstrated proficiency with the grade-level essentials they are working with right now. This approach broadens the focus of extensions, ensuring that all learners, not just a select few, are challenged.

The good news for educators is that providing meaningful extensions for high-achieving students isn't a complicated task. It is, however, a task that requires creativity and a commitment to individual potential. Figure 4.3.1 offers a comparison of language between ineffective groups and highly effective teams around this topic.

The Language of Ineffective Groups	The Language of Highly Effective Teams
"Wow, our students are low this year. Really low."	"I wonder how we can gather more targeted data so we know exactly what skills our students have already mastered."
"We need to do a better job planning harder work for our academically gifted students. They deserve it."	"We need to do a better job planning rigorous work for all our students. They deserve it."
"I know that my top performers are bored in my room sometimes, but at least they get to go to the academically gifted teacher for an hour every week. She challenges them."	"What if we tried creating an extension group during our school's daily intervention period? Then, we could provide the students who are ready with regular chances to be challenged in addition to the work they are doing with our academically gifted teacher."
"We are too busy trying to get our bubble kids up to passing to worry about our high achievers. They are going to be fine, anyway."	"If we develop rigorous lessons for our high achievers first and then scaffold our instruction to make those lessons approachable for all learners, won't that benefit more of our students?"

FIGURE 4.3.1: Language comparison.

Notice that the priority for ineffective groups is getting students to proficiency. That is a dangerous trap that schools often fall into in a world where success in education is defined by the percentage of students who pass standardized tests. Highly effective teams, on the other hand, recognize that proficiency is *a minimum standard of mastery* and that our goal is to always move students forward from where they currently are. Highly effective teams also recognize that planning for advanced students can help increase the overall rigor in their day-to-day instruction. Finally, highly effective teams understand that extension isn't just something that happens in pull-out classes designed and delivered by specialists in gifted and talented education. Instead, highly effective teams understand that providing additional time and support for learning includes designing opportunities for students to work beyond grade-level expectations.

How Highly Effective Teams Do This

Schools that have embraced both the PLC and RTI processes as outlined in *Learning by Doing, Fourth Edition* (DuFour et al., 2024), and *Taking Action, Second Edition* (Mattos et al., 2025), often differentiate student learning struggles as follows.

- Students who know how to complete a task, but other behaviors—attendance, work completion, demonstration of appropriate behaviors in the classroom, persistence in the face of challenge—prevent them from showing us what they know
- Students who lack the necessary knowledge to perform the tasks assigned to them and require specifically designed instruction to understand the essentials being introduced

Building on those ideas, we argue that most collaborative teams struggle with providing extensions not because they don't believe in the importance of challenging high achievers, but because they don't have the training to create extensions that are both meaningful and manageable.

The first knowledge gap that many teams struggle with is understanding the types of activities that can count as extensions. While there are many ways to design extensions, *Learning by Doing* (DuFour et al., 2024) specifically endorses three strategies: (1) introducing students to more of the nonessential grade-level curriculum, (2) asking students to demonstrate mastery beyond grade-level expectations, and (3) delivering instruction to students in above-grade-level curriculum.

Introduce More of the Nonessential Grade-Level Curriculum

The first critical question of learning that teams answer when learning together in a PLC is, "What knowledge, skills, and dispositions should every student acquire as a result of this unit, this course, or this grade level?" (DuFour et al., 2024, p. 44). Whether teams realize it or not, these conversations can be starting points for extension planning. Here's how: Small handfuls of standards that teams identify as "important but not essential" for learning at grade level or higher—sometimes called *nice-to-knows* in PLCs—can be set aside and used to extend learning (DuFour et al., 2024, p. 208). This makes extension doable because team members are likely to already have the resources and professional expertise necessary to teach these standards.

Ask Students to Demonstrate Mastery Beyond Grade-Level Expectations

As we detailed in action 2.1 (page 67), studying essential standards together—an important planning step for collaborative teams—involves "developing a deep, rich understanding of what the standard means, along with a clear understanding of what the standard, if met, would look like in student work" (Eaker, 2020, pp. 63–64). The second part of that process—developing a clear understanding of what mastery would look like in student work—can also provide teams with opportunities to develop extensions. If we can define what mastery looks like, we can also design demonstrations of mastery that go beyond grade-level expectations.

Here's an example: In mathematics, third-grade students are generally expected to use strategies to fluently multiply and divide within 100. A team may decide that to master this grade-level essential, students must be able to accurately solve ten problems and explain the reasoning used to come up with each answer. The same team might also develop an additional set of five problems that have been solved incorrectly and ask high-achieving students to first identify and then explain the errors that led to the incorrect solutions. For this team, identifying errors isn't a grade-level expectation. In fact, most students will never engage in that work. However, it can serve as an extension task for students working beyond grade-level expectations.

Deliver Instruction in Above-Grade-Level Curriculum

Highly effective teams in PLCs recognize the importance of preparing students to succeed in the next grade level or course. As a result, they spend some of their collaborative time *vertically aligning* their curriculum—identifying how learning progresses and concepts develop from one year to the next. Teams can use their understanding of these learning progressions in their curriculum to create extension tasks that give high-achieving students the chance to explore concepts and skills that go beyond grade-level expectations.

Apply Learning to Real-World Situations

Education author Michael Roberts (2019) introduces a fourth extension strategy worth considering: Students can "apply their learning on [an] extension standard to a real-life situation not addressed in class" (p. 14). Students of all ages have an innate need to understand why the content and skills they are learning matter (Ferlazzo, 2023). Collaborative teams can leverage this need when developing extensions by giving high-achieving students opportunities to study real-life examples of essential outcomes or to apply their knowledge to solve real-world problems.

What can this look like in action? Imagine that you are a first-grade teacher responsible for introducing students to community helpers as part of your social studies curriculum. The next time that the local news spotlights an event where community helpers made a difference—after a natural disaster or local emergency or as part of a service project designed to support community residents, for example—ask students working beyond grade-level expectations to study the event, identify the helpers involved, and evaluate the importance of their contributions to the community. Consider asking them to create a bulletin board that spotlights the top ten helpers in their community, and to update the board based on the events they are exploring and their evaluations of the importance of the contributions helpers made in each event.

Or imagine that you are a high school teacher responsible for introducing students to the concept of eminent domain in the Takings Clause of the Fifth Amendment in the U.S. Constitution. To extend learning, you could ask high-achieving students to research three different examples of when eminent domain was used in your local community to take private property for a public use, and then to determine whether the government's interest was justified and whether the private citizen was fairly compensated for the seized property. Finally, students could develop a set of criteria for determining when a government's right to support the public good is more important than an individual's right to private property, and you could encourage them to continue using their criteria to evaluate future instances of eminent domain that appear in news stories.

Another skill gap that many collaborative teams struggle with is addressing the logistic challenges of managing instruction in academically diverse classrooms. After all, high-achieving students often demonstrate mastery of grade-level expectations quickly and then have little left to do. Navigating this "ragged time" can be one of the most demanding aspects of providing extensions to students (Tomlinson, 2017, p. 92). How do we ensure that class time is productive for every student when some need more time and support than others? If teachers are busy reteaching concepts or providing extra practice to students who haven't yet demonstrated proficiency with essentials, how can they also ensure that students working beyond grade-level expectations are challenged?

The answer is to carefully design anchor activities that high-achieving students can automatically turn to when they are ready to move beyond mastery (Tomlinson, 2017). Good anchor activities meet three criteria. First, they are tied to the essential outcome, concept, or topic you are studying in class. All too often, we waste the instructional minutes of high-achieving students by asking them to read a book, play a review game on the web, or complete assignments for other classes when they are finished with their grade-level work. While these tasks may have some academic value, the goal of extension should be to move students forward in exploring your curriculum. That is only possible when the anchor activities we develop are tied directly to our current units of study.

Second, good anchor activities are tasks students can complete independently. If students struggle to understand the anchor activities you develop, they will either avoid the tasks completely or interrupt you frequently to ask for directions. Neither option results in additional learning for any of the students in your classroom. Instead, the directions for anchor activities are carefully delivered to students on "task cards or assignment sheets" or in recordings that can be revisited and reviewed when students get stuck and aren't sure what to do next (Tomlinson, 2017, p. 93). Furthermore, teams should use the same format for most anchor activities to establish extension routines. If high-achieving students have repeated experiences with the types of tasks they are going to encounter when working independently, they are more likely to use extension time productively.

Third, good anchor activities—like all good instruction—should be high-interest tasks. Our expertise as educators is knowing the parts of our curriculum that are the most engaging to our students. We know the elements of our essentials that cause controversy or spark debate. We know the kinds of questions students like to wrestle with in class. Just as importantly, we understand the characteristics of motivating assignments. Through trial and error, we have identified task types that students complete *because they want to*, not because they are required to. We need to rely on that content expertise and pedagogical expertise when developing anchor activities for extensions. High-achieving students are more likely to lean into extensions if the tasks tap into their interests.

Tools and Resources for Highly Effective Teams

The following tools and resources will help you accomplish the work for this essential action.

- **"Tool: Analyzing Your Team's Extension Reality" (page 219):** Creating a culture where educators consistently include extensions in their instruction starts with examining your team's beliefs about the value of extension as a classroom practice. If teams don't see extensions as essential, they are unlikely to invest the time and effort needed to develop strategies for advancing high-achieving students. Use this tool to start a conversation with your team about why prioritizing extensions matters.

- **"Tool: Creating a Tiered Task Card to Extend Student Learning" (page 220):** Tiered task cards are a simple example of the kinds of tasks that teams can use as anchor activities to extend student learning (Ferriter, 2020; Ferriter, Mattos, & Meyer, 2025). Like a choice board, tiered task cards give students a set of academic tasks to complete. What makes tiered task cards different is that students work through the tasks on a tiered task card sequentially, and each new task asks students to work at increasing levels of cognitive complexity (Ferriter, 2020; Ferriter et al., 2025). Designing a set of tasks that increase in cognitive complexity ensures that all students are challenged. Use this tool and its corresponding student tool and samples to develop a tiered task card for one of your upcoming units of study.
  - **"Student Tool: Creating a Tiered Task Card to Extend Student Learning" (page 221)**
  - **"Sample: Tiered Task Card—High School Sculpture (Assemblage)" (page 222)**
  - **"Sample: Tiered Task Card—High School History (The First Global Age)" (page 223)**
  - **"Sample: Tiered Task Card—Middle School Mathematics (Slope)" (page 224)**
  - **"Sample: Tiered Task Card—Middle School Science (Fossils)" (page 225)**
  - **"Sample: Tiered Task Card—Kindergarten Family Version (Counting and Cardinality)" (page 226)**

- **"Tool: Using AI Tools to Develop Extension Tasks" (page 227):** AI chatbots like ChatGPT (https://chat.openai.com) and Gemini (https://gemini.google.com) can generate first drafts of extensions like tiered task cards, RAFT activities, and badging tasks for classroom teachers. Teams can use the prompts in this tool to begin experimenting with AI in their efforts to plan more meaningful extensions for learners.

- **"Sample: RAFT Activity for an Infectious Disease Unit" (page 228):** Ask any veteran teacher to describe their initial efforts with designing activities that give students some measure of voice and choice, and they are likely to describe RAFT activities. First introduced as a strategy for encouraging creative thinking and improving writing in *Project CRISS®: Creating Independence Through Student-Owned Strategies* (Santa, Havens, & Maycumber, 1988), RAFT activities guide students in writing or speaking from the perspective of a defined *role*, to a specific *audience*, in a particular *format*, and about a certain *task*, encouraging creative and critical thinking by placing them in varied scenarios. Those same RAFT activities can serve as high-interest anchor activities in a differentiated classroom. Examine this sample to see how a middle school science teacher used the format to design extensions for students studying the spread of infectious diseases, and then discuss how to best adapt RAFT activities to the work you are doing with students.

- **Video "Creating Badging Activities for Extensions" (https://b.link/biotasks):** Anyone who grew up in Boy Scouts or Girl Scouts knows that both programs are built around earning merit badges. Scouts choose topics they are interested in and work through independent studies of those topics. When finished, they meet with a counselor to certify their mastery of the topic. When that certification is complete, students earn a physical badge to add to their uniform as a visible token of their learning. The notion of badging will also be familiar to anyone who plays video games, where players earn achievements for completing specific tasks outside of regular gameplay. For many players, these achievements are essential because they cannot fully complete a game until they earn all achievements. Teachers can build on this notion of badging and achievements to design extensions for high-achieving students. Visit https://b.link/biotasks and click play in the first slide to view a video introduction to badging tasks as extension activities and to explore a sample badging task created by career classroom teacher Bill Ferriter for fourth-grade students studying biology.

- **"Tool: Critical Issues for Team Consideration—Highly Effective Team Actions" (page 230):** This tool provides teams an opportunity to reflect on their progress, celebrate strengths, and identify next steps worth taking. At the conclusion of each set of actions, teams use a portion of this tool to dialogue about their current practices, to identify strengths and areas of focus, and to identify next steps on their pathway to becoming a highly effective collaborative team.

Tool: Analyzing Your Team's Extension Reality

Instructions: For the first three questions in the following tool, work with your learning team to circle an indicator that best represents your current extension reality. Then, use the reflection questions at the bottom of this template to analyze your team's readiness to begin providing extensions for question 4 students.

Question 1: On a scale from 1 to 5, *how important* do you think it is for teams to provide extension opportunities to students who are already proficient with essential outcomes?

Not Important	1	2	3	4	5	Very Important

Question 2: On a scale from 1 to 5, *how often* does your team provide extension opportunities to students who are already proficient with essential outcomes?

Not Often	1	2	3	4	5	Almost Always

Question 3: On a scale from 1 to 5, *how prepared* do you feel to provide extension opportunities to students who are already proficient with essential outcomes?

Not Prepared	1	2	3	4	5	Very Prepared

Questions to Consider	Your Response
Why is it so important for learning teams to provide extension opportunities to students who are already proficient with essential outcomes?	
What challenges make it difficult for learning teams to provide extension opportunities to students who are already proficient with essential outcomes?	
What strengths does your team have when it comes to providing extension opportunities to students who are already proficient with essential outcomes?	
What support will your learning team need in order to make providing more extension opportunities to students who are already proficient doable?	

PART FOUR
Providing Extra Time and Support

Source: Ferriter, W. M. (2020). The big book of tools for collaborative teams in a PLC at Work. *Solution Tree Press.*

Tool: Creating a Tiered Task Card to Extend Student Learning

Instructions: To create a tiered task card to extend student learning, review the following key, which outlines Norman L. Webb's (2002) Depth of Knowledge (DOK) levels. Then, use those descriptions to create four leveled tasks connected to your current grade-level essentials. Record those tasks in "Student Tool: Creating a Tiered Task Card to Extend Student Learning" (page 221). When you finish, you will have a tiered task card to engage students ready for extensions.

Depth of Knowledge Key

DOK Level 1	DOK Level 2	DOK Level 3	DOK Level 4
Recall and Reproduction	**Skills and Concepts**	**Strategic Thinking**	**Extended Thinking**
DOK 1 tasks involve the simple recall of information. Answers to DOK 1 tasks are either right or wrong. No reasoning is required to complete these tasks. Instead, students gather facts and information or apply simple formulas.	DOK 2 tasks involve applying knowledge. Students explain, describe, categorize, or interpret acquired information. DOK 2 tasks always require students to decide how to approach the problem.	DOK 3 tasks involve higher levels of reasoning than the two previous task types. Students develop logical arguments based on evidence, draw conclusions based on data, or provide justifications and reasoning to defend their positions.	DOK 4 tasks involve the highest level of cognitive demand. Students make connections within or between content areas, evaluate several possible solutions, or explain alternative perspectives from multiple sources. DOK 4 tasks may also ask students to apply what they have learned to real-life contexts.
Sample task: Can you list the four primary pathogens that cause human diseases?	*Sample task: What are the similarities and differences between the two main types of pathogens that cause human diseases: viruses and bacteria?*	*Sample task: Rank the four main types of pathogens that cause human diseases in order from "most dangerous" to "least dangerous." Defend your rankings with reasoning.*	*Sample task: Find an example of a disease outbreak in the world. Research the reasons for the outbreak and offer recommendations about how the outbreak should have been treated.*

Reference

Webb, N. L. (2002, March 28). *Depth-of-Knowledge levels for four content areas.* Accessed at http://ossucurr.pbworks.com/w/file/fetch/49691156/Norm%20web%20dok%20by%20subject%20area.pdf on December 13, 2023.

Source: Ferriter, W. M., Mattos, M., & Meyer, R. J. (2025). The big book of tools for RTI at Work. Solution Tree Press.

Student Tool: Creating a Tiered Task Card to Extend Student Learning

Tiered task card for: _____

(Name of our current unit of study)

Instructions for students: When you have demonstrated mastery of our grade-level essentials through your classroom assessments or work products, you are ready for extension tasks that push your thinking beyond grade-level mastery. This card includes the extension activities for our current unit of study. To complete it, follow these steps.

1. Unless your teacher gives you different instructions, start with the activity labeled DOK Level 1.

2. When you have completed the first activity, move to the task labeled DOK Level 2, DOK Level 3, and DOK Level 4.

3. You may choose any work product from the list at the end of the task card to demonstrate mastery of each task.

4. Your teacher will use your completed work to replace scores on classroom assignments that you place out of because you are working beyond grade-level expectations *or* as reworks for any assignments with scores you are trying to raise.

Tasks to Complete

DOK Level 1	DOK Level 2	DOK Level 3	DOK Level 4
Recall and Reproduction	**Skills and Concepts**	**Strategic Thinking**	**Extended Thinking**
Task:	Task:	Task:	Task:

You may choose to demonstrate what you know in any of the following ways.

Write a paragraph	Create a set of Google slides	Record a video	Make a podcast or audio recording
Develop a Venn diagram	Make a graphic organizer	Create a cartoon	Have a debate with a friend

Source: Ferriter, W. M., Mattos, M., & Meyer, R. J. (2025). The big book of tools for RTI at Work. *Solution Tree Press.*

Sample: Tiered Task Card—High School Sculpture (Assemblage)

Over the past two weeks, we have been studying sculptures in class. Specifically, we have been looking at the following.

- How artists use found objects, composition, and texture to create meaning in assemblage sculptures
- How to construct an assemblage sculpture that communicates a personal or social theme
- How to evaluate the effectiveness of assemblage sculptures by using artistic criteria such as materials use, emotional impact, complexity, or historical significance

To extend your learning about assemblage, spend some time exploring the assemblage resources found on the Museum of Modern Art's (MoMA's) website (www.moma.org/collection/terms/assemblage). Then, see if you can complete each of the following tasks.

Tasks to Complete

DOK Level 1	DOK Level 2	DOK Level 3	DOK Level 4
Recall and Reproduction	Skills and Concepts	Strategic Thinking	Extended Thinking
Task: Watch the video introduction to Alfonso Ossorio's *Empty Chair or The Last Colonial* at the bottom of MoMA's assemblage resources. In the video, the docent explains that Ossorio saw assemblages as "congregations" of objects. Summarize what he meant by that analogy.	**Task:** Assemblage is often used by artists to communicate a personal or social theme. Ossorio's *Empty Chair or The Last Colonial* is no different, communicating themes from his Filipino heritage. Some of those themes are briefly introduced by the docent in the video introduction on MoMA's website. Choose two of the objects Ossorio used in the piece to communicate themes, research more about how those objects are important in Filipino culture, and explain how their arrangement in *Empty Chair or The Last Colonial* advances those themes.	**Task:** In addition to *Empty Chair or The Last Colonial*, select three more assemblage pieces on display at the MoMA website, and rank them based on materials use, emotional impact, complexity, or historical significance. Justify your rankings, explaining how each artist's choices—such as object selection, arrangement, and scale—contribute to the overall effect of the piece.	**Task:** Working with a partner, design and create a small-scale assemblage sculpture using found objects that represent a specific theme (such as identity or time). Together, create a short artist statement explaining how the objects you chose and their arrangement communicate your theme. Then, reflect on how teamwork and shared ideas influenced your final product.

You may choose to demonstrate what you know in any of the following ways.

Write a paragraph	Create a set of Google slides	Record a video	Make a podcast or audio recording
Develop a Venn diagram	Make a graphic organizer	Create a cartoon	Have a debate with a friend

Source for DOK levels: Webb, N. L. (2002, March 28). Depth-of-Knowledge levels for four content areas. Accessed at http://ossucurr. pbworks.com/w/file/fetch/49691156/Norm%20web%20dok%20by%20subject%20area.pdf on December 13, 2023.

Sample: Tiered Task Card—High School History (The First Global Age)

Over the past two weeks, we have been studying the First Global Age in class. Specifically, we have been looking at the following.

- How advancements in science and technology contributed to exploration, trade, and cultural exchange during the First Global Age

- The positive and negative effects of technological innovations on global interactions during the First Global Age

- The similarities and differences in how innovations transformed societies in the First Global Age and how they are transforming societies today

To extend your learning about these concepts, see if you can complete each of the following tasks.

Tasks to Complete

DOK Level 1	DOK Level 2	DOK Level 3	DOK Level 4
Recall and Reproduction	**Skills and Concepts**	**Strategic Thinking**	**Extended Thinking**
Task: First, define key terms related to the First Global Age. What do we mean when we say *global age*, *science*, and *technology* within the context of this topic? Then, list three scientific or technological advancements from the First Global Age, and identify their regions of origin.	**Task:** Compare two key technological advancements from the First Global Age—(1) the printing press and (2) the astrolabe. Explain how each contributed to global exploration and cultural exchange. How do these compare to two modern technologies like the internet and GPS in terms of their impact on global connectivity?	**Task:** Create a graphic organizer that categorizes the positive and negative effects of advancements in science and technology on global trade, exploration, and cultural exchange during the First Global Age. Then, address how these effects are similar to or different from the effects of science and technology on globalization today.	**Task:** Artificial intelligence (AI) is clearly an advancement in science and technology that will have an impact on societies today. Using what you have learned about the First Global Age, predict potential impacts (positive or negative) that we are likely to face because of advancements in AI. Finally, what lessons can we learn from the First Global Age to navigate the technological impacts that AI will have on society today?

You may choose to demonstrate what you know in any of the following ways.

Write a paragraph	Create a set of Google slides	Record a video	Make a podcast or audio recording
Develop a Venn diagram	Make a graphic organizer	Create a cartoon	Have a debate with a friend

Source for DOK levels: Webb, N. L. (2002, March 28). Depth-of-Knowledge levels for four content areas. *Accessed at http://ossucurr.pbworks.com/w/file/fetch/49691156/Norm%20web%20dok%20by%20subject%20area.pdf on December 13, 2023.*

Source for tasks: Adapted from OpenAI. (2025). ChatGPT (GPT-4) [Large language model]. Response to "Can you create a set of four tasks leveled by DOK that I can use to teach world history students about the first global age?" *Accessed at https://chat.openai.com on January 29, 2025.*

Sample: Tiered Task Card—Middle School Mathematics (Slope)

We have studied slope and how it relates to relationships in class over the past two weeks. Specifically, we have been looking at the following.

- How to identify the slope given a graph, table, and equation
- What the slope means in the context of the input-output relationship
- How direction is essential to consider when finding the slope of a line

Slope Dude has been our source of information when talking about slope. Here is a video from Slope Dude himself.

Watch Slope Dude explain the slope of a line: www.youtube.com/watch?v=ZcSrJPiQvHQ

Then, see if you can complete each of the following tasks.

Tasks to Complete

DOK Level 1	DOK Level 2	DOK Level 3	DOK Level 4
Recall and Reproduction	**Skills and Concepts**	**Strategic Thinking**	**Extended Thinking**
Task: List the four different types of slopes that Slope Dude mentions in his video.	**Task:** Opposite slopes are not the same. Provide a rationale for why a slope of (−1) and a slope of 1 are not the same using your understanding of the four different types of slopes.	**Task:** Create a real-life scenario incorporating each slope ratio between the input (x) and output (y). Remember that the x value must remain the same for undefined relationships while the y value changes.	**Task:** Slope Dude created a metaphor to help mathematicians understand slope, using phrases like "puff, puff positive" and "the side of a mountain." Please create your own analogy to describe the different types of slopes and present it in a fashion that will help mathematicians understand slopes.

You may choose to demonstrate what you know in any of the following ways.

Write a paragraph	Create a set of Google slides	Record a video	Make a podcast or audio recording
Develop a Venn diagram	Make a graphic organizer	Create a cartoon	Have a debate with a friend

Source: Ferriter, W. M., Mattos, M., & Meyer, R. J. (2025). The big book of tools for RTI at Work. Solution Tree Press.

Sample: Tiered Task Card—Middle School Science (Fossils)

We have been studying fossils in class over the past two weeks. Specifically, we have been looking at the following.

- The difference between the main types of fossils
- What index fossils are and why they are important
- How scientists use fossils to understand the development of life on Earth better

A major fossil discovery was made in Northern Canada in early 2020.

Read more about that discovery here: https://bit.ly/3SG0Gw6

Then, see if you can complete each of the following tasks.

Tasks to Complete

DOK Level 1	DOK Level 2	DOK Level 3	DOK Level 4
Recall and Reproduction	**Skills and Concepts**	**Strategic Thinking**	**Extended Thinking**
Task: Can you summarize the fossil discovery made in Northern Canada?	**Task:** Can you name the type of fossil discovered in Northern Canada? Defend your decision with reasoning. Remember, we have been studying mold fossils, cast fossils, petrified fossils, preserved fossils, carbonized fossils, and trace fossils.	**Task:** How would you rate the fossil discovery made in Northern Canada? Use a scale from 1 to 5—where one represents not very important and five represents most important fossil discovery ever. Defend your ranking with reasoning.	**Task:** Find an example of another significant fossil discovery in the last one hundred years. Then, explain why that fossil discovery was even more important than the discovery made in Northern Canada.

You may choose to demonstrate what you know in any of the following ways.			
Write a paragraph	Create a set of Google slides	Record a video	Make a podcast or audio recording
Develop a Venn diagram	Make a graphic organizer	Create a cartoon	Have a debate with a friend

Source: Ferriter, W. M., Mattos, M., & Meyer, R. J. (2025). The big book of tools for RTI at Work. Solution Tree Press.

PART FOUR Providing Extra Time and Support

Sample: Tiered Task Card—Kindergarten Family Version (Counting and Cardinality)

One of the mathematics ideas elementary students must know is the idea of counting and cardinality. That means your students should be able to do the following.

- Consistently use number words in the same order.
- Count every item in a set only once and use only one number word per item.
- Understand that the result is the same no matter the order in which the objects are counted.

Here are a few leveled tasks that you can ask your child to do around the house to practice those skills.

Challenge Level 1	Challenge Level 2	Challenge Level 3	Challenge Level 4
Foundational Skill	On Grade Level	On Grade Level	Above Grade Level
Task: After returning from the grocery store, give your child a set of like items (a bag of apples, a bunch of bananas, a six-pack of bottled water), and ask them to count the items for you. Make sure they are using the correct number words while counting and they use each number word only one time. **Common Errors You May See:** When reciting number words, your child may omit or repeat numbers. When counting a set, your child may omit items or count items more than once.	**Task:** Pull the spoons and the forks out of your silverware drawer. Put them into one pile, and ask your child to count them as one set. While this task may seem similar to the first challenge, it is specifically designed to remind your child that any collection of like or unlike items can be counted as a set. **Common Errors You May See:** When reciting number words, your child may omit or repeat numbers. When counting a set, your child may omit items or count items more than once.	**Task:** Take five glasses and five plates out of your cupboard. Put them in two separate spots, and ask your child to count them as separate groups. When finished, ask your child two questions: (1) "What is the total number of objects in each set?" and (2) "Which set of objects has more items in it?" **Common Errors You May See:** Your child may not recognize that the last number word they say while counting is also the total number of items in the set. Your child may think there are more plates simply because they are bigger items that take up more space.	**Task:** Lay out ten grapes and six cherry tomatoes on your kitchen table. Ask your child to count both sets as separate groups. Then, ask your child how many objects are in both sets. Finally, ask your child to tell you how many more grapes there are than cherry tomatoes. **Common Errors You May See:** Your child may make a prediction about the difference between the two sets based on the size of each arrangement. Your child may need to recount both sets, pairing items off one by one, to come up with an answer.
(If you are willing to share your child's performance with me, make a recording of your child working on a challenge task and post it to our classroom Padlet. I will record a video response for both you and your student so you can see if you are on the right track!)			

Tool: Using AI Tools to Develop Extension Tasks

Instructions: Ensuring high levels of learning for all students means we must develop extension tasks to challenge students who have already mastered grade-level essentials. Ask an AI chatbot like ChatGPT (https://chat.openai.com) or Gemini (https://gemini.google.com) the following prompts to help you with this work.

AI chatbots can create tasks at different Depth of Knowledge (DOK) levels. • Can you generate four tasks leveled by DOK that *[grade level and subject area]* students learning about *[grade-level concept or skill]* can complete? ***Sample:*** *Can you generate four tasks leveled by DOK that AP biology students learning about Mendelian genetics can complete?* **Pro tip:** You can also ask ChatGPT to generate materials lists or directions for each task that it generates for you.	**AI chatbots can generate metaphors for concepts.** • Can you give me three metaphors that can help *[grade level and subject area]* students understand *[grade-level concept or skill]*? ***Sample:*** *Can you give me three metaphors that can help sixth-grade students understand feudalism?* **Pro tip:** Once you have your metaphors, you can ask groups of students to rank them from *most accurate* to *least accurate* or *most valuable* to *least valuable*. You can also ask groups to "beat the bot" by coming up with a better metaphor than the ones generated by ChatGPT.
AI chatbots can generate badging tasks. • Can you give me a list of five badges *[grade level and subject area]* students can earn while learning about *[grade-level concept or skill]*? • Can you write a set of directions that students can follow to earn each of these badges? Please use bullets and student-friendly language. ***Sample:*** *Can you give me a list of five badges fourth-grade students can earn while learning about the structure and function of internal and external parts of plants and animals?* **Pro tip:** Want to see what a badging task for extension can look like? Visit https://b.link/biotasks to see the final product using the previous sample prompt.	**AI chatbots can generate role, audience, format, topic (RAFT) activities.** • Can you create four RAFT activities for *[grade level and subject area]* students learning about *[grade-level concept or skill]*? I want the roles to be: *[sample roles]*. ***Sample:*** *Can you create four RAFT activities for eighth-grade science students learning about the spread of infectious diseases? I want the roles to be: medical professional, politician, business owner, and person who caught the disease.* **Pro tip:** You can also give AI chatbots specific product types or formats that you want your students to create while working on RAFT activities (for example, infographics, songs, posters, or cartoons). Doing so allows you to reinforce products that you are already teaching or include products that you know your students enjoy making.
AI chatbots can spark debates. • I am a *[grade level]* teacher. I am teaching *[insert grade-level concept]* and I want to engage my students in a debate. Can you tell me what aspects of this concept are controversial? ***Sample:*** *I am a third-grade teacher. I am teaching ecosystems and I want to engage my students in a debate. Can you tell me what aspects of this concept are controversial?* **Pro tip:** Consider using Flip (https://info.flip.com) to create an online discussion forum for your students to argue the pros and cons of the controversial ideas that AI chatbots generate for you.	**AI chatbots can help you connect your curriculum to the real world.** • Can you give me a bulleted list of examples of where I might see *[concept students are studying]* in current events? ***Sample:*** *Can you give me a bulleted list of examples of where I might see the science concept of substance density in current events?* **Pro tip:** Students are drawn to current events because it helps them feel knowledgeable in family discussions. Finding current events connected to your essentials is one of the best ways to create extension tasks.

Source: Ferriter, W. M., Mattos, M., & Meyer, R. J. (2025). The big book of tools for RTI at Work. Solution Tree Press.

PART FOUR Providing Extra Time and Support

Sample: RAFT Activity for an Infectious Disease Unit

Over the next few weeks, we will be studying the spread of infectious diseases in class. Our anchor activity for this unit will be this RAFT activity. When you demonstrate mastery of our grade-level essentials and are looking to push your learning forward, complete one of the following tasks, and then share your final product with your teacher.

Remember that you are working on this task independently—but you may brainstorm with other students who are working on the same task, and you may use your devices while researching and creating your final products. Finally, remember that there is a blank row at the bottom of every RAFT activity that you can use to create your own role, audience, format, and task for this unit. If you have an idea that is better than the ones that I've created for you, you are welcome to use it!

Role	Audience	Format	Task
You are a **medical expert**.	You are speaking to **local community members**.	You need to create **an infographic**	. . . that **explains the spread of disease**.
You are a **politician**.	You are speaking to **your constituents**.	You need to deliver **a speech**	. . . that **promotes public health measures** to keep everyone safe.
You are a **business owner**.	You are speaking to **your employees**.	You need to write **a memo**	. . . that **explains changes and challenges to your business** because of the disease.
You are a **person who caught the disease**.	You are speaking to your **family, friends, and close contacts**.	You need to write **a personal letter**	. . . that **shares your experience** and promotes awareness about the disease.

Source for RAFT concept: Santa, C. M., Havens, L. T., & Maycumber, E. M. (1988). Project CRISS: Creating independence through student-owned strategies. Kendall/Hunt.

Source for activities: OpenAI. (2023). ChatGPT (GPT-4) [Large language model]. Response to "Can you create four four R.A.F.T activities for eighth grade science students learning about the spread of infectious diseases? I want the roles to be: Medical Professional, Politician, Business Owner, and Person who caught the disease." Accessed at https://chat.openai.com on November 13, 2023.

Tool: Critical Issues for Team Consideration— Highly Effective Team Actions

Your honest evaluation is critical!

Please thoughtfully discuss your team's reality in each of the highly effective team indicators. Use the scale to rate your team in each area. At the conclusion of each section, identify areas to celebrate and areas for your team to intensify efforts.

+   This is very true of our team. This belief or action is embedded in our beliefs and actions.

✓   This is sometimes true of our team. We are not consistent about this belief or action.

–   This is rarely or never true of our team. We need to work on implementing this belief or action.

Rating	Part 1: Highly Effective Teams Have a Common Foundation
	Action 1.1: We identify team roles, norms, and protocols to guide us in working together.
	Action 1.2: We have a process for addressing moments when personalities interfere with the team's work.
	Action 1.3: We use SMART goals to drive our work.
	Action 1.4: We regularly evaluate our team's effectiveness.

Celebrations:

Next steps:

Rating	Part 2: Highly Effective Teams Focus on Learning for All Students
	Action 2.1: We collectively identify essential learnings and define what success looks like in student work.
	Action 2.2: We identify the prerequisite knowledge and skills needed to master our essentials.
	Action 2.3: We identify course content and topics we can minimize or eliminate to devote more time to our essentials.
	Action 2.4: We agree on how to sequence content and pace our course.

page 1 of 2

Celebrations:

Next steps:

Rating	Part 3: Highly Effective Teams Effectively Use Assessments and Data
	Action 3.1: We develop and deliver frequent common formative assessments throughout our units of instruction.
	Action 3.2: We use team assessment data to identify high-impact instructional strategies.
	Action 3.3: We teach students the criteria we will use to judge their work.
	Action 3.4: We create exemplars students can examine to evaluate their own progress toward mastery.

Celebrations:

Next steps:

Rating	Part 4: Highly Effective Teams Provide Extra Time and Support for Learning
	Action 4.1: We create flexible time during our units of instruction to provide extra time and support to learners.
	Action 4.2: We deliver targeted interventions to support students who have not yet reached grade-level expectations.
	Action 4.3: We deliver targeted extensions to students working beyond grade-level expectations.

Celebrations:

Next steps:

Source: Adapted from DuFour, R., DuFour, R., Eaker, R., Many, T. W., Mattos, M., & Muhammad, A. (2024). Learning by doing: A handbook for Professional Learning Communities at Work (4th ed.). Solution Tree Press.

PART FOUR
Providing Extra Time and Support

A Beacon of Hope

The actions of highly effective teams outlined in this book—the work of building a common foundation, ensuring clarity, getting clear on what *all* students must know and be able to do, effectively using team formative assessments and data, and providing extra time and support for learning—are more than a pathway to high levels of learning for all students. They represent a shared commitment in the belief that every student, regardless of their starting point, is capable of high levels of learning and that highly effective teams are the key to realizing this goal. Yet, even with the clearest actions and effective strategies, we believe the true power of a collaborative team's work lies in something more compelling: *hope.*

Each day, highly effective teams stand as beacons of hope for our students. We believe in their unlimited potential, that their efforts do matter, and in their ability to overcome challenges. When we come together to learn, grow, and collaborate, we model and increase this hope for our students. We show our students—and our team—what is possible when we refuse to settle for *This is how we've always done this* and instead strive to improve our collective practices.

- Part 1 of this book describes how highly effective teams build a common foundation through clarifying roles, developing norms to guide a team's collective work, establishing a process to address personality differences, and evaluating a team's effectiveness. *We organize and make commitments to each other to make our collaborative efforts powerful!*

- Part 2 focuses on the actions teams take to ensure high levels of learning for all students. By identifying those essentials that all students need to know to succeed, giving curricular priority to those essentials, and establishing shared pacing for the instruction of these essentials, teams build capacity for effectively assessing together and learning from their shared data. *We get crystal clear on what* all *students need to know and be able to do in our grade level or course!*

- Part 3 focuses on utilizing common formative assessments to drive instruction and to turn data into actionable steps that can improve student outcomes. *We use frequent common formative assessments as tools for learning together!*

- Part 4 emphasizes the critical responsibility of providing extra time and support for students who need it while also ensuring meaningful extension opportunities are available for those ready to go further. In providing extra time and support for learning, we send a clear and unmistakable message: *We will not give up on any student!*

But perhaps the most important message of all is that the work of highly effective teams in a PLC is not *only* about increasing student achievement. The work is grounded in teachers learning together. We are *professional* educators, in a school *community*, *learning* together—a *professional learning community*. Working as a member of a highly effective team reminds us that our professional growth matters, and that we have the ability to increase our collective efficacy and impact. When we learn together, think differently, and grow from our mistakes, we increase our team effectiveness and in turn, find deeper satisfaction in our professional work as educators. Most importantly, we create a culture of unwavering optimism—not just for students, but for ourselves.

As fellow practitioners, we know this work can be challenging. Education can often seem difficult and complex! We encourage you to remember that, in the middle of the classroom's occasional clutter and chaos, you represent *a beacon of hope* for the students you serve.

Let *The Handbook of Highly Effective Teams in a PLC at Work* serve as a guide for your team's collaborative work. More importantly, let your combined belief in students and each other be the energy that drives your team forward. In the end, it is not just the actions you take, but the hope you represent, that will leave a lasting mark on your learners. Make no mistake. As educators, we are not just changing classrooms. ***We are, and always will be, beacons of hope!***

References & Resources

Almarode, J., Fisher, D., Thunder, K., & Frey, N. (2021). *The success criteria playbook: A hands-on guide to making learning visible and measurable, grades K–12*. Corwin.

Anderman, E. M., Sheng, Y., & Cha, W. (2024). "Why do I have to learn this?" *Phi Delta Kappan, 105*(5), 8–12.

Arkansas Department of Education. (2015). *Arkansas K–12 science standards: Grade 3*. Accessed at https://dese.ade.arkansas.gov/Files/3rd_Grade_20231221143054.pdf on February 5, 2025.

Arkansas Department of Education. (2022). *Grades K–4 social studies academic standards*. Accessed at https://dese.ade.arkansas.gov/Files/AR_Grades_K-4_Social_Studies_Standards_2022_LS.pdf on February 5, 2025.

Arkansas Department of Education. (2023a). *Arkansas English language arts standards: Grades K–12*. Accessed at https://dese.ade.arkansas.gov/Files/AR_2023_K-12_ELA_Standards_LS_7.2023_LS.docx on February 3, 2025.

Arkansas Department of Education. (2023b). *Arkansas mathematics standards: Grades K–12*. Accessed at https://dese.ade.arkansas.gov/Files/AR_2023_K-8,_Alg,_Geo_Math_Standards_LS_6.21.23_LS.docx on February 5, 2025.

Bailey, K., & Jakicic, C. (2017). *Simplifying common assessment: A guide for Professional Learning Communities at Work*. Solution Tree Press.

Bailey, K., & Jakicic, C. (2019). *Make it happen: Coaching with the four critical questions of PLCs at Work*. Solution Tree Press.

Bailey, K., & Jakicic, C. (2022). *Formative tools for leaders in a PLC at Work: Assessing, analyzing, and acting to support collaborative teams*. Solution Tree Press.

Bailey, K., & Jakicic, C. (2023). *Common formative assessment: A toolkit for Professional Learning Communities at Work* (2nd ed.). Solution Tree Press.

Brooks, C., Carroll, A., Gillies, R. M., & Hattie, J. (2019). A matrix of feedback for learning. *Australian Journal of Teacher Education, 44*(4). Accessed at https://ro.ecu.edu.au/ajte/vol44/iss4/2 on August 6, 2024.

Brown, B. (2018). *Dare to lead: Brave work. Tough conversations. Whole hearts.* Random House.

Brown, T., & Ferriter, W. M. (2021). *You can learn! Building student ownership, motivation, and efficacy with the PLC at Work process*. Solution Tree Press.

Bureau of Legislative Research. (2022, May 2). *Learning expectations in Arkansas schools* (Handout D2). Arkansas State Legislature. Accessed at https://arkleg.state.ar.us/Home/FTPDocument?path=%2FAssembly%2FMeeting+Attachments%2F410%2F5093%2FHandout+D2+Learning+Expecations+Report+BLR+18.pdf on January 18, 2025.

Cancellieri, P. (2020a, June 11). Creating a Culture of Feedback *book study: Session two—How am I doing?* [Video file]. Accessed at https://solutiontree.wistia.com/medias/ra3371pryg on June 27, 2020.

Cancellieri, P. (2020b, July 17). *What does "meaningful feedback to students" look like in a remote environment?* [Video file]. Solution Tree Press.

Center for Parent Information and Resources. (2020, March). *Supports, modifications, and accommodations for students.* Accessed at www.parentcenterhub.org/accommodations on February 3, 2025.

Chappuis, J. (2015). *Seven strategies of assessment for learning* (2nd ed.). Boston: Pearson.

Chappuis, J., Stiggins, R., Chappuis, S., & Arter, J. (2012). *Classroom assessment for student learning: Doing it right—using it well* (2nd ed.). Pearson.

Chiprany, D. T., & Page, P. (2025). *Celebrating in a PLC at Work: A leader's guide to building collective efficacy and high-performing collaborative teams.* Solution Tree Press.

Conzemius, A. E., & O'Neill, J. (2014). *The handbook for SMART school teams: Revitalizing best practices for collaboration* (2nd ed.). Solution Tree Press.

Cornell University Center for Teaching Innovation. (n.d.). *Collaborative learning.* Accessed at https://teaching.cornell.edu/teaching-resources/active-collaborative-learning/collaborative-learning on January 7, 2025.

Covey, S. M. R. (2022). *Trust and inspire: How truly great leaders unleash greatness in others.* Simon & Schuster.

Cruz, L. F. (2024, December 11). *Utilizing the necessary context to understand and embrace the RTI at Work process* [Conference session]. RTI at Work Institute, Rogers, AR.

Cutler, C. (2017, February 11). *How the 60:1 rule helps you plan a perfect descent.* Accessed at www.boldmethod.com/learn-to-fly/navigation/how-the-60-to-1-rule-helps-you-plan-a-perfect-descent on January 18, 2025.

Dabrowski, J., & Reed Marshall, T. (2018). *Motivation and engagement in student assignments: The role of choice and relevancy.* The Education Trust. Accessed at https://edtrust.org/wp-content/uploads/2014/09/Motivation_Engagement_FINAL_LR.pdf on May 19, 2024.

Dagher, K. (2024, February 8). *Defining team roles and responsibilities: Benefits and tips* [Blog post]. Accessed at https://fellow.app/blog/productivity/how-to-effectively-define-team-roles-and-responsibilities on January 9, 2025.

Dimich, N. (2024). *Design in five: Essential phases to create engaging assessment practice* (2nd ed.). Solution Tree Press.

Dimich, N., Erkens, C., Miller, J., Schimmer, T., & White, K. (2022). *Concise answers to frequently asked questions about assessment and grading.* Solution Tree Press.

Donohoo, J. (2017, October 25). *Collective teacher efficacy: The effect size and six enabling conditions* [Blog post]. Praxis. Accessed at www.jennidonohoo.com/post/collective-teacher-efficacy-the-effect-size-research-and-six-enabling-conditions on April 3, 2024.

Doran, G. T. (1981). There's a S.M.A.R.T. way to write management's goals and objectives. *Management Review, 70,* 35–36.

DuFour, R., DuFour, R., Eaker, R., Many, T. W., Mattos, M., & Muhammad, A. (2024). *Learning by doing: A handbook for Professional Learning Communities at Work* (4th ed.). Solution Tree Press.

DuFour, R., DuFour, R., Eaker, R., Mattos, M., & Muhammad. A. (2021). *Revisiting Professional Learning Communities at Work: Proven insights for sustained, substantive school improvement* (2nd ed.). Solution Tree Press.

DuFour, R., & Reeves, D. (2016). The futility of PLC Lite. *Phi Delta Kappan, 97*(6), 69–71. https://doi.org/10.1177/0031721716636878

Eaker, R. (2020). *A summing up: Teaching and learning in effective schools and PLCs at Work.* Solution Tree Press.

Ferlazzo, L. (2022, December 14). Teacher expectations play a big role in the classroom. Here's how. *Education Week.* Accessed at www.edweek.org/teaching-learning/opinion-teacher-expectations-play-a-big-role-in-the-classroom-heres-how/2022/12 on June 2, 2024.

Ferlazzo, L. (2023). *The student motivation handbook: Fifty ways to boost an intrinsic desire to learn.* Routledge.

Ferriter, W. M. (2020). *The big book of tools for collaborative teams in a PLC at Work.* Solution Tree Press.

Ferriter, W. M. (2024a, April 2). *Ten minute team tip: Using badging tasks as extension activities* [Video file]. Accessed at www.youtube.com/watch?v=N3Emv5iM8sA&t=3s on February 3, 2025.

Ferriter, W. M. (2024b, April 12). *What does progress-driven leadership look like in action?* [Keynote presentation]. Effective Coaching Institute, Louisville, KY.

Ferriter, W. M., & Cancellieri, P. J. (2017). *Creating a culture of feedback.* Solution Tree Press.

Ferriter, W. M., Graham, P., & Wight, M. (2013). *Making teamwork meaningful: Leading progress-driven collaboration in a PLC at Work.* Solution Tree Press.

Ferriter, W. M., Mattos, M., & Meyer, R. J. (2025). *The big book of tools for RTI at Work.* Solution Tree Press.

Fisher, D., & Frey, N. (2012). Text-dependent questions. *Principal Leadership,* 70–73.

Fisher, D., & Frey, N. (2022). Show and tell: A video column/co-constructing success criteria. *Educational Leadership, 79*(8). Accessed at www.ascd.org/el/articles/co-constructing-success-criteria on May 19, 2024.

Fisher, D., Frey, N., & Gonzalez, A. (2023). 4 C's for better student engagement. *Educational Leadership, 81*(1). Accessed at www.ascd.org/el/articles/4-cs-for-better-student-engagement on May 19, 2024.

Fisher, D., Frey, N., Ortega, S., & Hattie, J. (2023). *Teaching students to drive their learning: A playbook on engagement and self-regulation, K–12.* Corwin.

Forbes Business Council. (2022). *15 daily habits that can keep your team productive and focused.* Accessed at www.forbes.com/councils/forbesbusinesscouncil/2022/07/14/15-daily-habits-that-can-keep-your-team -productive-and-focused on February 20, 2025.

Goodwin, B. (2021). Yes, you can motivate your students. *Educational Leadership, 79*(4). Accessed at https:// ascd.org/el/articles/research-matters-yes-you-can-motivate-your-students on July 4, 2024.

Goodwin, B. (2022). Getting their hopes up. *Educational Leadership, 80*(3). Accessed at https://ascd.org/el /articles/getting-their-hopes-up on July 4, 2024.

Goodwin, B., & Rouleau, K. (2022). *The new classroom instruction that works: The best research-based strategies for increasing student achievement* (2nd ed.). ASCD.

Hattie, J. (2018, May 1). *Collective efficacy* [Video file]. Accessed at https://vimeo.com/267382804 on January 7, 2025.

Hattie, J. (2023a). *Global research database.* Accessed at www.visiblelearningmetax.com/influences on March 5, 2024.

Hattie, J. (2023b). *Visible learning: The sequel.* Routledge.

Hattie, J., & Clarke, S. (2019). *Visible learning: Feedback.* Routledge.

Holloway, M. E., Martin, J., & Shaddix, L. (2007, July). *Under construction: Building communities from the ground up* [Presentation]. National Staff Development Council Third Annual Summer Conference for Teacher Leaders and the Administrators Who Support Them.

Holt, J. (1964). *How children fail.* Pitman.

Hurst, L. T. (2022). *Reading and mathematics growth patterns of high-achieving students: An investigation of school-year and summer trends* [Doctoral dissertation, University of North Texas]. UNT Digital Library. https://digital.library.unt.edu/ark:/67531/metadc2048628

Johnson, W. (2018, May 8). Why talented people don't use their strengths. *Harvard Business Review.* Accessed at https://hbr.org/2018/05/why-talented-people-dont-use-their-strengths on April 4, 2024.

Kraft, M. A., & Novicoff, S. (2023). *Time in school: A conceptual framework, synthesis of the causal research, and empirical exploration* (EdWorkingPaper No. 22-653). Annenberg Institute at Brown University. Accessed at https://files.eric.ed.gov/fulltext/ED639072.pdf on January 18, 2025.

Kramer, S. V., & Schuhl, S. (2023). *Acceleration for all: A how-to guide for overcoming learning gaps.* Solution Tree Press.

Lipnevich, A. A., Panadero, E., & Calistro, T. (2023). Unraveling the effects of rubrics and exemplars on student writing performance. *Journal of Experimental Psychology: Applied, 29*(1), 136–148. https://doi.org/10.1037/xap0000434

Lisitsa, E. (2024, June 26). *How to fight smarter: Soften your start-up* [Blog post]. Accessed at www.gottman.com/blog/softening-startup on September 30, 2024.

Maeker, P., & Heller, J. (2023). *Literacy in a PLC at Work: Guiding teams to get going and get better in grades K–6 reading.* Solution Tree Press.

Mandouit, L. W. (2020). *Investigating how students receive, interpret, and respond to teacher feedback* [Doctoral dissertation, University of Melbourne]. https://minerva-access.unimelb.edu.au/items/a044d981-879d-50f6-8427-ba1266b81af7

Many, T. W., & Horrell, T. (2014). Prioritizing the standards using R.E.A.L. criteria. *TEPSA News, 71*(1), 1–2.

Marzano, R. J. (2017). *The new art and science of teaching.* Solution Tree Press.

Marzano, R. J., Pickering, D. J., & Pollock, J. E. (2001). *Classroom instruction that works: The best research-based strategies for increasing student achievement.* ASCD.

Mashek, D. (2022, June 23). Collaboration is a key skill. So why aren't we teaching it? *MIT Sloan Management Review.* Accessed at https://sloanreview.mit.edu/article/collaboration-is-a-key-skill-so-why-arent-we-teaching-it on February 5, 2024.

Mattos, M. (2022). *RTI at Work two-day workshop.* Solution Tree.

Mattos, M., Buffum, A., Malone, J., Cruz, L. F., Dimich, N., & Schuhl, S. (2025). *Taking action: A handbook for RTI at Work* (2nd ed.). Solution Tree Press.

Mattos, M., DuFour, R., DuFour, R., Eaker, R., & Many, T. W. (2016). *Concise answers to frequently asked questions about Professional Learning Communities at Work.* Solution Tree Press.

Nash, C., Ashford, M., & Collins, L. (2023). Expertise in coach development: The need for clarity. *Behavioral Sciences, 13*(11), Article 924. https://doi.org/10.3390/bs13110924

National Center for Education Statistics. (2020). *Table 1.1. Minimum number of instructional days and hours in the school year, minimum number of hours per school day, and school start/finish dates, by state: 2020.* Accessed at https://nces.ed.gov/programs/statereform/tab1_1-2020.asp on January 18, 2025.

National Governors Association Center for Best Practices & Council of Chief State School Officers. (2010a). *Common Core State Standards for English language arts and literacy in history/social studies, science, and technical subjects.* Authors. Accessed at https://corestandards.org/wp-content/uploads/2023/09/ELA_Standards1.pdf on September 29, 2024.

National Governors Association Center for Best Practices & Council of Chief State School Officers. (2010b). *Common Core State Standards for mathematics.* Authors. Accessed at https://corestandards.org/wp-content/uploads/2023/09/Math_Standards1.pdf on September 29, 2024.

National School Reform Faculty. (n.d.). *What are protocols? Why use them?* Accessed at https://nsrfharmony.org/whatareprotocols on April 4, 2024.

Nawaz, S. (2018, January 15). How to create executive team norms—and make them stick. *Harvard Business Review.* Accessed at https://hbr.org/2018/01/how-to-create-executive-team-norms-and-make-them-stick on April 4, 2024.

Next Generation Science Standards. (2013). *3-LS3-1 Heredity: Inheritance and variation of traits.* Accessed at www.nextgenscience.org/pe/3-ls3-1-heredity-inheritance-and-variation-traits on February 19, 2025.

Nielsen, M. (2016, July 19). Unpacking standards leads to confidence, not chaos, for teachers and students [Blog post]. *AllThingsAssessment.* Accessed at https://allthingsassessment.info/2016/07/19/unpacking-standards-leads-to-confidence-not-chaos-for-teachers-and-students on February 1, 2025.

Nottingham, J. A. (2024). *Teach brilliantly: Small shifts that lead to big gains in student learning.* Solution Tree Press.

OpenAI. (2023). ChatGPT (GPT-4) [Large language model]. *Response to "Can you create four R.A.F.T activities for eighth grade science students learning about the spread of infectious diseases? I want the roles to be: Medical Professional, Politician, Business Owner, and Person who caught the disease."* Accessed at https://chat.openai.com on November 13, 2023.

OpenAI. (2024). ChatGPT (GPT-4) [Large language model]. *Response to "Can you help me generate exemplars of responses to a question about the Magna Carta?"* Accessed at https://chat.openai.com on November 19, 2024.

OpenAI. (2025). ChatGPT (GPT-4) [Large language model]. *Response to "Can you create a set of four tasks leveled by DOK that I can use to teach world history students about the first global age?"* Accessed at https://chat.openai.com on January 29, 2025.

Page, C. (2019, December 30). *What do pilots do during the cruise?* The Points Guy. Accessed at https://thepointsguy.com/airline/what-do-pilots-do-during-cruise on January 18, 2025.

Rambo-Hernandez, K. E., & McCoach, D. B. (2015). High-achieving and average students' reading growth: Contrasting school and summer trajectories. *Journal of Educational Research, 108*(2), 112–129. https://doi.org/10.1080/00220671.2013.850398

Roberts, M. (2019). *Enriching the learning: Meaningful extensions for proficient students in a PLC at Work.* Solution Tree Press.

Rockwell, D. (2017, March 16). *How to K.I.S.S. lousy operational meetings goodbye* [Blog post]. Accessed at https://leadershipfreak.blog/2017/03/16/how-to-k-i-s-s-lousy-operational-meetings-goodbye on August 5, 2019.

Ruiz-Primo, M. A., & Brookhart, S. M. (2018). *Using feedback to improve learning.* Routledge.

Russell, T. (2019). *Why is teamwork so difficult?* Accessed at www.quora.com/Why-is-teamwork-so-difficult/answer/Toby-Russell-25 on April 3, 2024.

Sadler, D. R. (1989). Formative assessment and the design of instructional systems. *Instructional Science, 18*(2), 119–144. https://doi.org/10.1007/BF00117714

Saka, A. O. (2021). Can teacher collaboration improve students' academic achievement in junior secondary mathematics? *Asian Journal of University Education, 17*(1), 33–46.

Santa, C. M., Havens, L. T., & Maycumber, E. M. (1988). *Project CRISS: Creating independence through student-owned strategies.* Kendall/Hunt.

Saphier, J. (2005). *John Adams' promise: How to have good schools for all our children, not just for some.* Research for Better Teaching.

Schimmer, T. (2024, February 24). *Panel discussion.* Solution Tree PLC Summit. Phoenix, AZ, United States.

Schuhl, S. (2022, November 12–13). *PLC associate retreat presentation* [Conference presentation]. Solution Tree. New Orleans, LA.

Schuhl, S., & Kanold, T. D. (2024). *Mathematics assessment and intervention in a PLC at Work* (2nd ed.). Solution Tree Press.

Schuhl, S., Toncheff, M., Deinhart, J., & Buckhalter, B. (2024). *Mathematics Tier 1 and 2 interventions in a PLC at Work.* Solution Tree Press.

Simms, J. A. (2024). *The Marzano synthesis: A collected guide to what works in K–12 education.* Marzano Resources.

Sonju, B., Powers, M., & Miller, S. (2024). *Simplifying the journey: Six steps to schoolwide collaboration, consistency, and clarity in a PLC at Work.* Solution Tree Press.

Tomlinson, C. A. (2015, January 18). Differentiation does, in fact, work. *Education Week.* Accessed at www.edweek.org/teaching-learning/opinion-differentiation-does-in-fact-work/2015/01 on April 1, 2024.

Tomlinson, C. A. (2017). *How to differentiate instruction in academically diverse classrooms* (3rd ed.). ASCD.

Venables, D. R. (2011). *The practice of authentic PLCs: A guide to effective teacher teams.* Corwin Press.

Visible Learning Meta^X. (2023, June). *Teacher clarity.* Accessed at www.visiblelearningmetax.com/influences/view/teacher_clarity on May 19, 2024.

Vygotsky, L. S. (1978). *Mind in society: The development of higher psychological processes.* Harvard University Press.

Webb, N. L. (1997). *Criteria for alignment of expectations and assessments in mathematics and science education* (Research Monograph No. 6). Council of Chief State School Officers.

Webb, N. L. (1999). *Alignment of science and mathematics standards and assessments in four states* (Research Monograph No. 18). Council of Chief State School Officers.

Webb, N. L. (2002, March 28). *Depth-of-Knowledge levels for four content areas.* Accessed at http://ossucurr.pbworks.com/w/file/fetch/49691156/Norm%20web%20dok%20by%20subject%20area.pdf on December 13, 2023.

White, K. (2022). *Student self-assessment: Data notebooks, portfolios, and other tools to advance learning.* Solution Tree Press.

Wiliam, D. (2017). *Embedded formative assessment* (2nd. ed.) Solution Tree Press.

Will, M. (2024, March 29). Dear administrators: Teachers want you to get these 8 tasks off their plates. *Education Week.* Accessed at www.edweek.org/teaching-learning/dear-administrators-teachers-want-you-to-get-these-8-tasks-off-their-plates/2024/03 on April 3, 2024.

Williams, K. (2016, August 17). *How to use common formative assessments to help teachers reflect on practice* [Video file]. Solution Tree. Accessed at www.youtube.com/watch?v=9p3Fp5rBdz8 on January 30, 2025.

Wisniewski, B., Zierer, K., & Hattie, J. (2020). The power of feedback revisited: A meta-analysis of educational feedback research. *Frontiers in Psychology, 10,* Article 3087. https://doi.org/10.3389/fpsyg.2019.03087

Wood, D., Bruner, J. S., & Ross, G. (1976). The role of tutoring in problem solving. *Journal of Child Psychology and Psychiatry, 17*(2), 89–100.

Index

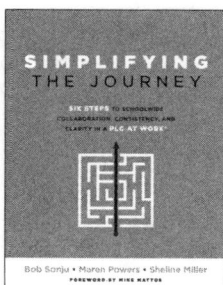

Simplifying the Journey
Bob Sonju, Maren Powers, and Sheline Miller
Successfully implement the PLC at Work® process and strategies with this straightforward guide. Step-by-step actions for teachers, school leaders, and coaches focus on answering each of the four critical questions of a PLC so you can be confident you are doing the right work.
BKG118

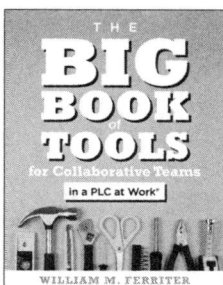

The Big Book of Tools for Collaborative Teams in a PLC at Work®
William M. Ferriter
Build your team's capacity to become agents of change. Organized around the four critical questions of PLC at Work, this comprehensive resource provides an explicit structure for collaborative teams. Access tools and templates for navigating common challenges, developing collective teacher efficacy, and more.
BKF898

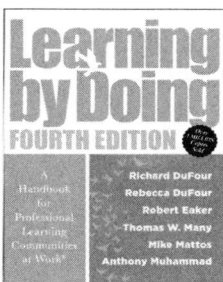

Learning by Doing, Fourth Edition
Richard DuFour, Rebecca DuFour, Robert Eaker, Thomas W. Many, Mike Mattos, and Anthony Muhammad
In this fourth edition of the bestseller *Learning by Doing*, the authors use updated research and time-tested knowledge to address current education challenges, from learning gaps exacerbated by the COVID-19 pandemic to the need to drive a highly effective multitiered system of supports.
BKG169

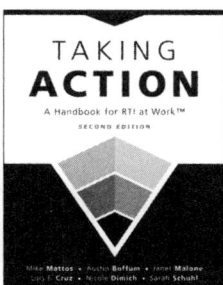

Taking Action, Second Edition
Mike Mattos, Austin Buffum, Janet Malone, Luis F. Cruz, Nicole Dimich, and Sarah Schuhl
The second edition of the bestseller *Taking Action* delves deeper into the essential actions needed to create a highly effective multitiered system of supports. New recommendations and tools are included to better target assessments, engage students, and proactively address resistance.
BKG136

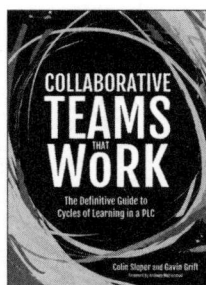

Collaborative Teams That Work
Colin Sloper and Gavin Grift
Collaborative Teams That Work is the ultimate guide to excellent collaboration. Rely on this resource as you set up collaborative teams within your PLC, and then refer back to it before, during, and after meetings to maintain focus on the right work.
BKB012

Solution Tree | Press

a division of
Solution Tree

Visit SolutionTree.com or call 800.733.6786 to order.